The Garrick Stage

'The Downfall of Shakespeare on a
Modern Stage.' Oil painting by Philip
Dawes, exhibited 1765.

Allardyce Nicoll

EDITED BY *Sybil Rosenfeld*

The Garrick Stage

THEATRES AND AUDIENCE IN THE EIGHTEENTH CENTURY

Manchester University Press

Published by
Manchester University Press
Oxford Road, Manchester M13 9PL

First issued in paperback 1981

*British Library
cataloguing-in-publication data*

Nicoll, Allardyce
    The Garrick stage.
    1. Theatre—England—History
        —18th century
    I. Title
    792'.0942   PN2593

    ISBN 0-7190-08581

Printed in Great Britain
by Butler & Tanner Ltd
Frome and London

Contents

Foreword

I was honoured and delighted at the invitation from the Manchester University Press to edit the last posthumous work of Professor Allardyce Nicoll. He had been my lecturer on drama when I was an undergraduate at King's College, London, and later was a stimulating and careful supervisor of my MA thesis. For nearly twenty years he was President of the Society for Theatre Research when I was acting as Hon. Secretary. We became not only colleagues but friends sharing a passion for the theatre and its history. I owe him an incalculable debt for inspiring my life-long interest in the subject which has afforded me so much delight. Professor Nicoll was fascinated by all aspects of the theatre and his range was, therefore, astonishingly wide. His books cover Greek and Roman theatre, medieval, Italian Renaissance, commedia dell' arte, theory of drama, modern drama and film. His immense industry enabled him to produce his *History of English Drama 1660 to 1900* and its sequel *English Drama 1900 to 1930* with their basic lists of plays and their productions which must always remain a foundation on which other scholars can build. It was his knowledge of the theatre of other countries which illuminated his books on his own; a fact which is evident in his last script on the Garrick era. This knowledge provided him with insights unpenetrated by other workers in the field.

My contribution has been mainly on the illustrations which I selected from over 700 which he possessed on the period. Quite a number he had himself indicated for inclusion, others had to be supplied from blanks or added. This task I could not have performed without the patient assistance of Mrs Nicoll who looked out the photographs together with the notes on them and made useful suggestions as to choice. She was also most kind in inviting me to stay with her so that we could collaborate in deciding what to include.

The text was complete and needed only a little up-dating as a result of research since the book was written. I have not considered it necessary to add any sections of material which has been dealt with elsewhere but have indicated where such work may be found.

I am sure that Professor Nicoll would have wished to make acknowledgments to those libraries, collections and people who assisted him. I should like to add my thanks to the owners of the illustrations for permission to reproduce them and particularly to Mr Richard Leacroft who has kindly allowed me to use his new and hitherto unpublished plans of Drury Lane. I am indebted to the following for supplying or helping me and the publishers to trace photographs: Miss Ann Brooke

Barnett, Curator of the University of Bristol Theatre Collection; the Victoria and Albert Museum, Theatre Collection; the British Library; the British Museum; the Folger Shakespeare Library; the John Rylands University Library of Manchester; the Scarborough Public Library; the Witt Collection at the Courtauld Institute; Paul Mellon Centre for Studies in British Art (London); Signora Murano of the Fondazione Cini, Venice, who obtained the photographs from the Museo Correr; Mrs Lumsden, librarian of the Garrick Club; Mrs Constance Fletcher; Messrs Sotheby Parke Bernet; the Leger Galleries; the John Freeman Group; the Greater London Council; Mr Iain Mackintosh and Mr John Baskett. In a few cases we have been unable to discover the sources of prints obtained by the late author. The publishers and I have made every effort to do so. We trust that if works have been reproduced without the permission of their present owners being received and recorded, this omission will be seen in the light of the special circumstances surrounding the book's preparation for press and that our sincere apologies will be accepted.

Sybil Rosenfeld

London 1979

The Age of David Garrick: an introduction

The hero of John Balderston's *Berkeley Square* was mysteriously swept back in Time's invisible chariot to dwell for a space in the eighteenth century. If we were thus similarly privileged to sojourn in London for weeks or months or years between 1741 and 1776, and if our principal interest lay in the theatre, inevitably we should have found that the playhouse world, despite its teeming variety, was dominated in spirit and in practice by one man—David Garrick. We might have listened to sharp adverse comments made upon him by his enemies; glancing at the periodicals, we might have read satirical paragraphs concerning his acting and his behaviour; we might have met some gentlemen and ladies who claimed to have greater admiration for other performers or who asserted that they derived richer enjoyment from the offerings of his rival manager, John Rich; yet in the end we should have been forced to acknowledge that no theatre-man of his time succeeded, so powerfully and so firmly, in stamping the contemporary stage with his own image.

Nor did he labour hard and long to secure his position of pre-eminence. Perhaps the most widely familiar record in the entire range of the theatre's annals is that of Garrick's sudden advent and immediate success in the autumn of the year 1741. The announcement of his first appearance in London is there for us to see—*King Richard III*, at an outlying playhouse in Goodman's Fields, with 'The part of King Richard by a Gentleman (Who never appeared on any Stage)' (plate 1). The performance was on Monday 19 October: on the following day *The London Post and General Advertiser* informed its readers that the anonymous actor's 'Reception was the most extraordinary and great that was ever known upon such an Occasion', and Garrick himself was writing excitedly to his brother: 'Last Night I play'd Richard ye Third to ye Surprize of Every Body & as I shall make very near £300 p Annum by It & as it is really what I doat upon I am resolv'd to pursue it' (plate 2).[1] Within a day or two he was able to announce that his interpretation of the role was bringing 'crowded Audiences every Night'; before a month had passed by, he could declare that 'We have greater Business than Either Drury Lane or Covent Garden', 'As to Company ye Best in Town are desirous of Mine, & I have rec'd more

GOODMAN's FIELDS.
AT the *Late Theatre* in *Goodman's-Fields*, this Day, will be perform'd a CONCERT of VOCAL and INSTRUMENTAL MUSICK. Divided into TWO PARTS.
Tickets at Three, Two, and One Shilling.
Places for the Boxes to be taken at the Fleece-Tavern near the Theatre.
N.B. Between the Two Parts of the Concert will be presented an Historical Play, call'd The LIFE and DEATH of
King RICHARD the Third.
Containing, The Distresses and Death of King Henry VI.
The Artful Acquisition of the Crown by King Richard.
The Murder of young K. Edward V. and his Brother, in the Tower.
The Landing of the Earl of Richmond.
And the Death of King Richard, in the memorable Battle of Bosworth-Field; being the last that was fought between the Houses of York and Lancaster.
With many other True Historical Passages.
The Part of King Richard by a GENTLEMAN;
(*Who never appear'd on any Stage*;)
King Henry, by Mr. Giffard; Richmond, Mr. Marshall; Prince Edward, by Miss Hippisley; Duke of York, Miss Naylor; Duke of Buckingham, Mr. Peterson; Duke of Norfolk, Mr. Blakes; Lord Stanley, Mr. Paget; Oxford, Mr. Vaughan; Tressel, Mr. W. Giffard; Catesby, Mr. Marr; Ratcliff, Mr. Crofts; Blunt, Mr. Naylor; Tyrrel, by Mr. Pattenden; Lord-Mayor, Mr. Dunstall. The Queen, Mrs. Steel; Dutchess of York, Mrs. Yates;
And the Part of Lady Anne, by Mrs. Giffard.
With Entertainments of Dancing by Mons. FROMENT, Madem. DUVALL, and the two Masters and Miss GRANIER.
To which will be added a Ballad-Opera of One Act, call'd
The VIRGIN UNMASK'D.
The Part of Miss Lucy by Miss Hippisley.
Both which will be perform'd gratis, by Persons for their Diversion.
The Concert will begin exactly at Six o'Clock.

1

Announcement of David Garrick's first appearance in London

Civilities & favours from Such Since my playing than I ever did in all my Life before'.[2] Possibly we might have been inclined to discount some of these statements, treating them as exaggerated self-praise designed to disarm the hostility of his family towards his proposed choice of profession; and we might likewise have been prepared to regard as an inspired 'puff' a paragraph in *The London Daily Post* of 27 November: 'Last Night there was a great Number of Persons of Quality and Distinction at the Theatre in Goodman's Fields, to see the Play of Richard the Third, who all express'd the highest Satisfaction at the whole Performance, several hundred Persons were obliged to return for want of room, the House being full soon after Five o'clock.' Our reservations and doubts, however, would have been unjustified: Garrick's triumph was a real one. Among those who came to see him was Charles Fleetwood, then manager of Drury Lane; immediately he engaged this Richard for his own theatre; and only a few years later Garrick was to find himself in Fleetwood's place, controlling London's Theatre Royal.

All these facts are so well-known as hardly to require or even to

2
David Garrick as Richard III in the tent scene, 1741–42. Oil painting by William Hogarth.

bear repetition, yet an understanding of the playhouse world during this period demands that due attention be paid to several significant aspects of this actor's sudden rise to fame: they may, indeed, be permitted to serve as an introduction to the whole of the mid-eighteenth-century theatre.

THE LONDON PLAYHOUSE WORLD

At the very start, we realise that the records of his career, from its beginning until its close, lead us directly into almost all the various kinds of theatrical activity operative at that period. Even before he made his appearance as an actor at Goodman's Fields he had written his first play, *Lethe*; this 'Dramatic Satire' was first produced at Drury Lane on Tuesday, 15 April 1740 (sixteen months before his success as an actor at Goodman's Fields), and his later long series of writings made him almost as important a dramatist as he was a performer. His fame is most closely associated with the Theatre Royal, Drury Lane, but for two seasons before he became its manager he had also been associated with the rival house at Covent Garden; and thus he had connections with both of those twin 'patent' houses which theoretically alone had the right to present plays in the metropolis. His first introduction to the city's public, moreover, had been at Goodman's Fields, and this fact immediately brings to our notice one of the peculiarities of the eighteenth-century playhouse world.

Just four years previously, in 1737, the famous Licensing Act had sought to ensure that all new dramas should be sent for approval to the Lord Chamberlain and that no other places of entertainment save those provided with formal 'patents' should be allowed to operate. At first, alarmed by the provisions of the Act, the various theatres which did not possess such patents hurriedly shut their doors and for a time hardly anyone dared to make a move. Yet, as we are all well aware, there is scarcely a single piece of legislation which cannot be circumvented by the wit of man; and the re-establishment, in London's East End, of Goodman's Fields was responsible for launching the 'minor' stage on its not inconsiderable career. Barely twelve months before the epoch-making production of *King Richard III*, its manager, Henry Giffard, had reopened the doors so rudely closed in 1737, and he carefully devised that its offerings were advertised in such a way as to maintain a polite fiction: this erstwhile theatre now was no longer a theatre, and the spectators were not really being asked to pay any money at all for the privilege of witnessing the performance of a play. Goodman's Fields was described as 'the late Theatre'; there, said the play-bills, would be given a 'Concert of Vocal and Instrumental Music, divided into two parts. Tickets at three, two, and one shilling.' Payment, then, was specifically for a musical entertainment, but the division of this entertainment into two parts was all-important, since those who cared to buy tickets were informed that between these sections of the concert *The Recruiting Officer*, or *The Constant Couple*, or *All's Well that Ends Well*, or *Hamlet*, or *Richard III* would be 'performed gratis by persons for their diversion'. In first putting himself before a London public, therefore, Garrick was performing in a house which was not only outside the recognised theatrical area but was operating in a manner which was more or less surreptitious.

Paradoxically, his appearance on that stage at once helped to curb for a time the semi-illegal productions and encouraged further developments within the sphere of the minor playhouses. The immediate result of his success was that the authorities, forced to take notice of what was happening at Goodman's Fields, brought pressure to bear on its manager to close his house. By an ironic twist, the actor's triumph there was thus responsible for the theatre's disappearance. More important, however, was the longer-term effect. Giffard had suggested a method by which ingenious persons might wind adroitly round the strict provisions of the law, and Garrick had demonstrated that, if the performances were good, an unlicensed playhouse could reap handsome profits. Others soon sought to follow similar courses. In the spring of 1744, the actor Charles Macklin, having established a kind of informal acting school, announced the performance of several plays by his pupils at the former Little Theatre in the Haymarket—thus, incidentally, bringing the notorious Samuel Foote before the public. Apparently he also was compelled to cease his activities, but the harassed authorities found themselves plagued and perplexed by other diverse schemers. During the following September, Theophilus Cibber, son of the famous Colley Cibber, leased the same theatre in order to introduce his daughter Jenny as a youthful Juliet; this production was followed by several others before the Lord Chamberlain succeeded in bringing the series to a close. A month or so later Theophilus popped up again with the 'concert' device, but this also was suppressed. Another of his attempts to wriggle into the theatrical scene was by means of 'rehearsals' to be given by members of his dramatic 'Academy', while his sister, the erratic Charlotte Charke, had the bright idea of offering to sell pints of ale, with a play thrown in for nothing; she was also responsible for inventing a 'Queen of Hungary's Company of Comedians'. Amid all these sporadic efforts, duly thwarted by the forces of the law, one playhouse, a second theatre at Goodman's Fields, somehow managed to keep its doors open; it seems possible that, while rivalry from a Haymarket close to Drury Lane and Covent Garden stimulated the 'patentees' to put pressure upon the Lord Chamberlain, the rivalry of a theatre in outlying Whitechapel did not seem to call for such urgent action. Whatever the reason, the performances at the 'New

Wells' provided an exception, and its company, headed by members of the Hallam family, were soon to win fame by being the fount from which the first English professional troupe was formed to carry the works of Shakespeare and other dramatists across the Atlantic. Numerous performances of a like kind multiplied in later years, the most important being those organised by Macklin's pupil Samuel Foote, Garrick's intermittent friend and almost constant annoyance. This irrepressible mimic and pin-pricking satirist, after finding that the old 'concert' formula would not work, cleverly devised a novel trick: knowing that the two Theatres Royal were less concerned with matters of principle than with fears of having their profits affected, he invented the matinée and added to this the fiction of inviting his public to a 'tea' or 'chocolate' party. 'This Day at Noon,' he informed the newspaper readers, 'exactly at Twelve o'Clock … Mr. Foote begs the favour of his Friends to come and drink a Dish of Chocolate with him.' The chocolate, of course, was duly charged for, and such entertainment as he chose to offer was, also of course, provided entirely gratuitously. Through these activities Foote occupies a double position in English theatrical history:

3 left
Samuel Foote in *The Diversions of the Morning, or, a Dish of Chocolate,* 1747.

4 right
Ipswich playbill announcing David Garrick's appearance there under the name of Lyddal, 1741.

For the Benefit of
Mr. MARR and Miss HIPPESLEY,
By a Company of Comedians
From the Theatres in LONDON.

At the Playhouse in TANKARD STREET,
On *Tuesday*, the 21st of July.
Will be performed a COMEDY, call'd
The INCONSTANT,
Or, The WAY To WIN HIM.
Young *Mirabel*   by   Mr. GIFFARD,
Captain *Duretête*   by   Mr. LYDDALL,
Bisarre   by   Miss HIPPESLEY,
At the End of the Second Act, a *Pantomine Dance.* call'd
The DRUNKEN PEASANT,
Peasant   by   Mr. YATES,
Clown   by   Mr. VAUGHAM,
To which will be added a New *Dramatic Satire,*
(as it was Performed last Winter at the Theatre in Goodman's Fields,
with great applause), call'd
L E T H E,
Or, ÆSOP in the SHADES,
Æsop   by   Mr. GIFFARD,
Ventrebleu and Sir Roger Rakeit, by Mr. LYDDALL,
Sir Wittling Rattle Mr. MARR, Macboggin Mr. YATES,
Scrape the Attorney Mr. PAGET, Mercury Mrs. DUNSTALL,
Charon Mr. DUNSTALL, Lady Rakeit Mrs. YATES,
Mr. Thomas Mr. CROFTS, Miss Lucy Miss HIPPESLEY,
That Scene being a Sequel to the VIRGIN UNMASKED,
With an Epilogue, by Miss HIPPESLEY,
To begin exactly at SEVEN o'Clock.
Tickets to be had, and Places to be taken, at Mr. ROOK'S,
Opposite to the Theatre.

the 'matinée', which later became so familiar a playhouse occasion, owned its being to him, and the fact that his polite fiction was suffered to endure, ultimately led to his obtaining, in the year 1766, a special summer 'patent' for his Haymarket theatre (plate 3).

These, it may be added, were not the only attempts made to add to London's entertainments. All through the forty years from 1740 to 1780 the citizens of the metropolis were given the opportunity, from time to time, of going elsewhere than to the regular seasonal performances at Drury Lane and Covent Garden. Already in 1761 Foote, associating himself with he dramatist Arthur Murphy, had rented the former theatre for summer shows; there were sporadic productions at Sadler's Wells; open-air presentations of Italian burlettas at Marybone Gardens succeeded in slipping through the net; periodically, 'benefit' performances were advertised at unlicensed playhouses; in 1766 English plays were actually given at the King's Opera House in the Haymarket; and, although they were eventually put out of action, the theatres at the London fairs for long were able to attract their customers.[3]

FIRST APPEARANCES

In considering this aspect of the eighteenth-century theatrical scene, the irony inherent in Garrick's initial appearance at Goodman's Fields must become ever more and more apparent: in fact, after he had assumed the management in 1747, a fair amount of his time and energy was consumed in trying, as best he could, to suppress the activities of those very 'minors' which had offered him the chance of soaring from obscurity to fame and fortune. Not only the appearance, however, attracts our attention; the way in which he was made to appear may also seem peculiar. Yet here it should be borne in mind that, in being announced as an anonymous 'Gentleman' prepared to essay the role of Richard III, he was not in any exceptional position. The announcement was both familiar in form and, in so far as Garrick was concerned, cast in a somewhat dishonest shape. Among the strange conditions of the eighteenth-century stage not least noticeable is the frequent advent of unnamed gentlemen and ladies prepared to essay notable tragic or comic roles, sometimes—although not always—being described in the advertisements as doing so for their own diversion. The device, then, was common; but the manager of the late theatre in Goodman's Fields—perhaps because he thought that it might aid him in maintaining his polite fiction—seems to have had a particular liking for it. On 27 January 1741 the part of Polly in *The Beggar's Opera* was thus taken by a 'Gentlewoman'; on 21 April a 'Gentleman' played Falstaff in *Henry IV*; less than three weeks before Garrick's introduction to the public, Aimwell in George Farquhar's *The Beaux Stratagem* was represented by a 'Gentleman who never appear'd

on any Stage before'; while just five days preceding the production
of *King Richard III* another 'Gentleman' assumed the role of the
Ghost in *Hamlet*. There was, obviously, no novelty here of a kind
likely to attract interest and attention.

We may be reasonably sure that many of such actors and
actresses had, in fact, performed previously elsewhere; and certainly
the statement, 'never appeared on any Stage', was false when
applied to Garrick. Three years earlier, he had come to London
as a wine-merchant, working in partnership with his brother, and
there is ample reason to believe that some of his business troubles
may have been caused or aggravated by the time he spent in seeking
the acquaintanceship of persons engaged in theatrical affairs. The
production of his *Lethe* in 1740 must have brought him into touch
with a number of professional players, and by the beginning of the
following year he must have been talking over his plans with Henry
Giffard, since this manager took him, in the summer, to play, under
the pseudonym of 'Lyddal' or 'Lyddall', in his company at Ipswich
(plate 4). Clearly, therefore, he had spent more than a little time in
self-training before he appeared as Richard in London, and clearly,
too, he had strutted on a stage before his entry upon the boards of
Goodman's Fields.

The fact has particular interest because it associates Garrick with
almost the entire range of the contemporary theatre realm: he began
in a small summer provincial company, he won his first success at
a minor unlicensed house in the east end of London, he acted for a
brief spell at Covent Garden, he soon became manager of Drury
Lane, while later we find that he had connections with the theatre
in Dublin and with those at Bath and Bristol. If we leave out the
King's Opera House in the Haymarket and the various booths at
the fairs, always humble and, in his days, sinking into decline, we
can well say that during the course of his career he touched every
corner of the eighteenth-century stage.

LONDON'S 'PLAY FOLLOWERS'

In noting Garrick's initial triumph, we have to remember that
the Goodman's Fields theatre in which he appeared was a very small
house, with a total capacity of perhaps some 700 persons, and we
may well guess that the spectators fortunate enough to have seen
him on that first exciting night in October 1741 constituted but a
meagre audience. His contemporary biographer observes that,
because 'so many idle persons, under the title of gentlemen acting
for their diversion, had exposed their incapacity at that theatre...,
no very large company was brought together to see the new performer', most of those present being men 'of his own acquaintance'.[4]
This is significant on account of what happened immediately thereafter: by word of mouth mainly, this tiny audience spread the news

of the actor's extraordinary skill, so that, as we have seen, hardly a month had passed before Drury Lane and Covent Garden were suffering from the competition of Goodman's Fields. The inevitable conclusion is that the playgoing public of London in 1741 was relatively small and compact—so small that the drawing-away of a few hundred spectators each night could at once affect the takings at the two 'patent' theatres, and so compact that, without the application of anything like our modern advertising devices, the verbal praises of those lucky few who had witnessed Garrick's performance could lead the whole Town in his direction.

Attempts to assess the scope and qualities of theatrical audiences at various selected periods are always difficult, and sometimes hazardous, but maybe the mid-eighteenth-century auditorium offers material for a clearer picture than many others.[5] About the year 1750 it has been estimated that the population of London, including the areas of Westminster and Southwark, amounted to some 676,000 and that steady increases raised this number to nearly 900,000 at the close of the century.[6] A contemporary author, who, although he preferred to remain anonymous, was in all probability the actor Samual Foote, in penning *A Treatise on the Passions, so far as they regard the Stage* (1747), asserted in his introductory pages that, 'upon the least favourable Calculation, the Number of those called Play-Followers, cannot be rated at less than twelve thousand in this Metropolis';[7] and his figure is more or less corroborated, in general terms, by detailed scrutiny of relevant documentary material. If we are prepared to accept these figures and if we engage in a certain amount of guessing in order to allow for the gradual increase in the population as a whole, perhaps we may be allowed to assume that the 'Play-Followers', those whom we should now style regular play-goers, numbered about 9,000 at the start of the Garrick period, rose to about 12,000 at the time when this actor took over the manage-ment of Drury Lane, and no doubt gradually expanded during the succeeding years. If the calculated population in 1750 is set against the figure of 12,000, this means that the theatres attracted, at that time, some 1·7 per cent of the citizenry. Such an estimated proportion is markedly less than the 13 per cent which has been proposed as the corresponding figure about the year 1605,[8] but maybe it comes near to the truth: obviously the theatres in the middle of the eighteenth century, even although they attracted so much attention in books, pamphlets and newspapers as well as in pictorial representations of scenes and actors, were not so widely 'popular' as were the playhouses around the year 1600.

It is true that the theatre buildings themselves offered accom-modation in their galleries for the poorer sections of the community, and we must suppose that many of these poorer persons, even if they did not or could not afford to attend the whole of an evening's entertainment, flocked in to view the pantomimes and other 'afterpieces' at the hour when admittance might be secured at half the regular charges.[9] At the same time, we shall probably be correct if we regard the theatrical public who witnessed the main tragedies and comedies as consisting, for the most part, of 'persons of quality', reasonably prosperous tradesmen and those belonging to the professional classes: the folk who had less money in their pockets could no doubt obtain more of the value they sought by paying their sixpences at one or other of the outlying places of entertainment. Still further, it may well be supposed, first, that only those members of the upper and middle classes who resided reasonably close to the playhouses formed the core of the 'Play-Followers' and, second, that by no means all whose houses were within easy walking distance of Drury Lane and Covent Garden were regular frequenters of those buildings. Theatrical affairs were quite clearly matters of prime interest to a central group in London, yet that central group was in fact rather strictly limited.

Bearing this in mind, it is easy to imagine how rapidly, like a fire on a laid train, theatrical news could be carried through the relatively small body of 'Play-Followers' by word of mouth: one hundred or two hundred excited spectators at Goodman's Fields could readily draw crowds into Whitechapel. The smallness and compactness of the audience during the Garrick period must ever serve as the basis for any imaginative reconstruction of the Georgian theatre world.

THE 'NATURAL' STYLE

The excitement experienced by the first tiny audience at Goodman's Fields and by the thousands who later were privileged to witness Garrick's interpretation of diverse roles, both tragic and comic, had, as it were, a double force. Fundamentally, the spectators, from the beginning of his career to its close, associated him with the concept of 'Nature', but what they precisely felt has to be examined carefully. In our own days a new actor or actress may suddenly create a stir; but spectators in general will think of the performer simply as an individual artist whose personality and skill, in voice, movement, gesture, imaginative power of character projection, will be the dominant object of attention. So far as Garrick's reception was concerned, however, there was more than that. Assuredly he made his impact as an individual, but the excitement was largely generated by something else, by something, in fact, which was intimately related to the whole of the period's culture. The eighteenth century, in life, painting, music and literature, was dominated and enriched by ideas of taste and style; and those who watched Garrick derived their pleasure not only from appreciating the skill of the performer but also from recognising that his entire approach was founded on a style which, quite apart from his own excellence, could be savoured and defined in and for itself.

Perhaps the best way of coming to an understanding of what he meant to these spectators is to put ourselves in the company, not of an experienced theatre-goer, but in that of an eighteenth-century youth who was making one of his earliest entries into the auditorium. By doing so we, as strangers to the time, may thus more readily grasp the essentials than we would if we had accompanied a man better versed and more expert. The youth of our choice is Richard Cumberland, later to become one of the most prominent dramatists of his age, but, in the year 1746, as yet merely an eager sixth-form boy at Westminster School. On 14 November he found his way into a front gallery seat at Covent Garden when a new production of Nicholas Rowe's *The Fair Penitent* was being presented with the veteran actor James Quin as Horatio, Mrs Cibber in the heroine's role and the youthful David Garrick as Lothario. Looking back on that occasion, Cumberland tells us that Quin

> presented himself upon the rising of the curtain in a green velvet coat embroidered down the seams, an enormous full bottomed periwig, rolled stockings and high-heeled, square-toed shoes: with very little variation of cadence, and in a deep full tone, accompanied by a sawing kind of action, which had more of the senate than of the stage in it, he rolled out his heroics with an air of dignified indifference, that seemed to disdain the plaudits, that were bestowed upon him. Mrs Cibber in a key high-pitched but sweet withal, sung or rather recitatived Rowe's harmonious strain, something in the manner of the improvisatores: it was so extremely wanting in contrast, that, though it did not wound the ear, it wearied it; when she had once recited two or three speeches, I could anticipate the manner of every succeeding one: it was like a long old legendary ballad of innumerable stanzas, every one of which is sung to the same tune, eternally chiming in the ear without variation or relief.

And then something unexpected happened. There came the moment of Garrick's entry—'little Garrick', Cumberland calls him, 'young and light and alive in every muscle and feature'—and in a moment,

> heavens, what a transition!—it seemed as if a whole century had been stept over in the transition of a single scene: old things were done away, and a new order at once brought forward, bright and luminous, and clearly destined to dispel the barbarisms and bigotry of a tasteless age, too long attached to the prejudices of custom, and superstitiously devoted to the illusions of imposing declamation.[10]

Such, no doubt, would have been our sentiments too, had we also been watching the scene from the Covent Garden gallery— although, in making this acknowledgment, we must be on our guard. The early eighteenth century was by no means the 'tasteless age' which Cumberland imagined it to have been: its culture was likewise based on a consciousness of style. By the 'forties, however, the time had arrived for a change, and what once had been applauded as grace was now being castigated as barbarism; yet

5 opposite page
David Garrick as Richard III. Oil painting by Francis Hayman, dated 1700.

barbarism it was not, and, as Cumberland's words indicate, there were still men who regarded it with approval. The excited boy had praise only for Garrick, but Quin still received a fair share of the evening's acclamation: both men had their own particular personal abilities, and to a large degree the basic difference between them was a difference in style.

In exploiting the new style, which contemporaries defined in terms of 'Nature', Garrick wrought a transformation: that is certain. At the same time it has to be recognised that actually his success arose from the fact that he simply gave the age what it wanted (plates 5, 6 and 7). For a number of years before his advent various potent attacks had been directed against the conventional and rhetorical method of interpretation which, once fresh, was so rapidly losing its power and appeal.[11] One diligent dramatist and would-be trainer of actors, Aaron Hill, had for at least a decade previously been seeking to establish a fresh basis for the histrionic art, setting forth a system of interpretation which he based on four fundamental principles. First, he declared, 'The imagination must conceive a *strong idea* of the passion'; but, secondly, 'that idea cannot *strongly* be conceived, without impressing its own form upon the muscles of the *face*'; nor, thirdly, '*can* the look be muscularly stamp'd, without communicating, instantly, the same

6 left
David Garrick as Abel Drugger in *The Alchemist*. Water colour by J. Roberts.

7 right
David Garrick as Sir John Brute. Water colour by J. Roberts.

impression, to the muscles of the *body*'; so that, finally, 'The muscles of the body, (brac'd, or slack, as the idea was an active or a passive one) must, in their natural, and not to be avoided consequence, by impelling or retarding the flow of animal spirits, transmit their own conceiv'd sensation, to the sound of the *voice*, and to the disposition of the *gesture*.'[12] This meant, of course, that, instead of putting stress on the words, the actor should start with the concept of character. Particularly significant is the emphasis which he places on the force of muscular reactions: the performer, he insists, who wishes to convey a passion ought to start from the bodily expression of that passion: if an actor begins by looking like hate, he will begin to feel like hate, the muscular movement stimulating the imagination.

Aaron Hill by no means stood alone as a theorist pleading for a fresh approach, and concurrently several performers were beginning to feel their way towards the new conception. Only eight months before Garrick's appearance as Richard, for example,

8
Charles Macklin as Shylock. Oil painting by J. Zoffany.

Charles Macklin had won sudden fame for his novel and vigorous treatment of Shylock (plate 8); and Sir John Hill's account of the way in which this actor trained his young pupils recalls in its wording Cumberland's contrast between the methods of Quin and Garrick:

> It was his manner to check all the cant and cadence of tragedy; he would bid his pupil first speak the passage as he would in common life, if he had occasion to pronounce the same words; and then giving them more force, but preserving the same accent, to deliver them on the stage. Where the player was faulty in his stops or accents, he set him right; and with nothing more than this attention to what was natural, he produced out of the most ignorant persons, players that surprized everybody.[13]

We may, therefore, best see Garrick as sweeping to popularity on the crest of a great wave which had slowly been gathering force during the immediately previous decade. Still further, we probably ought to recognise that, although contemporaries acclaimed his method as 'natural', it might not seem so natural to us. In looking at the numerous paintings and prints depicting him in his several parts, we begin to realise that an imaginative conception of his acting may most effectively come from placing him within the realm proper to himself: his style was assuredly 'natural', but, turning the phrase, we shall go wrong if we do not admit that it was natural in the style of the eighteenth century. Unquestionably he gave his audiences the illusion of reality; he invested his lines with passionate delivery; and he possessed, to a supreme degree, the ability to move from emotion to emotion with supple ease and rapidity. 'His great aim,' declared *The Gentleman's Magazine*[14] at the time of his retirement, 'in all his performances was to follow *Nature*'; and numerous contemporaries indicate that by this word 'Nature' they had particularly in mind the actor's expressive face and eyes, the speech variety he so imperiously commanded, the speed with which he passed from passion to passion, and the way he immersed himself in the character he was portraying. As Richard III (see plates 2 and 5), for example,

> His soliloquy in the tent scene discovered the inward man. Everything he described was almost reality; the spectator thought he heard the hum of either army from camp to camp.—When he started from his dream, he was a spectacle of horror: He called out in a manly tone,
>   'Give me another horse;'
> He paused, and, with a countenance of dismay, advanced, crying out in a tone of distress,
>   'Bind up my wounds,'
> and then falling on his knees, said in a most piteous accent,
>   'Have mercy heaven.'
> In all this, the audience saw an exact imitation of *nature*.[15]

They certainly *thought* they saw an exact imitation of nature, but we may be sure that, were we now able to witness a Garrick performance, we should have been highly conscious of the conventional gestures, part of the equipment of his age, which he employed. Macklin and he were revolutionaries, but they were revolutionaries within the scope of the century's decorum.

THE SHAKESPEARE VOGUE

If we had been enabled to interview members of his audiences in a free association test, 'Nature' would have been undoubtedly the first reaction to the naming of 'Garrick'. If we had been able to continue the test, asking for a second reaction, almost certainly the word 'Shakespeare' would have come to our ears—and here again caution is demanded.

Without any possibility of doubt, Garrick was a Shakespeare lover. Quite apart from the fact that his greatest roles were heroes from the tragedies and histories—Richard III, Hamlet, Macbeth, Lear—he sought always to keep his repertory rich in plays by the Elizabethan master. The name of Shakespeare was constantly on his lips, and the delight he took in organising the ill-fated Jubilee at Stratford-upon-Avon in 1769 was inspired by a deep-felt emotion (plates 9, 10 and 11). The story of this Jubilee has been told so many times that no detailed account of its episodes needs to be given here.[16] We all have heard about the trouble it caused him, about the torrential rains which ruined his best effects, about the ridicule which was meted out to him by envious enemies. What we must remember, on the other hand, is that this Jubilee was, for its time, an extraordinary creation and that its impress proved truly international: in France and Germany it became the very symbol of romantic philosophy, giving 'substance to the vision of the Poet as creator, prophet and national hero'.[17] That it resulted in considerable financial loss is true, although Garrick himself, with his customary humorous ebullience, restored his credit by the amazing success with which his little afterpiece, *The Jubilee*, including the

9
David Garrick as Steward of the Shakespeare Jubilee at Stratford-upon-Avon, 1769.

10
The Shakespeare Jubilee, Stratford-upon-Avon, 1769: (*left*) procession of characters outside Shakespeare's Birthplace; and (*right*) ticket for the Oratorio and Ode.

picturesque procession of Shakespearian characters, was greeted the following season at Drury Lane (plates 12 and 13). What matters in the end, however, is its image and not its execution: no doubt we may find amusement in reading cynically caustic accounts of what happened at Stratford; but the fact remains that Garrick, in this his pet venture, was expressing the spirit of his time.

We may, of course, if we are not careful, run into danger here. We can allow ourselves to be led into the trap of assuming that, often in spite of adverse criticism, he himself was solely responsible for establishing the Shakespeare vogue. The real truth is that, just as with his 'natural' style of acting, he was rather the inspired consolidator than the lonely inventor. In so far as the popularity of Shakespeare is concerned, if we want to find a prime innovating force we have only to go back a few years, to the theatrical season of 1736–37, and observe the activities of a group of 'Ladies of Quality' who, banding themselves into a 'Shakespeare's Club', persuaded the managements of Drury Lane and Covent Garden to engage in a significant series of Shakespearian revivals.[18] Not only were several interesting productions resultant from their efforts, contemporaries freely acknowledged their force and heartily congratulated them. Typical is a comment in *The Grub Street Journal* for 3 March 1737: ''Tis a great Pleasure for us to hear, that the Ladies begin to encourage Common Sense; which makes us in hopes that the Gentlemen will follow their Example.' And apparently the gentlemen, given their partners' lead, were prepared to support the appeal; not only

11
The processions arranged for the Shakespeare Jubilee, 1769.
The chief characters shown are Mrs Ford, Falstaff, Pistol, the Witches, Hecate, Aguecheek, Caliban, Richard III, Edgar, Hamlet's Ghost, the Gravedigger, Friar Lawrence, the Apothecary, Shylock, Henry VIII and Wolsey.

12 opposite page, above
David Garrick reciting the Ode at the Shakespeare Jubilee, 1769. He repeated this at Drury Lane (see plate 13).

13 opposite page, below
The stage of Drury Lane, 1769: 'Mr. Garrick delivering his Ode'.

did the series of revivals continue during the succeeding seasons, there soon came, as a further offshoot of their endeavours, the idea of raising a fund for the erection of a Shakespeare Monument in Westminster Abbey. Symbolically, that monument was set up in the very year when Garrick first appeared at Goodman's Fields.

Nor were the ladies of the Shakespeare Club simply a set of lonely enthusiasts: when we look at the printing of Shakespeare's plays during those years we realise that the publishers were well aware of a general public interest. Up to the close of the seventeenth century most of these plays could be read only in bulky folio form; and a folio, apart from being expensive, is not the easiest kind of volume to balance on one's knees. The first decade of the following century had not closed before something new, still dignified but much more manageable, made its appearance in Nicholas Rowe's ten-volume octavo edition, with its series of pictorial illustrations—and this was followed by numerous other similar collections from that edited by Alexander Pope onwards.[19] Even these octavo editions, however, remained expensive, and a further move towards a 'popular' Shakespeare was effected when, in 1714, Rowe's text was re-issued in nine smaller (duodecimo) volumes. Still another mighty change came when some publishers had the bright idea of printing the dramas separately as cheap booklets—in fact, providing their readers with the eighteenth century's equivalent of today's ubiquitous 'pocket books'. From the earlier years, for instance, we can pick up a *Hamlet*, 'As it is now Acted by his Majesty's Servants', printed by J. Darby for A. Bettesworth and F. Clay in 1725, or an *Othello, The Moor of Venice*, with its simple imprint 'LONDON, Printed for the Company' without a date, which we now know to have been set up in The Hague by T. Johnson and imported into England. Obviously, a need was being met. Then, in the middle of the seventeen-thirties came the culmination of this movement: two publishers, Andrew Walker and Jacob Tonson, competitively vied with each other in producing the texts at ever decreasing prices: fourpence a play soon was lowered to a penny.

Thus were Shakespeare's dramas brought before a widening public, and that public became anxious to see the printed texts interpreted in stage form. By 1740 Shakespeare had become essentially a popular dramatist: to realise how popular, indeed, we require to do no more than glance at Drury Lane's offerings during the very months when Garrick was attracting so much attention at Goodman's Fields. From its seasonal opening on 1 October until the end of December, audiences at the Theatre Royal could have seen *Macbeth*, the first part of *Henry IV, As You Like It, Othello, The Merchant of Venice, The Comedy of Errors, Julius Cæsar, Hamlet* and *Richard III*—no mean Shakespearian repertory within the space of three months. Instead of assuming that the vogue was due to Garrick, we may rather say that Shakespeare's popularity never seriously declined in the English theatre, that a definite upsurge in this popularity became obvious during the thirties of the eighteenth century, and that Garrick's enthusiastic activities were its appropriate culmination.

NOTES TO CHAPTER ONE

[1] *The Letters of David Garrick*, edited by David M. Little and George M. Kahrl (1963), vol. i, p. 28.

[2] Id. vol. i, pp. 30 and 32.

[3] The relevant volumes of *The London Stage* amply illustrate and statistically record the diverse theatrical activities of those years, while the introductions to Parts III and IV, written by A. H. Scouten and G. W. Stone Jr. respectively, provide excellent general surveys. Sybil Rosenfeld admirably deals with *The Theatre of the London Fairs* (1960).

[4] Thomas Davies, *The Life of David Garrick* (new edition, 1808), vol. i, p. 39

[5] H. W. Pedicord, in *The Theatrical Public in the Time of Garrick* (1954), has carefully surveyed the evidence, and his conclusions may be accepted as coming as near to the truth as is now possible. The figures given in the text are largely based on his findings.

[6] M. D. George, *London Life in the Eighteenth Century* (1925), pp. 24–38.

[7] Sig. A2.

[8] Alfred Harbage, *Shakespeare's Audience* (1941), pp. 40–1.

[9] See page 90.

[10] Richard Cumberland, *Memoirs* (1806), pp. 59–60.

[11] Lily B. Campbell, in 'The Rise of a Theory of Stage Presentation in England during the Eighteenth Century', *PMLA*, xxxii, 1917, pp. 163–200, ably and concisely surveys theories of acting from the end of the seventeenth century to the development of the 'Grand Style' at the close of the eighteenth, relating these to various forces operating in the realms of poetry and pictorial art. A later informative essay is Alan S. Downer's 'Nature to Advantage Dressed: Eighteenth-Century Acting', *PMLA*, lviii, 1943, pp. 1002–37. See also the excellent summary by G. W. Stone Jr. in *The London Stage*, IV, i, 1961, pp. xcii–xciii.

[12] Aaron Hill, 'An Essay on the Art of Acting', in his *Works* (1755), vol. iii, p. 356. Already in *The Prompter* (1734–6), he had developed these arguments more fully, both in general and particular terms.

[13] Sir John Hill, *The Actor* (revised edition, 1755), pp. 239–40. As far back as 1725, apparently, Macklin had attempted to introduce the more 'natural' style, but the age was at that time not yet ready to accept it.

[14] xlvi, 1776, p. 304.

[15] Arthur Murphy, *Life of David Garrick* vol. i (1801), p. 23. For Garrick's acting style see *The Revels History of Drama in English* ed. Clifford Leech and T. W. Craik, vol. VI Pt ii by Frederick and Lise-Lone Marker pp. 96–106.

[16] Martha Winburn England, *Garrick and Stratford* (1962), Christian Deelman, *The Great Shakespeare Jubilee* (1964), Johanne M. Stochholm, *Garrick's Folly* (1964).

[17] Martha Winburn England, 'Garrick's Stratford Jubilee', *Shakespeare Survey*, ix, 1956, pp. 90–100.

[18] The fullest account of the work achieved by the 'Ladies of Shakespear's Club' or 'The Ladies Subscription' is that given by Emmett L. Avery in *Shakespeare Quarterly*, vii, 1956, pp. 153–8.

[19] Arthur Brown, 'The Great Variety of Readers', *Shakespeare Survey*, xviii, 1965, pp. 11–21 provides an excellent general account of the changing styles in the printing of the plays. See also Giles E. Dawson, 'Robert Walker's Editions of Shakespeare' in *Studies in the English Renaissance Drama*, ed. J. W. Bennett, O. Cargill and V. Hall Jr. (1959), pp. 58–81, and 'Three Shakespeare Piracies in the Eighteenth Century', *Papers of the Bibliographical Society of the University of Virginia*, i. 1948–49, pp. 49–58.

The idea of the mid-eighteenth-century theatre   2

In all aspects of playhouse ventures within the forty years from 1740 to 1780 a combination of past and present, similar to that we have seen in the last chapter, is clearly evident—not least so, perhaps, in the structures of those theatres with which Garrick was most closely associated. When he moved from Goodman's Fields to Drury Lane, he stepped into a house which, apart from relatively minor alterations and occasional redecoration, continued to remain much as it had done at the start of his career. The interior structure of the old playhouse, indeed, vanished only a few months before his retirement in 1776. The architect of the Theatre Royal had been Sir Christopher Wren; the redesigning of the auditorium and the stage front was executed by Robert Adam. Thus Garrick had been content to perform, throughout almost his entire active life, in a theatre belonging basically to the reign of King Charles II, while towards the very close of his management he was responsible for opening another playhouse which, even although its earlier plan remained unchanged, was prophetic of things to come.

This may be taken as a kind of symbol of these forty years, and with Garrick's guidance we may now start a journey, front-stage and back-stage, into the Georgian playhouse realm.

In approaching this and in seeking to grasp its inherent characteristic quality, one thing is essential: we must banish entirely from our vocabulary the word 'apron'.

At first glance such a statement may appear absolutely absurd. Does not this playhouse, we may ask, differ from the nineteenth-century theatre precisely because it included in its architectural form an 'apron' or 'forestage' which jutted out from the curtain line well into the auditorium? Even slight reflection, however, will serve to persuade us that the very question itself is likely to lead us astray. The term 'apron', used in a theatrical sense, is purely modern; so far as we can tell, it did not come into familiar parlance until about the year 1900; and, when we examine its use at that time, we realise that it was a term invented to describe a deviation from what was then regarded as the playhouse norm—a structure composed of two basic parts, one reserved for the audience and the other for the actors, two virtually separate worlds divided almost literally by an iron curtain, with a solid and substantial framework marking off the stage from the area in which the spectators were seated. During the nineteenth century this had come to be generally accepted as the common theatre plan, and only a few odd eccentrics paused to consider other possibilities. Men knew about the ancient Greek stage, of course, but these vast open-air structures were so distant in time and so utterly unlike the contemporary indoor theatres in form that the two could hardly be brought into mental conjunction. Only towards the close of the century did something fresh come into being, partly—indeed perhaps largely—inspired by the discovery in 1888 of the famous sketch of the Swan playhouse, when a little group of scholars and theatre-men began to interest themselves in earlier and almost forgotten theatre forms, from the stage for which Shakespeare had penned his plays on to Garrick's Drury Lane. In these, they discovered, no curtain formally separated the spectators from the performers, and under the enthusiastic direction of William Poel they proceeded to experiment in the production of early plays on open stages. The Elizabethan Swan and Globe were so entirely distinct in concept from the ordinary Lyceums and Drury Lanes of their own time, that no real difficulty arose in the pursuit of their historical reconstructions; but the eighteenth-century playhouse presented a problem since obviously its form had a distinct and direct connection with the later familiar playhouse structures: Garrick's Drury Lane did have a curtain and it did have scenery— and yet existing prints showed that its stage jutted out towards the audience.

Dominated by the image of the bi-partite theatre of their own times, these men, who were prepared to think of the Elizabethan playhouse in its own terms, hence tended to regard the eighteenth-century forestage as an archaic anomaly, they inclined to regard the forestage itself as something strung on to the playhouse model with which they were familiar, and hence the term 'apron' was invented to describe it: by simply taking off the apron, the Drury Lane of 1750 could be seen, properly dressed, as a theatre akin to the Drury Lane of 1890. Even those few who dimly saw a connection between the forestage and the open stage of the Elizabethan period were inclined, subconsciously, to regard it as part of a primitive theatre structure which, in the style of Darwin's theory of evolution, was in the process of developing into a higher form.

This procedure was, no doubt, eminently understandable and excusable; but for our purposes it is basically wrong; instead of leading us to approach the eighteenth-century playhouse in and for itself, it induces us to move towards the age of Garrick from the viewpoint of the Victorian era. For the moment, therefore, we have to forget what happened during the nineteenth century in a free endeavour to accept Garrick's stage as his contemporaries saw it; they obviously could not anticipate what was to develop in later years, and not one of them had any notion of how this theatre of theirs had been shaped out of previously invented models: consequently, like their descendants a hundred years later, they simply accepted the fact before them, with little or no desire to introduce changes and modifications.

Here it is imperative that we should remember three things. The first is that, although the theatre manifestly flourished during the four decades from 1740 to 1780, there was virtually no new playhouse built in London during those years. This leads to a complementary second observation, that, with the partial exception of the King's Opera House in the Haymarket, the various theatres used by Garrick and his companions were all designed according to one single established plan. And, finally, to these facts must be added a third—that such theatres as were constructed outside of London within the period all followed the same pattern.

A brief comparison with two preceding ages may help to emphasise what all of this implies. If we cast our minds back to the forty years from 1600 to 1640, for instance, we can be in no doubt but that the chief theatrical interest of that period rests in its variety: characteristically, the chief acting company, the King's Men to which Shakespeare belonged, operated two entirely different houses, the open-air Globe and the indoor Blackfriars;[1] at court Inigo Jones was experimenting with perspective scenery, and soon even the professional players were at least toying with similar devices. Were we at present seeking to explore the playhouse of the Jacobean and Caroline periods, therefore, it would clearly be our business to examine and to stress the diversity of models which it embraced. From those forty years, we may next turn to a second set of four decades, from 1660 to 1700. Here something different confronts us. Although the resumption of acting immediately after the Restoration meant that the players for a time were forced to make use of whatever accommodation they could secure—a disused tennis-court hastily equipped with a stage or an old open-air structure which had escaped complete destruction at the hands of the Puritans—it is quite obvious that the age was intent upon securing uniformity rather than in practicising variety: it was, indeed, during this time that the theatrical model so unquestioningly accepted in the mid-eighteenth century was developed and set up as an established form.

The years 1740–80, accordingly, differ from both of these earlier ages—from the Jacobean and Caroline in rejecting diversity, and from the period of King Charles II in simply accepting what had previously been invented. Hence we are confronted here by a peculiar paradox: the very lack of divergence, the very absence of experimental designing, gives to the theatres of 1740–80 their peculiar interest and quality. Although it goes without saying that, in scrutinising plans and interior views of the various playhouses operative during the Garrick period, our eyes should be alert constantly to note particular variations, however slight, the acceptance and persistence of the prevailing model ought certainly to be the chief guiding image in our minds.

This being so, our best plan, at the start, will be to ignore the individual houses—Drury Lane and Covent Garden and Goodman's Fields—where the examination of incidentals might distract and probably confuse us: instead, we may profit most by imagining ourselves taken by a knowledgeable guide to *any* of the larger theatres, looking at it as though it were a model or mould for all the others.

It will, no doubt, assist us if, before our actual visit to this playhouse, we glance briefly at a very simple ideal plan. Let us suppose that the theatre of our choice is about 120 feet long by some 50 feet wide, and, further, let us suppose that, in entering it, we decide to go in by the ordinary front doors, selecting an hour when no performance is impending. Our guide will probably take us along an alley-way leading off a main street, with houses, inns and pawnshops at its sides; and, on reaching the end of the theatre building, he will direct us to a small doorway beyond which is a small vestibule containing a tiny cubicle for the use of the ticket-seller. Past this, he will lead us along a tortuous, dark and uninviting tunnel which slopes downwards until at its end it suddenly makes a sharp right-hand turn, revealing a few steps with light beyond. We ascend these steps and find ourselves in a kind of well—and indeed it *was* then named the 'well'—at the front of the stage.[2]

THE 'HOUSE'

Here we turn round to look first at the accommodation provided for the spectators, at what was familiarly known as the 'house'.[3]

Together with a contracted vestibule at the entrance end of the structure, it obviously takes up about half the total length of the theatre-building as a whole. As we stand at the side of the well we see the pit immediately before us, an area shaped in an elongated U-form, heavily raked and provided with some nine or ten or a dozen backless benches. What particularly excites our interest is the fact that this part of the 'house' does not proceed backwards under a superimposed gallery, as was the usual practice in the nineteenth century and as it frequently appears even in some of our latest theatre plans: rising on its inclined floor so that its rear is almost on a level with the stage, it is bounded all round by a wooden palisade which forms the front of a curving row of boxes so constructed that the seats in those boxes which face the stage are set only a foot or so above the rearmost bench in the pit.[4] The result of this arrangement, of course, is that, although separated in one sense, the pit and the lower row of boxes combine to form one single unit: the spectators seated in that rearmost pit bench could easily greet and talk to their friends in the boxes behind them. (See plate 36.)

The boxes opposite to, and directly facing, the stage are called, as our informant tells us, the 'front' boxes; and we observe that, instead of being small, compact, cosy and self-contained, they are relatively large, each equipped with several benches capable of accommodating some twenty persons, or more. We notice, also, that these 'front' boxes are continued, as 'side' boxes, along the walls of the house so that they serve to enclose the pit in its elongated U-form. Later, there will be an opportunity for us to see that some other individual playhouses modify this arrangement by inclining the side-boxes in the shape of a magnet or horseshoe, or of a fan, without, however, changing essentially or modifying the principle exhibited in the particular typical theatre which for the moment we are engaged in examining.

Our gaze now travels upwards. Above the lower tier of boxes comes another tier of upper side-boxes, and over the front-boxes is a 'middle' gallery, in which sets of curving benches form what was familiarly called an 'amphitheatre'. Looking still higher up towards the ceiling, our eyes finally come to rest on a similarly shaped upper gallery which extends itself along the walls of the house in two open balconies. Our informant explains that these balconies are named the 'slips' and that in some playhouses they are divided into sections called 'green boxes' in London and, in Dublin, 'lattices'.[5]

In gazing round at all these basic features of the auditorium, no doubt our eyes would also have been attracted towards their rich decoration, and we should have been tempted more closely to examine some details, such as the sconces and branches for the candles; but since our immediate object is to concentrate upon the essential structural elements in the building, we may wisely decide to leave the details for further scrutiny later and to proceed now to look at the other main parts of the playhouse.

BACK-STAGE AND THE 'SCENE'

Instead of asking us to turn round and mount the stage, our guide advises us that it will be more profitable for us to retrace our steps along the gloomy pit passage. Once we have come back to the entrance door from which we had started our tour, he conducts us round the whole building to a stage-door at its opposite end. Here he brings us into an area, extending from side-wall to side-wall and perhaps some 25 feet deep, honeycombed with dressing-rooms, storage rooms, offices and the inevitable greenroom with, in their midst, a long open hall-like space leading from the rear wall of the theatre up towards the stage. Through this space our guide directs our steps, threading his way past and around various items of theatrical paraphernalia—bits of scenery, property chairs and tables and thrones, suits of armour, spears and targes. A few candles have been kindled for our visit, and by their glimmering light we grope onto a raked stage, which, from the inner end of the hall-like space up to the curtain, is some 40-odd feet wide and about 15 feet deep. As we stand thus, and as our eyes become accustomed to the gloom, we realise that this area is set with three pairs of wings backed by a large pair of shutters. The shutters are cut out to form a kind of archway, and the guide explains that, while they might well have been one unbroken flat, terminating the vista, for this particular scene they are so constructed in profile or 'relief' as to permit the audience to look beyond them into the hall-like space at their rear, where suitable backings will be set up to give an impression of depth.

Once more, we might be inclined to linger here in order to examine the scenic apparatus more minutely, but again, as in the auditorium, we decide to confine ourselves to essentials. Until a later opportunity arises for a visit back-stage, we leave over our scrutiny of the wings and shutters, the machines and the lighting fixtures. Instead of pausing here, we step over to the curtain and ask if it can be raised.

THE PLATFORM

One of the stage-hands obligingly causes it to ascend—and suddenly we realise to the full why the word 'apron', and even the word 'forestage', is utterly inadequate when applied to this playhouse. The term 'apron' suggests a fairly shallow extension of the stage beyond the curtain-line; but here, as we move forwards, we find ourselves standing upon an acting-area as wide as the auditorium and fully as deep as the space reserved for the scenery. At once we understand why our guide has been calling the area behind the curtain the 'scene' and using the word 'platform' to apply to the area in front of the curtain; and, thinking of Garrick's theatre in this way, we recognise clearly that, while the Victorian playhouse was fundamentally bi-partite, the only way of appreciating the mid-eighteenth-century playhouse is to think of it in terms of three parts, the 'house', the 'scene' and the 'platform', or stage proper.

In identifying the platform with the stage, however, we must observe that it has in fact a double function. Clearly it is designed for forward movement on the part of the actors; but it is also designed for a corresponding forward movement, in an opposite direction, on the part of the spectators—the two groups, as it were, meeting in the one location. Glancing round, we see in a moment how this is effected. If we place ourselves midway between the curtain-line and the further edge of the platform, we note that a firm separation between players and pittites is established by two means: first, there is a long trough containing a batten of footlight lamps

14
A proscenium door from the Stamford Theatre, Lincolnshire.

extending from side to side, and, secondly, at each front edge of the stage are set up two ornamental spiked railings somewhat similar to those which still may be seen at the corners of old-fashioned London basement areas: in some theatres, indeed, we shall find that the rows of spikes are carried on along the whole front of the stage, thus making the separation even more emphatic. When these lamps and spikes are taken in conjunction with the space in the pit-well which has been palisaded off for the use of the musicians in the orchestra, it seems at first as though an absolutely clear line of demarcation has been drawn between audience and actors.

Then we turn round to look at the sides of the platform. Starting from the curtain-line, we see that what has come to be styled the 'proscenium arch' is here a relatively flimsy affair, and not the deep, three-dimensional, heavily-moulded structure so common in many contemporary continental theatres. When Robert Adam in 1775 designed a new frame for Drury Lane (plate 15), he lettered his

15
Design by Robert Adam for the frontispiece or proscenium frame of Drury Lane, 1775.

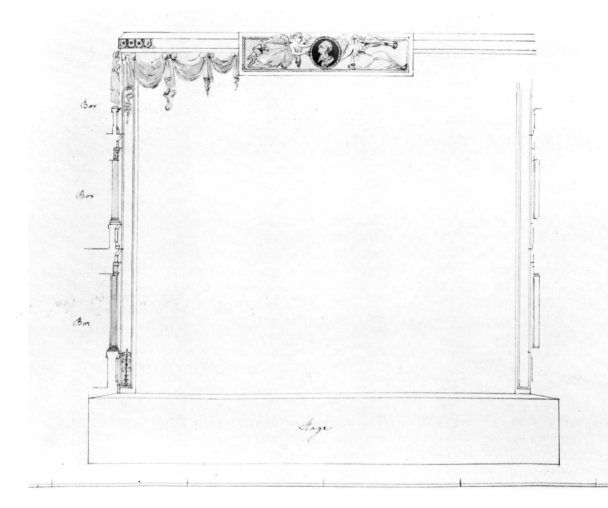

sketch 'Front of the Stage which covers the front Curtain and is never changed'—and that indeed is what it is, not a structural part of the building, but rather the foremost piece of scenery, masking what lies beyond it and separating the platform from the scene. Moreover, immediately in front of this frame, at each side are set two substantial stage-doors, fitted with handles and knockers and we hardly need any guide to inform us that through these the actors made most of their entrances and exits (plate 14): it was on the platform that normally they delivered their lines and carried out the business of the play.

Casting our eyes still further forward, we see that at each side the stage-doors are flanked by stage-boxes, their floors at stage level or little higher; while above them come upper stage-boxes: the former carry on to the platform the lines of the side-boxes in the house, and the latter continue on from the middle tier. We realise that, when these are occupied during the performance, members of the audience thus have, as it were, mounted the stage, where the players have stepped forward to join them (plates 16 and 17).[6] As the century advanced, there was no doubt a slow, tentative mov-

16 left
The intimacy between the performer and the audience in the boxes. Undated, anonymous eighteenth-century engraving. Note should be taken of the stage-door beyond the boxes.

17 right
'John Bull at the Italian Opera', coloured engraving by Thomas Rowlandson, published 1805 and 1811.

ing back of the action, largely due, as we shall see, to the introduction of improved methods of lighting; but up to the very end of this period the platform was the preferred location for the majority of scenes, and actors rejoiced in the opportunities provided by the doors for effective stage entrances and climactic exits.

THE TRI-PARTITE PLAYHOUSE

Full and proper appreciation of the impression produced upon the spectators in this tri-partite house of entertainment demands from us free use of the imagination, especially in view of the facts that, during this age, we have extraordinarily few representations of theatrical interiors and that most of those which have come down to us may well have the effect of leading us astray. One such illustration may serve as an example. Two prints depicting the notorious 'Fitzgiggo' riots at Covent Garden have frequently been reproduced (one here, plate 18); indeed, it may be said with some assurance that on these our image of the mid-eighteenth-century theatre has mainly been based. Certainly they might well appear to be faithful pictures of what we should have seen had we been present in the playhouse during those rowdy demonstrations in 1763. They show clearly the front platform over which the

18
The interior of Covent Garden Theatre, 1763 during the 'Fitzgiggo' riot.

rioters are clambering, the stage-boxes and the actors' entrance doors, the framework separating the platform from the scene, the wings and the back-shutters behind. It is only when we consider them more carefully that we detect a basic error in the engravings. The artist has drawn no distinction between what lies beyond the curtain-line and what comes in front: instead, we are shown a single stage area which extends from the orchestra well backwards to the last piece of scenery. The pictorial element lacking here becomes immediately apparent if we turn to a hitherto unknown little oil-painting of the same playhouse (plate 19). This picture has assuredly not been executed by a master in his art, but its very simplicity may well lead us to believe that it suggests, much more plainly than a master's work might have done, what would have met our eyes had we been spectators of the performance of *Macbeth* which is depicted in action. More will have to be said about this little painting later; but for our present purpose its essential features must briefly be noted here. The appearance of the

19
Performance of *Macbeth* at Covent Garden about 1765.

Witches to Macbeth and Banquo takes place well in front, thus
emphasising that the erroneously-styled 'apron' is in fact the main
stage; and, even more significantly, the artist has successfully
attempted to indicate a patent difference between the visual values
of what is taking place on the platform and what lies beyond the
curtain-line. Whereas the actors are clearly visible, the setting of
mountain and moor behind them remains dim and indistinct. The
platform and the scene may have appeared to contemporary spectators to be a single unit of the kind shown in the 'Fitzgiggo' engravings; but actually they remained fundamentally distinct areas. The
artist, of course, has omitted a view of the 'house', but, if we imaginatively add this 'house' to what he has drawn, the tri-partite form
of Garrick's playhouse comes forcibly before us.

That the conclusions drawn from consideration of the small
anonymous painting of Covent Garden are not false or misleading
seems proved by examination of another much larger canvas which
also has only recently come to light (see *frontispiece*). This is a satirical picture entitled 'The Downfall of Shakespeare on the Modern
Stage', painted by Philip Dawes and exhibited at the Free Society
of Artists in 1765. Although it does not profess to depict exactly
any particular theatre, there are ample indications that Covent
Garden was in the artist's mind. Certainly, in the interests of his
design and of its content, he has foreshortened the platform, omitting the stage-doors entirely, but despite this the general impression
is the same as that in the smaller painting discussed above. The performers are carrying on their business at the very edge of the platform, with spectators seated and standing at each side, and, while
they are in full illumination, the scene, with its three pairs of tree
wings, its clearly marked set of blue cloud borders, its (apparently)
free-standing pyramid piece and its back drop or back shutter of
a hilly landscape, remains in comparative gloom.

One further matter should be considered before we turn to look
at the individual playhouses of this period. If we examine the
ground-plans of some contemporary continental theatres, we may
be struck by the fact that there, too, on occasion the actors seem
to be given the opportunity of coming forward towards the
audience, while at the same time provision is made for the seating
of spectators at the sides of the stage. At the Parisian Comédie
Française (plate 20), for example, open benches for a selected public
lined the sides of a forestage which extended outwards from the
curtain-line; and the same, or a similar, arrangement is to be found
in a few other theatres (plate 21, Lyon; plate 22, Montpellier). Occasionally, also, a playhouse or an opera-house, such as that at Stuttgart (plate 23), has a proscenium arch so enlarged as to leave a
considerable stage area enclosed within the confines of a deepened
archway or opening; thus actors and singers might advance far
forward of the wings, and some spectators might be given seating

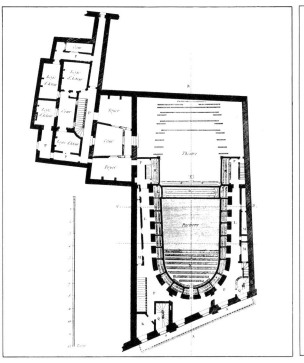

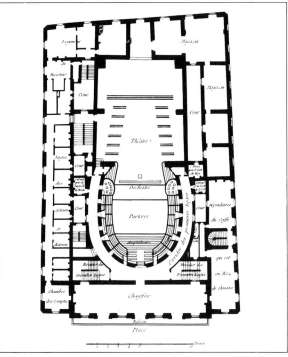

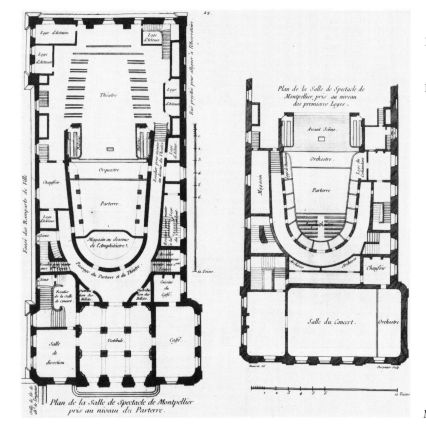

20 *above left*
Ground-plan of the Comédie
Française, Paris.

21 *above right*
Ground-plan of the Theatre at
Lyon.

22
Ground-plans of Theatre at
Montpellier.

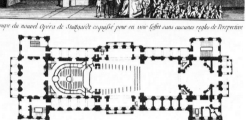

Coupe du nouvel Opéra de Stuttgardt esquissé pour en voir l'effet sans aucunes regles de Perspective

or standing space within the architectural framework. Another variant of the same plan is excellently illustrated in a painting by P. D. Olivero of a performance in the Teatro Regio at Turin (plate 24) where the players are standing close to the edge of a forestage while members of the public are seated in boxes between the columns at each side. Perhaps the most emphatic expression of this tradition in theatre architecture is to be found in an album of designs executed in 1787 by Pietro Bianchi for a projected Venetian playhouse (plate 25); here the scenic area, with seven pairs of wings, has an extension nearly half as deep, with twelve boxes, arranged in four tiers, set left and right.

Obviously, then, the use of a forward acting area which could also be provided with accommodation for spectators was not confined to English playhouses during the course of the eighteenth century. On the other hand, in relating the continental to the English tradition, we must be careful to make a distinction. In France and elsewhere in Europe, the 'idea' of the theatre was based on a bipartite model; the proscenium arch was designed fundamentally to frame a stage picture which was separate and distinct from the auditorium. When, therefore, in some structures provision was made for a forward extension of the stage, quite properly this extension may be thought of as an 'apron'. The essential distinction between

23 left
Stage-boxes in the Theatre at Stuttgart.

24 right
Teatro Regio, Turin. Painting by P. D. Olivero *c.* 1740.

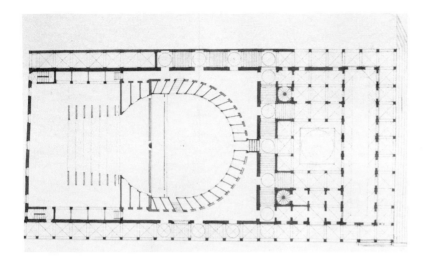

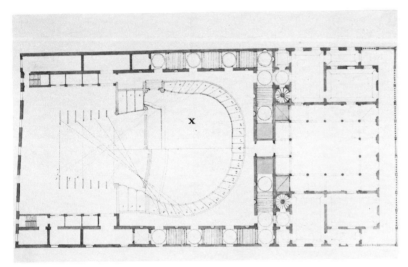

25
Ground-plans and section of a theatre project by Pietro Bianchi, 1787.

the continental plans and those of English invention remains firmly in the region of basic principle. The former, even when they deviate in practice, are founded on a two-part concept, so that the forestage is treated, as at Turin, in such a manner that it becomes almost part of the setting while the boxes are deliberately arranged so that they do *not* carry on the lines of the side-boxes in the auditorium; or else, as in the Venetian project, they are tucked away behind concealing pillars. In contradistinction, the English tradition tends to emphasise the extension of the 'house' onto the platform, while at the same time that platform is deliberately kept distinct from the setting. The difference in approach is firmly and amply indicated by the fact that, whereas stage-doors are virtually unknown in France and Italy, in England they formed an obligatory element in the theatre plan.

Only by holding fast to the fundamental tri-partite idea can we hope to appreciate fully the way in which performances in Garrick's time were built—only so can we aim at an imaginative understanding of what the actors sought to provide and of what the audiences received. The 'house', the 'platform' and the 'scene' have to be held distinct in our minds.

NOTES TO CHAPTER TWO

[1] The Blackfriars, during the first years of the seventeenth century, was used by children's companies, but it was taken over by the King's Men about the year 1609: despite this, however, when the first Globe was destroyed by fire in 1613, a second Globe was immediately erected to take its place.

[2] Since room had to be made in this volume for as many illustrations as possible, and since a passage can be nothing else than a passage, no representation of any of these uninviting entrance-ways has here been included. Excellent examples can be found in Richard Southern, *The Georgian Playhouse* (1948), fig. 13 (Richmond, Surrey), pl. 28 (Bristol), pp. 35, 36 and 38 (Richmond, Yorkshire).

[3] As in modern times, the word 'house' could be applied in two senses—one referring to the theatre building in general (as in 'play house'

and 'opera house'), and the other specifically alluding to the auditorium (as in the still current phrase 'house full').

[4] One of the few known exceptions seems to have been the Drury Lane theatre opened at Liverpool in 1749 or 1750, where the gallery is said to have extended over the pit: this playhouse did not originally have any boxes (See R. J. Broadbent, *Annals of the Liverpool Stage* (1908), p. 20).

[5] There seems to be little doubt concerning the position of the green-boxes: in describing, for example, the new theatre at Winchester, *The Hampshire Chronicle* for 23 May 1785 states that the 'pillars that support the green boxes and the gallery are superbly painted', implying that these were in one tier (Arnold Hare, *The Georgian Theatre in Wessex* [1958], p. 105). Some uncertainty, however, arises from a few references to the Dublin lattices.

Tate Wilkinson declares that the first play he saw there was from 'the lattices ... which lattices are what is called in London, the green-boxes' (*Memoirs* (1790), vol. i, p. 169); on the other hand, John O'Keeffe states emphatically that in Dublin 'the upper boxes, in a line with the two-shilling gallery, were called lattices; and over them, even with the shilling gallery, were the slips, called pigeon-holes' (*Recollections* (1826), vol. i, p. 287); and in a survey of Dublin prepared in 1818 by J. Warburton, J. Whitelaw and R. Walsh, an account of the theatre about the year 1793 speaks of it as being separated 'into three compartments—pit, boxes, and lattices, which were without division'; the prices are given as 5s/5d for the boxes, 4s/4d for the lattices, 3s/3d for the pit and 2s/2d for the gallery (*History of the City of Dublin*, vol. ii, pp. 118 and 1113).

[6] See pp. 86.

The playhouses

3

The exploration of a new city or district is always made easier and more profitable if a map has been scrutinised beforehand: by its aid we are enabled not only to keep our orientation unconfused, but also to direct our attention towards those things which are of greatest significance. With just such an object in view the preceding chapter has aimed at outlining the chief principles operative in the mid-eighteenth-century theatre so that we may now proceed, with its assistance, to look more particularly at some of the more important individual playhouses of the age.

Before setting out on this tour, it may be advisable to make reference once more to the somewhat peculiar fact that virtually all London's theatres active between the years 1740–80 did not in fact belong to that period: they were earlier structures, accepted, as a heritage from the past, by audiences and actors without any widespread desire for change. When Garrick first became a manager, the Theatre Royal at Drury Lane was thus about seventy years old; Sir John Vanbrugh's theatre or opera-house in the Haymarket had been opened in 1705; Covent Garden and Goodman's Fields both had arisen, within a few months of each other, in 1732. The old houses, certainly, were freshly decorated from time to time, and occasionally some alterations were carried out in them; but the sole really significant reconstruction in any one was that directed by Robert Adam at Drury Lane in 1775, the year before Garrick's retirement—and even that affected only the interior, leaving the basic structure of the Theatre Royal untouched.

This extraordinary fact, that one of the greatest periods in the history of the English stage witnessed no new theatre building in London, clearly raises a serious problem, since any endeavour to describe these playhouses necessitates a backward movement into preceding years. Such a backward movement cannot be escaped, and yet we must remember that our primary concern here is with the four decades which almost exactly extended from Garrick's sudden rise to his tearful retirement. Information deriving from earlier periods has, therefore, been restricted here as much as possible and, furthermore, has been presented in very summary form.

THE THEATRE ROYAL, DRURY LANE, FROM 1674 TO 1774

In writing his life of Garrick, the dramatist Arthur Murphy declared that there were four estates in London—'King, Lords, and Commons, and Drury-Lane playhouse';[1] and this emphatic statement immediately directs us to what must be the first object of our attention. Drury Lane was Garrick's home; it was admittedly the outstanding theatre in the metropolis; when playhouse enthusiasts in the provinces set about the erection of theatrical structures in their own cities, Drury Lane was selected as their model; it was by far the oldest of London's houses of entertainment; the foundation upon which all the others rested.

In 1674, during the reign of King Charles II, Sir Christopher Wren had designed it for the King's Men, and, despite a number of alterations, it may be confidently asserted that the playhouse which Garrick took over in 1747 was fundamentally the same as that in which his distinguished predecessor Thomas Betterton had won popular and critical acclaim.

The theatre itself stood in the middle of an irregularly-shaped plot of ground which was bounded by Bridges Street on the west, Russell Street on the north and Drury Lane on the east. Passages leading out of the first and last of these gave access respectively to its main public entrance and to its stage door; later, in 1750, a third passage was opened up from Russell Street, offering special facilities for the patrons of the boxes.

Somewhat strangely in view of its exceptional position, there is an almost complete lack of exact evidence relating to its planning and decoration, so that particular interest attaches to a design in the hand of Sir Christopher Wren which may be a sectional view of the theatre as it was originally constructed (see plate 26): although no proof can be brought forward to establish the connection with absolute certainty, the measurements in the plan are so close to the known measurements of the Drury Lane site, and the main features of the drawing correspond so aptly with what we know of Drury Lane at a later date, as to make it most probable that in this design we have a representation of the Theatre Royal in its first form—and consequently with it a start must be made.[2]

The length of the rectangular structure is some 114 feet. On the left, space is provided for a narrow vestibule equipped with stairways leading up to the boxes and gallery; from the rear of the back wall to the centre of the curving stage-front is a distance of about 66 feet. There are two large side-boxes, each with four rows of benches; three front-boxes face the stage in an elliptical or semi-circular line at the rear of the auditorium. A second tier of boxes carries its lines over the sides of the platform, while an open 'amphitheatrical' gallery is placed close to the ceiling on a third level. The small pit has nine benches, although it remains uncertain whether these originally ran straight from side to side or were curved to harmonise with the stage-front. Just below the innermost of the two side-boxes the entrance to the pit is clearly shown.

If we follow the procedure adopted in considering the 'ideal' plan, and if consequently we now move to the opposite end of the building, we note that an appreciably large area has been reserved for the various rooms assigned to the actors and the management. The 'scene', extending from the back-shutters to the curtain-line, has a depth of about 15 feet; the platform, some 20 feet deep, is flanked by columned pilasters, similar to those used as supports for the boxes; between them are set two entrance doors at each side of the stage, with small boxes above them. Looking at these pilasters more closely, we observe that they are so placed and fashioned as to make the side-boxes slope slightly upwards towards the acting area, while at the top they correspondingly slope downwards, the result being a kind of perspective effect in the planning of the auditorium.

Wren's sectional drawing tells us much concerning the general design of his theatre, but unfortunately it cannot provide us with any precise concept of the basic ground-plan. The perspective lines of the side-boxes might well suggest that they were also intended to incline inwards towards the platform in a horseshoe, fan or magnet shape: on the other hand, they may have been placed, more simply, parallel to the outside walls of the playhouse. That, in fact, the latter was the form adopted at Drury Lane seems to be indicated, if not made absolutely certain, by a rough plan of the interior made some time during the period of Garrick's management, probably about 1760. The precise purpose for which this drawing was made is not known but it is interesting as showing a) the position of Garrick's box, b) the arrangement of the musicians, presumably for some special occasion, and c) the pit with side-walls extending at right-angles from the stage-front, back to a curved rear. Differing modern reconstructions of the Wren plan are illustrated in plates 26, 27, 28 and 29.

Also a number of provincial theatres seem to have taken their forms from this source. Here, however, we must bear in mind that over the course of many years several alterations of various kinds were carried out in the Theatre Royal, chiefly for the purpose of increasing its seating capacity. In 1674 Drury Lane probably could not accommodate more than about seven hundred persons,[3] and we need feel no surprise on finding that repeated attempts were made to enlarge such a tiny house. The first of these attempts, and the only one concerning which there exists precise information, was, in fact, carried out, before the seventeenth century had drawn to its close, when the theatre's astute patentee and manager, Christopher Rich, cut off four feet from the front of the platform, provided more bench room in the pit and replaced the foremost stage-doors with boxes.[4] This meant that the depth of the platform was

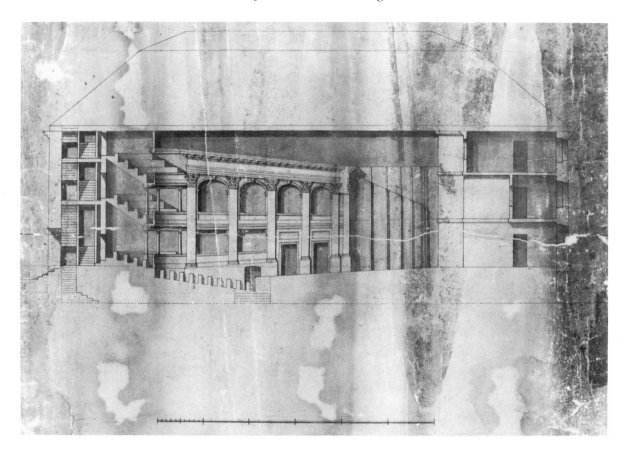

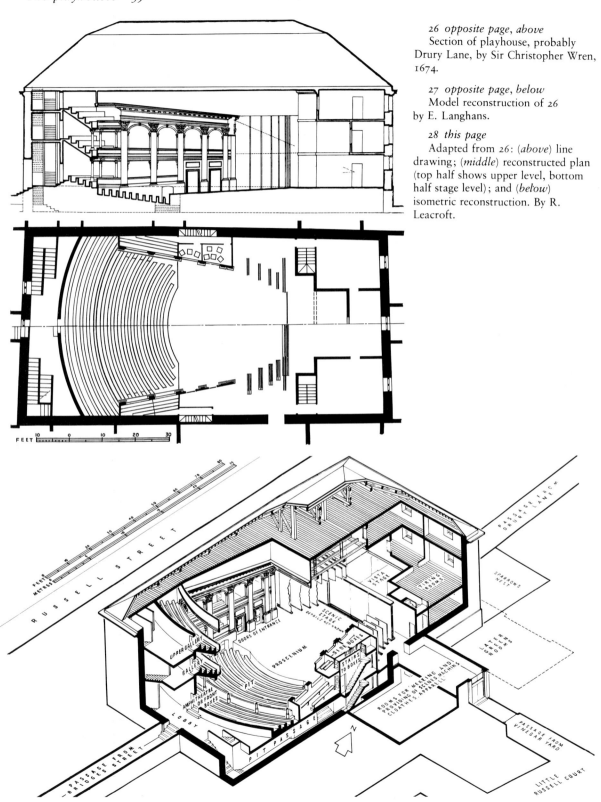

26 *opposite page, above*
Section of playhouse, probably Drury Lane, by Sir Christopher Wren, 1674.

27 *opposite page, below*
Model reconstruction of 26 by E. Langhans.

28 *this page*
Adapted from 26: (*above*) line drawing; (*middle*) reconstructed plan (top half shows upper level, bottom half stage level); and (*below*) isometric reconstruction. By R. Leacroft.

FEET 10   0   10   20   30

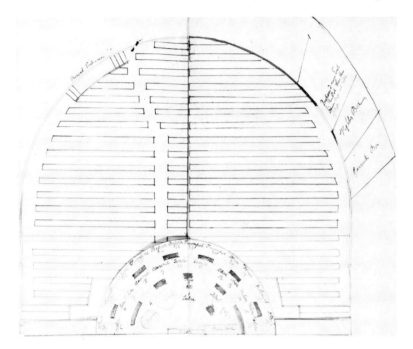

29
Plan of the pit at Drury Lane:
anonymous sketch showing Garrick's
box and musicians.

reduced to about sixteen feet, that the actors were moved slightly back from the main body of spectators, but that, at the same time, a definite step was taken towards establishing on the stage some formal accommodation for at least a small section of the public.

In all probability other modifications in the interior of the playhouse were made during the first part of the eighteenth century, although these perhaps amounted to no more than the devising of means for squeezing the public in more tightly; and thus we may believe that by 1740 Drury Lane had its seating capacity increased so as to admit a total of some nine hundred or one thousand persons, or even slightly more. When Garrick decided to assume its management, he must have fully realised that even this nightly intake was not sufficient to offer a reasonable profit, and accordingly he made some changes which, we are informed, could add receipts of some £40 for a full house—the possible capacity total being now raised to £190; and in 1762, maybe after some further unrecorded adjustments, a remodelling is said to have raised the total intake to nearly £350, a sum which has been interpreted to mean that accommodation was then provided for a capacity audience of well over two thousand spectators. Exactly what were the means by which Garrick achieved this objective are not certain, but we do know that the pit and boxes were enlarged by dispensing with one of the side lobbies, that the galleries were extended and that the topmost tier was provided with 'slips' along the walls.

It is, of course, possible that all of these diverse efforts to increase the theatre's accommodation may have involved some modifica-

tions in the original ground-plan; on the other hand, it would seem
to be most likely that the basic outlines of the house erected in 1674
were permitted to remain more or less in their primal form. If we
are prepared to accept such a conclusion, then something very valuable comes to our aid as we attempt to form an imaginative reconstruction of the building in which Garrick won his greatest
triumphs. Indeed, this something might well be regarded as a kind
of mirror of Drury Lane.

THE THEATRE AT BRISTOL, 1766

In 1764, just ninety years after the opening of Wren's playhouse,
a number of worthy Bristol citizens decided that the time had arrived
for the erection in their city of a playhouse likely to vie with the
best. Not for a moment did they pause to think of any novel architectural design: the best, in their minds, was London's pre-eminent
Theatre Royal. Having appointed a local architect, James Paty,
a committee set forth by stage-coach to London for the specific
purpose of having conferences with Garrick's master-carpenter.[5]
Returning home with a plan and elevation, they set immediately
to work, but within a month or two it was discovered that a mistake
had been made in their calculations, so a 'Model' of Drury Lane
was hurriedly sent for. Eventually, in 1766, the structure was completed, its length 99 feet, and width a few inches over 48 feet; the
stage area had the full width of the auditorium, with a depth of
29 feet; the opening of the frontispiece was 25 feet wide by 18 feet
high. Under the direction of the City Painter, a local artist named
Michael Edkins decorated the interior.

Everything indicates, therefore, that, although its measurements
were not exactly the same, a determined effort was made to design
this playhouse (which itself became a Theatre Royal some fourteen
years later) as a somewhat reduced replica of the most famous
theatre in London. This being so, it is of unquestioned interest to
observe that its capacity was 1,600—750 in the boxes, 320 in the
pit and 530 in the gallery; and still greater interest arises from an
examination of its interior arrangements (plates 30, 31 and 32). In
all, there were nine boxes on the first tier—two stage-boxes, four
side-boxes and three front-boxes, each of the last group capable of
accommodating fifty-one spectators. All these boxes were named
after famous English dramatists ancient and modern. The centre
front-box was 'Shakespeare', flanked by 'Fletcher' and 'Jonson'; to
the left came 'Congreve', 'Otway' and 'Cibber', to the right 'Vanbrugh', 'Rowe' and 'Steele'; upper boxes seem to have been
assigned, on the left, to 'Wycherley', 'Addison' and 'Farquhar', and,
on the right, to 'Dryden', 'Lee' and 'Shadwell'; on the stage itself
places of honour were reserved for 'Garrick' and 'Colman', the two
friends and partners at Drury Lane (plate 33). The signalling out

of Garrick and Colman, the securing of the London model, added
to the facts that Garrick himself visited Bristol to inspect the theatre
just before its opening and that he penned its special inaugural prologue and epilogue, amply prove that in 1766 the Bristol playhouse
was indeed designed to be a mirror of Drury Lane.

During the course of its by no means undistinguished history
from that date on to the time when, in the forties of the present
century, it narrowly escaped being bombed out of existence and,
a short time afterwards, was almost demolished in the name of our
current modern shibboleth, 'development', it certainly witnessed
several alterations. In 1800, for example, it was enlarged by having
the original gallery turned into boxes and a new top gallery thrust
up towards the roof; at the same period its ceiling was replaced
by that which has remained into the present century. Later, the old
open boxes were split up and made more intimate, while the platform was cut back to the line of the entrance doors. Naturally, these
and other changes in the building have to be borne in mind, so that
we may avoid the error of assuming that the interior which existed
in 1945 was precisely the same as that which Garrick saw; yet we
may well be justified in believing that the basic ground-plan of pit
and boxes remained virtually unaltered. The significance of this
observation becomes apparent when we note that at Bristol the
arrangement of the boxes produces neither a U-shape nor a fan-
shape: the side-boxes do incline slightly inwards, but only slightly,
and maybe a similar compromise was present in the original Drury
Lane of 1674.

30 left
The stage of the Theatre Royal,
Bristol.

31 right
Side-boxes of the Theatre Royal,
Bristol.

32 opposite page, above
Auditorium of the Theatre Royal,
Bristol.

33 opposite page, below
Booking plan of the boxes at the
Theatre Royal, Bristol, 1773.

ROBERT ADAM'S DRURY LANE, 1775

Whatever was changed throughout the years in the Bristol theatre, one feature remained to the end—the two Corinthian pilasters framing the stage-boxes, imitative relics of the heavy columns in London's Theatre Royal. Towards the close of Garrick's active career, however, many changes in taste were becoming evident, and, in particular, the Wren style of architecture was beginning to seem somewhat old-fashioned and ponderous. As a result, it was decided that 'Old Drury' required to have a face-lifting.

The year 1774 was its centenary, and the thought of this centenary may well have been in Garrick's mind when he eventually determined upon a complete remodelling of his house. Turning the work over to the popular and distinguished architect Robert Adam, he was able, in 1775, to display to admiring spectators something entirely fresh. Nothing was done to add to the capacity of the building, but those who arrived on the opening night were delighted to see the imposing new entrance which took the place of the old insignificant alley-way which, running alongside the Rose Tavern, had previously led the public to pit and box doors. An enterprising publisher issued an attractive engraving of the newly designed front (plate 35), but perhaps the most faithful illustration is a small contemporary oil-sketch which shows it (a pawnbroker's shop on the left and an inn on the right) with the eighteenth-century's beloved green-coloured doorways standing out pleasantly against the greys of the stonework (plate 34).

This new entrance gave to the public a foretaste of what they

34 and 35 opposite page
Bridges Street front of Drury Lane
as designed by Robert Adam, 1775.

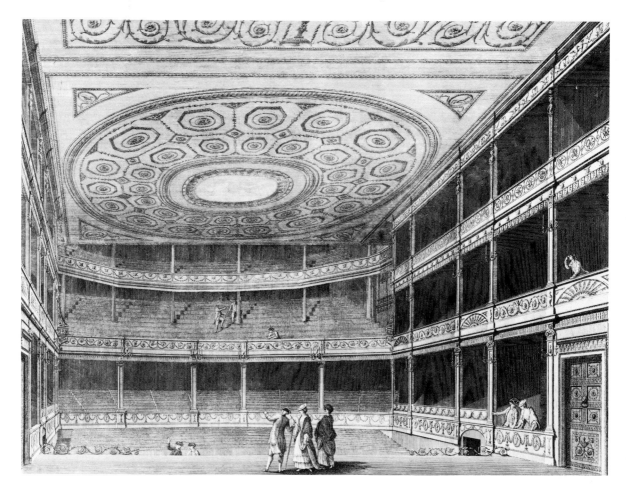

36
Auditorium of Drury Lane by
R. Adam, 1775.

were to view inside. Within the confines of the original outside walls
Adam had effected a startling change. Gone were the old heavy
pilasters, and in their stead were slender supporting posts, giving
an impression of grace and delicacy (plate 36). The ceiling had been
raised by 12 feet (plate 37), the fronts of the boxes had been
re-designed and lined with 'crimson spotted paper', their slender
pillars, 'inlaid with plate glass on a crimson and green ground',
creating an effect which was described as '*leste* and brilliant'.[6] All
combined, as contemporaries noticed, to suggest greater magnitude,
spaciousness and delicacy. That the effect was real we must believe,
yet it is still necessary to exercise due caution in accepting at face
value the charming print of the interior which was issued in 1775
(plate 36). This shows various visitors admiring the house during
an hour when no performance was in progress, and it has rightly
been pointed out that the proportions of the human figures do not
agree with the proportions of the house being represented too small,
they suggest vaster space than could have actually been present in
the reality—although maybe the engraving can still be regarded as

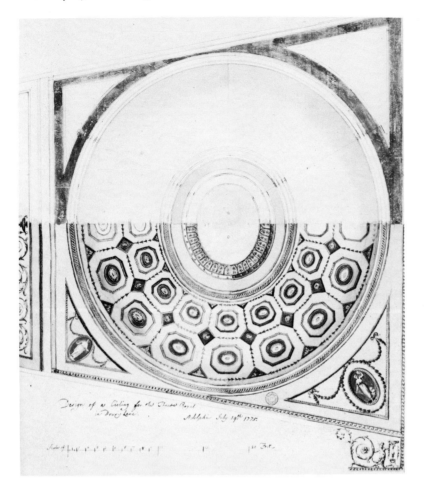

37
'Design of Ceiling for the Theatre Royal in Drury Lane', 1775 by Robert Adam.

fairly true to the impression produced on those spectators who, familiar with the older and weightier interior, gasped in wonder as they looked upon the transformation wrought by Garrick and his architect.

GOODMAN'S FIELDS AND COVENT GARDEN

Logically, it might have seemed proper to proceed directly from Drury Lane to its neighbouring great rival at Covent Garden, but there is some reason why we should first glance at the far-off playhouse, Goodman's Fields, where Garrick made his first appearance in London.

This theatre came into being originally, although not directly, because of the enormous success of John Gay's *The Beggar's Opera*. The story, of course, belongs to a period long before Garrick captured the public, yet its main features must be summarised. In 1714 Christopher Rich, at that time manager of an old house in Lincoln's Inn Fields, had been pursuing such profitable seasons as to make him decide to build a new and better structure. Rich himself died suddenly just before this was due to open, but it was taken over by his son John, lover of pantomime and later manager of Covent Garden. Some years afterwards, in 1728, the new Lincoln's Inn Fields playhouse witnessed the triumphant run of Gay's ballad opera—which, as everyone knows, made Rich Gay and Gay rich; and that run coincided with what was evidently a generally increasing public interest in the theatrical entertainment. Observing the current trend, and hoping to capitalise upon it, another enterprising manager, Thomas Odell, proceeded to open up a fresh playhouse area by converting an empty workshop in Ayliffe Street, Goodman's Fields, Whitechapel, into a theatre: despite numerous objections from local residents, he kept this in fairly regular use from 1729 until, in 1731, he handed it over to Henry Giffard. In all probability the stage and seating arrangements in Odell's building were somewhat makeshift, and, on taking it over, Giffard almost immediately issued proposals for the construction of an entirely new house on the same site (plate 38).[7] Engaging Edward Shepherd as architect, he succeeded in getting this completed for a first performance, of Shakespeare's *Henry IV*, on 2 October, 1732. In the meantime, John Rich, at Lincoln's Inn Fields, had been harbouring similar thoughts, although somewhat more grandiose in scope—nothing less than the setting up of a theatre quite close to Drury Lane, much larger than it and distinctly more 'modern' in its appointments. He too selected Edward Shepherd as his architect, and the opening performance at his Covent Garden theatre, William Congreve's *The Way of the World*, came only a few months later than that of Goodman's Fields, on 7 December 1732.

Giffard's theatre at Goodman's Fields virtually ceased to function immediately after Garrick's season there in 1741–42, but fortunately its derelict structure remained until the close of the century, when the scene-designer William Capon was able to scrutinise its shattered interior and to make plans of its seating accommodation (plate 39).[8]

The building itself appears to have been just under 90 feet long by a trifle over 47 feet wide. At the rear was a space intended for storage and dressing rooms; then came the stage and scene, about 47 feet deep,[9] and, if a later-recorded anecdote be correct, very heavily raked:[10] this story recalls a mishap of Garrick's when he was playing the Ghost in *Hamlet*; the stage, it is said, 'which rose very rapidly from the lamps, made it somewhat difficult for a performer to walk properly on it', and the young actor, clad in complete steel, unfortunately missed his footing, stumbled and clattered down, most unspiritually, in disgrace. Capon found signs of fitments for four sets of wings, the distance between the inner edges of the first pair being slightly over 20 feet. The inclined pit, only 30 feet wide and 15 feet deep, was supplied with 7 benches curved

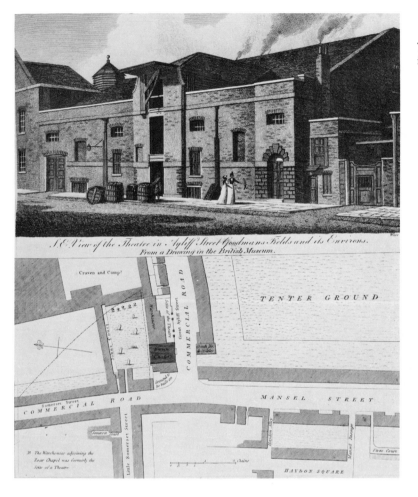

S.E. View of the Theatre in Ayliff Street Goodmans Fields and its Environs.
From a Drawing in the British Museum.

38
Exterior of Goodman's Fields Theatre, together with a plan showing its position.

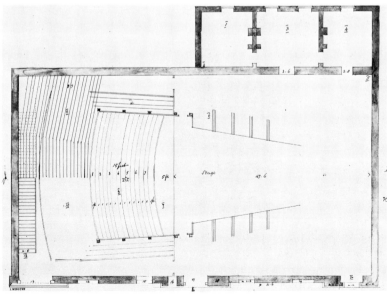

39
Ground-plan of Goodman's Fields Theatre.

round in harmony with the palisade of the orchestra well—and here we encounter our first undoubted example of a fan-shaped house, the fronts of the boxes widening out sharply until they meet the sweep of those at the rear. The boxes must have varied greatly in size, and Capon records that at least some of them were over 17 feet deep, equipped with 9 rows of benches: enough evidence remained for him to conclude that they were decorated inside in 'a light flesh colour or pink'.

It has been estimated that the pit probably could have accommodated about 120 persons, the front-boxes just over 200, the side-boxes 80 and the gallery 250—giving a total of approximately 700. A very small and intimate house, therefore, yet one to which Giffard devoted considerable embellishment. The ceiling was adorned with a large oval painting, loyally displaying the King's Majesty, attended by the allegorical figures of Peace, Plenty and Justice, 'trampling Tyranny and Oppression under his Feet'—the work of William Oram:[11] placed around this central panel were the heads of Shakespeare, Dryden, Congreve and Betterton: there were also selected scenes from Joseph Addison's *Cato*, Shakespeare's *Julius Caesar* and John Dryden's *All for Love*. The sounding board over the platform was enriched by another painting, the joint work of Francis Hayman and William Oram, depicting poetry's traditional patron, Apollo, surrounded by the Muses (see plate 40).

40
The ceiling of Goodman's Fields Theatre.

All the elegant decorations are now only a dim memory, and not a stick or stone of Goodman's Fields theatre has come down to us; but it does not require a great effort of the fancy to see Garrick captivating his meagre audience on that great night in October 1741 and to listen to the ecstatic words of praise which, buzzing busily round the Town, brought rank and fashion hurrying to greet the new star.

From this house we may now appropriately turn to the still more important theatre in Covent Garden, established so close to Drury Lane that playgoers, if they so desired, could step from the one house to the other within a few minutes.[12] John Rich having leased his plot of ground, 120 by 100 feet, Edward Shepherd applied himself

41
'Rich's Glory or his Triumphant Entry into Covent-Garden', 1732.

to the erection of the building, and the significance attached by contemporaries to its opening may well be gauged from the satirical print issued as 'Rich's Glory or his Triumphant Entry into Covent-Garden' (plate 41): the public evidently felt, although not without some twinges of trepidation, that theatrical history was being made.

Most fortunately a plan and section of the theatre has come down to us (plate 42), and even a rapid glance at their chief features indicates how advisable it was first to have looked at Goodman's Fields. At Covent Garden Shepherd has allowed his fan-shaped model to develop full scope. The eleven curving pit benches flare out from the front of the orchestra well, and these curves are further extended in the wide row of front-boxes at their rear. The side-boxes, together with those on the stage, correspondingly grow smaller as they recede, the stage-boxes having three benches, the next pair two and the remaining three but one bench each: in contrast, the front-boxes are all made to accommodate half-a-dozen.

The ground-plan further suggests that there has been a certain departure from tradition in making the boxes smaller than had hitherto been usual, with five on each side and no fewer than nine in the front; yet, on the other hand, an ancient tradition has peculiarly been retained, since the single large box, that in the centre immediately facing the stage, is described as 'the King's front box'. Thus had royalty been regularly placed in seventeenth-century playhouses. The peculiarity comes from the facts that evidence emanating from the first decades of the eighteenth century proves that these distinguished spectators were beginning to prefer seats in the stage-boxes and that kings and princes inclined to attend Covent Garden performances more frequently than those at Drury Lane precisely because in Shepherd's building, unlike Wren's Theatre Royal, provision had been made for easy and discreet access between one of these stage-boxes and the greenroom.

In the ground-plan we can see the familiar pair of stage-doors placed in front of the 'frontispiece', which is clearly a cut-out profiled frame, not a structural proscenium arch. Originally this frontispiece, painted (apparently in water colour) by George Lambert and Jacopo Amiconi, or Amigoni,[13] showed figures of Tragedy and Comedy on pedestals at each side; above, there seems to have been a painted representation of a looped-up, reddish brown curtain. No doubt the colours on the frame gradually, and sadly, faded with the passage of years, and in 1777 G. B. Cipriani was commissioned to design a new frontispiece which, incorporating the same emblematic figures, had a delicate surround of fruit, flowers and putti (plate 43). In addition, he designed, and partly painted, a new picture on the ceiling which introduced the inevitable Apollo, attended by the Muses, while an allegorical Genius of Reward offered 'the laurel to superior merit'.[14]

At this point it may be wise to pause for another note of caution. The plan at which we are looking was not published until in 1774 Dumont included it in his 'parallel' of playhouses,[15] more than forty years after Covent Garden had originally been opened. On the basis of a statement made by George Saunders,[16] that from the theatre's inception up to 1782 it had 'not undergone any material alterations, except in the decorations', it has generally been assumed that the 1774 plan can be taken to represent the house as it had first been designed by Shepherd—yet such an assumption cannot strictly be maintained. In this plan, for example, a building is to be seen behind the stage, and the open area within it is described as a 'Chambre servant à alonger le Théatre'. Now, on 15 September 1740, *The London Daily Post and General Advertiser*, after noting that the interior

42 opposite page
Cross-section and ground-plan of Covent Garden, 1774.

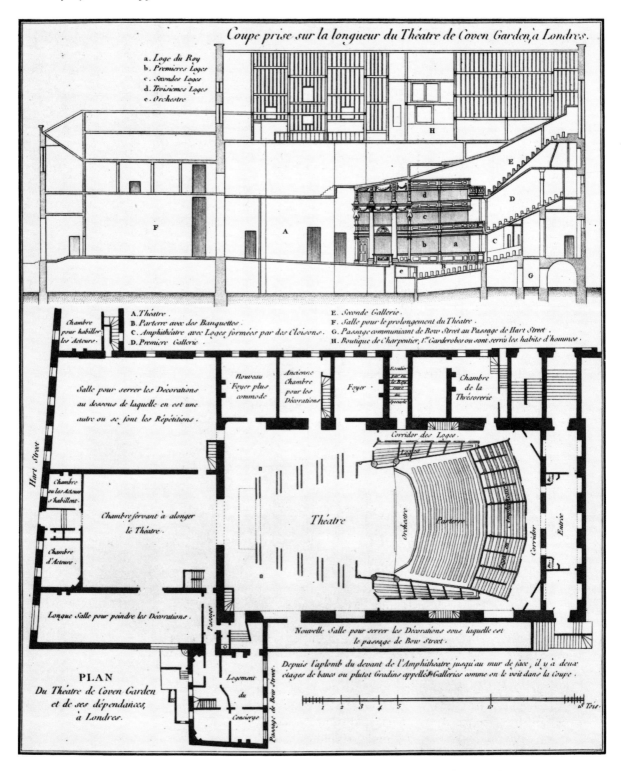

Coupe prise sur la longueur du Théatre de Coven Garden, à Londres.

a. Loge du Roy
b. Premières Loges
c. Secondes Loges
d. Troisièmes Loges
e. Orchestre

A. Théatre
B. Parterre avec des Banquettes
C. Amphithéatre avec Loges formées par des Cloisons
D. Première Gallerie
E. Seconde Gallerie
F. Salle pour le prolongement du Théatre
G. Passage communiant de Bow Street au Passage de Hart Street
H. Boutique de Charpentier, 1.re Garderobes ou sont serrés les habits d'hommes.

PLAN
Du Théatre de Coven Garden
et de ses dépendances,
à Londres.

Depuis l'aplomb du devant de l'Amphithéatre jusqu'au mur de face, il y a deux
étages de bancs ou plutot Gradins appellés Galleries comme on le voit dans la Coupe.

43
Frontispiece or proscenium frame designed by G. B. Cipriani for Covent Garden, 1777.

of Covent Garden had then been freshly re-decorated, refers to the provision of 'a large additional building ... whereby they will, on some Occasions, be enabled to add near 70 Feet to the length of the Stage, which was before the largest in England, but will now exceed in Depth any Theatre in Europe'. Presumably, therefore, the 'Chambre' depicted in the ground-plan was not built until eight years after the completion of Shepherd's work. Nor was this the only modification of the original design. With its tiers of side-boxes and its exceptionally deep upper and lower galleries, Covent Garden appears to have had seating for some 1,300 to 1,400 spectators when it was first opened to the public, but evidently, at some date before 1780, several changes had been made in an endeavour to accommodate still more. Maybe such changes were not introduced until after the appearance of Dumont's volume; on the other hand, we must be prepared to accept the possibility that, even apart from the addition of the 1740 'Chambre', the printed plan may not be a wholly faithful representation of Shepherd's original design.

This question assumes special significance when we turn to examine contemporary illustrations of the interior. The earliest of these is a print depicting a performance of Garrick's *Miss in Her Teens* in 1747 (plate 44). Although of decided interest, this is less informative than might have been desired since the engraver has obviously compressed some of his material; no entrance doors are shown, only the flanking boxes, the footlights, the platform and what appears to be a forward drop or shutter. Much more valuable are the two prints, already referred to, relating to the notorious 'Fitzgiggo' riots of 1763 (see plate 18): these embrace a wider area, taking in the first benches of the pit, and their proportions agree more or less with the outlines of the 1774 ground-plan, with a stage-door and a stage-box on each side of the platform. Recently, however, as has been noted above, another illustration of the interior has come to light (see plate 19). Clearly, its main features are the same as those of the 'Fitzgiggo' prints, but it differs from them in one particular respect—two stage-boxes are shown on each side of the platform instead of only one. Precisely when this little oil-painting was executed cannot be determined, but a date in the early sixties, perhaps earlier, may be suggested by the appearance of the sentinel guards and of the great chandeliers over the platform.[17] Unhappily, however, neither of these pieces of evidence is positively conclusive: Covent Garden, following the lead of Drury Lane, dis-

44
'The Modern Duel', a scene from Garrick's *Miss in her Teens*, Covent Garden 1747.

pensed with the chandeliers in 1765, but there is always the possibility that, after their removal in that year, they were later rein-
stated; and although the grenadiers seem to have been relieved of
their stage duties some time in the sixties, there is at present no
means of determining exactly when they ceased to be present at
Covent Garden. All that may be said is that the painting gives the
impression of being an attempt to depict accurately what the
audience saw during a performance of *Macbeth* and that, if indeed
it was executed about 1760, it may conceivably show the theatre
in its original form, with a platform so deep as to be capable of
permitting two boxes on each side. If this were so, then we might
believe that what Christopher Rich did to Drury Lane in 1697 was
repeated by his son at Covent Garden some sixty-odd years later.

45
View from front-boxes of Covent
Garden.

One further illustration may be briefly recorded here, although
it is both puzzling and perhaps suspect (plate 45). When included
by Saxe Wyndham in his *Annals of Covent Garden*,[18] it was described simply as 'c. 1770. From an Old Print'. Hitherto it has been
accepted without any question save that, from the evidence of the
costumes worn by the spectators, its date has been advanced to 1780
or later;[19] but it unquestionably raises doubts in our minds. The
original print, with a caption declaring it to be a 'View from the
Front Boxes of the THEATRE ROYAL Covent Garden', has several
peculiarities which must make us question its value as evidence. If
it could be authenticated as a faithful representation of the Covent
Garden interior around the year 1780, then it would prove that the
branches, or chandeliers, had been restored to their former posi-

tions; but in the absence of such authentication it may be best to put it aside as a later attempt at an early nineteenth-century historical 'reconstruction' of the house.

Under the management of John Rich, Covent Garden flourished until his death in 1761. Notable productions were to be seen there, although in general its companies of players rarely rivalled those at Drury Lane and although its popularity depended largely upon the pantomimic spectacles so dearly beloved by its Harlequin manager. It is true that Garrick, with the aid of Henry Woodward, frequently succeeded in out-doing Rich at his own game, but, even so, Covent Garden's scenic effects for long drew crowds to the rival house. That it had thus been able to cultivate its own clientèle was fortunate, since otherwise it might easily have foundered after Rich's departure. In 1761 his sons-in-law, James Bencraft and John Beard, took over the patent, but soon afterwards the shares were sold to an oddly associated quartette consisting of Thomas Harris, John Rutherford, George Colman and William Powell, whose extraordinary quarrels and law-suits were such as to leave us amazed that the playhouse managed to survive at all (see the satirical

46
'The Triumphal Entry of the Red Kings with the Expulsion of their Black Majesties', 1768.

print of 1768: plate 46). The dignity and skill of Garrick's control of Drury Lane appears the greater the more we consider the disorder among his professional rivals and the troubles that arose at his own house shortly after his retirement.

THE TWO THEATRES IN THE HAYMARKET

About ten minutes' walk westward from the Drury Lane–Covent Garden area was the Haymarket, once a shabby, dirty street cut off from the then fashionable quarters of London, but gradually assuming importance as the metropolis expanded. Here two theatres demand attention, although one was only rarely used for the performance of spoken drama, while concerning the shape of the other little evidence is available.

The first started life in 1705 as the Queen's Theatre in the Haymarket, and after the death of Queen Anne, became known as the King's Opera House.[20] Designed and built by Sir John Vanbrugh, dramatist and architect of Blenheim, it had several things against it from the very start: the roads around it were in such a wretched state that carriages could not travel there in comfort; few fashionable playgoers resided in the region; and, most serious of all, the actors found themselves confronted by an experience not unknown to the performers of our own days—the acoustics of the house were atrocious. Instead of following the typical English playhouse pattern, Vanbrugh created a huge structure, grandiose if nothing else, reminiscent of some contemporary Italian architecture. Within its heavy brick outer walls, 130 feet long by 60 feet wide, he set a semi-circular pit, the 'amphitheatrical' effect being further emphasised by other rows immediately above and behind. As might easily have been guessed, when the players first took over its stage, they found that the sound of their voices echoed and reverberated cavernously against the bare walls. Before three years had passed by, it became necessary to lower the high ceiling and to construct four tiers of boxes around the auditorium; and it is this 1708 reconstruction which is depicted in Dumont's plan published in 1774 (plate 47); other later additions included in the plan are the 'Escalier per lequel le Roi vient au Spectacle', the set of stage 'Loges de la Famille Royale', probably the 'Chambre servant à alonger le Théatre', and, since the building came to be freely used for masquerades, the extensive 'Salle pour les Assemblées' erected alongside the auditorium. In 1732 it was stated that the stage was no less than 100 feet deep, 40 feet broad and 32 feet high;[21] the 'house' seems to have been able to accommodate just under 1,000 ladies and gentlemen, with space for an indeterminate number of their footmen in the upper gallery.

The history of this building is almost entirely concerned with operatic performances, and, as we trace its fortunes, bearing in mind

47 opposite page
King's Theatre, Haymarket. Plan and section, 1774.

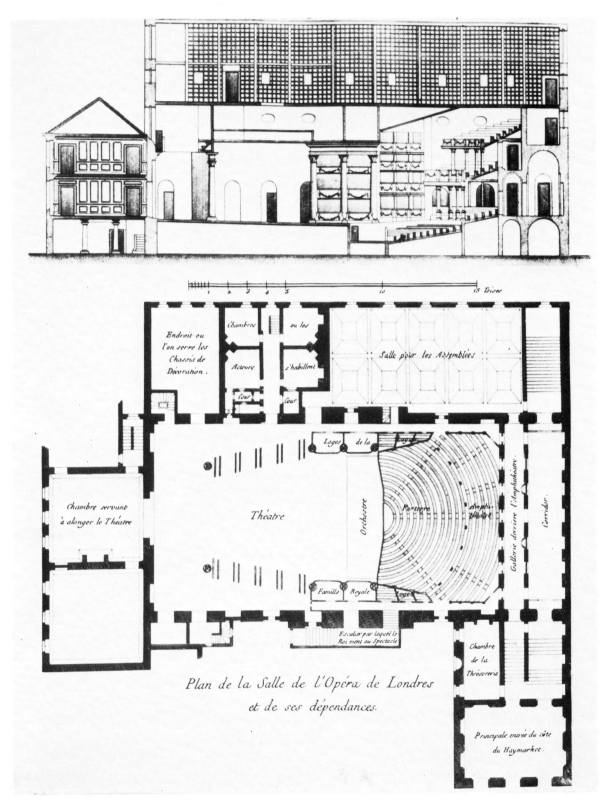

Plan de la Salle de l'Opéra de Londres
et de ses dépendances.

the vast development of the operatic form in almost all European countries, maybe what must chiefly strike us is the series of deficiencies associated with this King's Theatre. It had been planned by a gentleman-architect, but planned badly; it was patronised by royalty and the aristocratic set, yet it stumbled along its course, continually floundering into difficulties; although it did succeed in attracting the genius of one outstanding composer, George Frederick Handel, its offerings were frequently dull and sometimes ridiculous; it spent its money freely on the scenic spectacles which contemporary opera-lovers adored, and yet no relics of these have come down to us remotely comparable with the wealth of designs emanating from its Continental companions. The truth is that the Italian style of opera always seemed, in eighteenth-century England, somewhat awkward and out of its element—a fashionable toy, no doubt, but something indulged in rather because of the dictates of the prevailing mode than because of real interest.

Naturally, since Vanbrugh had aimed at erecting a nobly-planned, complete structure, this King's Theatre had, unlike Drury Lane, a fairly imposing entrance, which at the start must have seemed hardly in keeping with the Haymarket's tawdriness. Within a period of fifteen years, however, it was provided with a companion, the frontage of the 'New' or 'Little' playhouse, far less ornate and quite possibly looking like a pert alley-cat seated alongside a lion monarch. Built by John Potter in 1720, this Little Theatre's main early distinction arrived when it became the home of Henry Fielding's company of comedians and witnessed the presentation of his farcical satires. Apart from this, however, it made comparatively slight impact on London's theatrical world until another, very different, satirist took over its stage. Here Samuel Foote invited his friends to tea, and here in 1766, almost half a century after its opening, Londoners were provided with a third 'patent' house. The story has often been told of how Foote, badgered by a group of aristocratic gentlemen to mount a mettlesome horse, was thrown to the ground and so injured that his leg had to be amputated; one member of the group, and perhaps the chief instigator, was the Duke of York, and through his influence the lamed actor was recompensed by receiving a licence which allowed him to run a company during the summer season—a period of time originally defined as extending from the middle of May until the middle of September, but later discreetly widened at both ends.

Just what this house looked like inside in its earlier years we do not know, but in all probability its general arrangements conformed to the prevailing English mode.

THEATRES OUTSIDE LONDON

These, then, were the city's principal theatres, but, in their search for entertainment, Londoners were by no means entirely restricted to the houses which have already been briefly described.[22] Occasional 'benefit' and other single performances were given from time to time at diverse taverns; on various occasions the old Lincoln's Inn Fields playhouse and another playhouse which had been built in James Street, Haymarket, had some runs of, usually, brief duration; for a time there were interesting summer seasons of burlettas at Marybone, or Mary-le-bone, Gardens; entertainments of a mixed kind were provided at the popular Sadler's Wells and Vauxhall Gardens; and the booths at the fairs, even although they were rapidly declining, continued to function.[23] Although these are all worthy of the remembrance, however, we must believe that most of them operated under primitive conditions, and concerning all of them there exists but little evidence of the kind which can be assembled for the more important houses. They must, accordingly, be passed by.

Playhouse activities in the provinces occupy a vastly more important position. There can be no doubt but that London was the hub of the theatrical world during Garrick's active lifetime; but this fact should not draw our attention away from what was happening outside that limited area. Indeed, if our gaze is set on the theatre rather than upon the drama, we may occasionally discover more within this sphere than we can within the sphere of the metropolitan houses of entertainment. This can be demonstrated by one single, and rather startling, fact: already it has been observed that all the London playhouses had been erected before the year 1740; in contrast, the four decades between 1740 and 1780 witnessed a truly extraordinary development of theatre designing and construction both in the provinces and in the two other component parts of the British Isles—Ireland and Scotland.

The building of these playhouses depended upon a complete change after the middle of the century in the quality of dramatic performances beyond the periphery of London. Strolling actors, of course, since the distant days of the sixteenth century had been carrying the drama into almost every part of the kingdom, some of them even pursuing their profession erratically and dangerously during those decades when the Puritan Commonwealth suppressed theatrical activities in and around the seat of government; but until the middle of the eighteenth century they possessed hardly any regular homes of their own, and frequently their productions must have been deplorably wretched. On a few occasions some earlier provincial audiences may have had the good fortune to see interpretations exhibited by youthful stage aspirants of promise—as, for example, when Charles Macklin took to the road in 1716—while

Delivering Play Bills in the Country.
My first Appearance, 'pon my honour, Sir, in Hamlet the Great Prince of Denmark.

48
'Delivering Playbills in the Country'. Anonymous engraving late eighteenth century.

at certain centres, such as Richmond, Bath and Dublin, they were able periodically to applaud visiting players from London; but in general they can only have had the opportunity of being confronted with the mediocre and the shoddy, while the poor actors, for their part, lived a miserable nomadic existence (plate 48). Hogarth's well-known print of strolling actresses dressing in a barn was no doubt a fair representation of the common theatrical conditions operative during the earlier decades of the eighteenth century.[24]

In the very year when Garrick appeared first as Richard III, a pitiful little account-book recording the adventures of a tiny company of six provincial players suggestively indicates what must have been frequent in many districts. Starting about May 1741, these half-dozen performers were soon reduced to two men and one woman;

and yet, despite the defections, the remaining three undauntedly proceeded with their repertory. Occasionally, members of the local gentry kindly gave them some support by 'commanding' plays: at Malmesbury, for instance, at the request of a certain Mr Collins, the trio put on an evening's entertainment consisting of John Dryden's *The Spanish Friar* and *The Parting Lovers* (otherwise known as *Nancy*) by Henry Carey. For that performance—and it is typical—their takings amounted to no more than sixteen shillings: 'music' cost them 6*d*, candles 10*d*, ale 1*d*, rent of the 'theatre' (presumably a barn or a room at the local inn) 2*s*, nails and packthread 2*d*: when they came to share out at the evening's close, each of them received only five pennies.[25] In one respect this diminutive company was representative: they had agreed among themselves to share their poor, pitiful profits; but generally an actor-manager took four or five shows to recover his outlay. The actors would need to rely on their benefits but even when the manager did not do a midnight flitting with the cash, his starving followers were left with merely a pittance after the 'house-charges' had been deducted from the ticket-money taken in. There were exceptions, of course, but the overall picture is a dismal one, and in the circumstances little inducement could arise for the building of permanent stages, the more particularly since this provincial playing was largely unlegalised and performances depended entirely upon the whims of local justices.

A definitely marked change begins to make itself obvious as we approach the mid-century mark, and this, it would seem, was partly, if not wholly, resultant from the notorious Licensing Act. During the earlier years, London actors had often been accustomed to add to their salaries by appearing on stages at the summer fairs, but gradually this source of income began to decline. As a consequence, more and more metropolitan players became inclined to move further afield, seeking custom in the country, and their occasional presence there necessarily started to raise production standards. From this period onwards we begin to hear of new playhouses being set up at inns or converted out of barns, and by the time we reach the year of Garrick's retirement we find ourselves in a world wherein at least several major centres were graced by relatively imposing Theatres Royal and wherein the actors, no longer strollers, were engaged on terms not dissimilar from those operative in London.

In turning to look at these new playhouses, however, we must not delude ourselves into believing that the establishment of the Theatres Royal wrought a complete transformation. Up to 1780, and indeed for long after that date, strollers as miserable as any in 1740 continued to wander from town to town, from village to village. 'I don't know how it is,' Garrick wrote to his brother in 1762, 'but the Strollers are a hundred years behind hand—We in Town are Endeavouring to bring the Sock & Buskin down to Nature, but *they* still keep to their Strutting, bouncing & mouthing.' 'I dread a

Stroler,' he wrote three years later to James Love, 'they contract such insufferable Affectation that they disgust me—I never could account for the Country Actors being so very wide of yᵉ mark.'²⁶

And if the acting was generally bad, the places in which the poorer performers gave their shows often remained as wretched as any in the past. John Bernard in 1830 records how, as a stage-struck boy, he visited a 'theatre' run by a certain 'manager', Adam Winterton, who was then at Fareham:

> He had engaged the largest room at the ... Black Bull, suspended a collection of green tatters along its middle for a curtain, erected a pair of paper screens right-hand and left for wings; arranged four candles in front of said wings, to divide the stage from the orchestra, (the fiddlers' chairs being the legitimate division of the Orchestra from the Pit,) and with all the spare benches of the inn to form Boxes, and a hoop suspended from the ceiling, (perforated with a dozen nails, to receive as many tallow candles,) to suggest the idea of a chandelier; he had constructed and embellished what he denominated a Theatre! The scenery consisted of two drops, simply and comprehensively divisible into the inside of a house, and the outside of a house. The former (which was an original of about the same date as the manager) was a *bona fide* representation at bottom of a kitchen, with all the culinary implements arranged about it; but by the simple introduction of two chairs and a table, this was constituted a gentleman's parlour! And in the further presence of a crimson-cushioned, yellow-legged elbow chair, with a banner behind, and a stool in front, was elevated into a royal hall of audience! This was clever stage managing. The other drop (which I have termed outside of a house) was somewhat younger than its companion, and very ingeniously presented on its surface two houses peeping in at the sides, a hill, a wood, a stream, a bridge, and a distant plain; so that, from the general indistinctness of the whole, the eye of the spectator might single out a particular feature, and, agreeably to the locality of the scene that was passing, imagine himself in a street, a wood, by a stream, &c. alternately.²⁷

In connection with this may be taken another revealing glimpse of another country manager, 'Jemmy' Thornton, about the year 1776: when he visited a poor community, he was, Bernard tells us, prepared to receive 'public support in money or in "kind". He would take meat, fowl, vegetables, &c. value them by scales, &c. and pass in the owner and friends for as many admissions as they amounted to.'²⁸

Similar examples could readily be multiplied, but these instances may be enough to keep an image in our minds of the hundreds of performances presented during these years in similar circumstances. In thinking of the theatre in the provinces we must seek to keep a balanced picture which, like Winterton's outside setting, allows for almost everything.

The Theatres Royal outside of London started with Bath and Norwich in 1768; York and Hull hurried after them during the following year, Liverpool in 1771, Manchester in 1775, Bristol in 1778; and, in harmony with the distinction accorded to them by the Crown, their actors in 1788 won a new position for themselves by the passing of an act which formally legalised the practice of their profession.

In considering these playhouses, it must, of course, be remembered that the appellation 'Theatre Royal' did not necessarily serve to mark off one kind of theatre from another and that the title itself need not have been used when first any particular house was planned and directed. Thus, for example, the Bristol theatre, with which we have already dealt, was opened in 1766, although its elevation to the upper rank did not come until twelve years later.

The same was true in Bath, the very first of the Theatres Royal. In this city, charming and fashionably elegant, there had been a 'theatre' as early as 1705, and a 'new theatre' was contrived twenty years later—but both of these were no doubt simple affairs.[29] Vastly different was the Orchard Street playhouse, opened by John Palmer on 27 October 1750, with a production of Shakespeare's *Henry V*. The building was 60 feet long by 40 feet wide, and, after some alterations five years later, it was said to be 'esteemed in fancy, elegance, and construction, inferior to none in Europe'—although, in reading these words and other similar comments made elsewhere, perhaps it is wise to make due allowance for the possibility of 'puffing' or of the expression of local pride. After it had become dignified with the 'Royal' title, further alterations were carried out either in 1774 or in 1775. An undated water-colour by John Nixon depicting its interior suggests that, while evidently it could on occasion attract crowded audiences, its fittings were of the simplest (plate 49). No

49
Theatre Royal, Orchard Street, Bath, interior.

painted decorations are indicated here, and the lines of the house are uninteresting, rectangular, with two tiers of open side-boxes surmounted by an upper gallery. On the upper part of the stage stand four pairs of columned wings, combined in a wholly inappropriate manner with a back-shutter showing trees on one side and a castle-topped hill on the other. Apparently we are supposed to be on the battlements of Elsinore, since the performers, standing boldly on the platform, are almost certainly in the midst of the fourth scene in *Hamlet* when the Prince, with his companions, stare in amazement at the Ghost's visitation.

If the Bath newspapers went into ecstasies over their local theatre, *The Norwich Gazette* was even more fulsome in its praise of the

50
Norwich Theatre, exterior, 1758.

new playhouse built in that city in 1758 (plate 50), ten years before it became a Theatre Royal. This 'Grand and Magnificent THEATRE,' we read,

> is allow'd by all Connoisseurs and Judges to be the most perfect and compleat structure of the kind in this Kingdom. It is most admirably constructed for seeing and hearing;—the Stage is large and lofty;—and the Scenes so highly finish'd and executed, by the late ingenious Mr. COLLINS, that they are accounted far superior to any of the kind.[30]

More than a single grain of salt, clearly, is demanded here; although we have to remember that this playhouse, like that at Bristol, was designed by its architect, Thomas Ivory, on the model of Drury Lane. And still a greater quantity of salt is needed when we read the *York Courant*'s description, on 8 January 1765, of its local theatre as being 'by far the most spacious in Great Britain, Drury-lane and Covent Garden excepted, and for Convenience and Elegance it is thought to be equal, if not superior to either of them.' Very little is known about the construction of this house, but most probably its plan was similar to that of the others. The pattern, indeed, was wellnigh universal. If, for example, we look at the Ordnance Survey of Manchester prepared in 1849, we may experience considerable surprise on spotting the ground-plan of a theatre which well might have been that of the 'ideal' playhouse from which we started (plate 51). In the *Survey* this is marked as the Queen's Theatre, but when it was originally built in 1775 it had been Manchester's Theatre Royal: although the structure had been destroyed by fire, in 1789, the new playhouse erected on the same site had obviously copied exactly the plan of its forerunner. Roughly 102 feet long by 48 feet wide, its side-boxes ran parallel to the exterior walls, with the front-boxes curving round in an ellipse: so far as can be determined from the tiny plan, the former were fairly large whereas the latter had been divided into smaller compartments (although that may have been part of a later alteration). There would appear to be the possibility at least that Manchester followed the initiative of Bristol and Norwich in selecting Drury Lane as its model; on reading that its proscenium consisted of 'six Corinthian pillars' the image of Wren's playhouse certainly rises clearly in our minds.[31]

In fact, the solitary oddity in this theatrical gallery seems to be the playhouse opened at Liverpool in 1749 or 1750, and even here the spirit of Garrick's house was invoked: it was in fact, called Drury Lane Theatre. Probably an unpretentious building, its chief interest rests in the positioning of its gallery, which projected out over a pit not lined by the usual rows of boxes. In a reconstruction about a decade later the house was remodelled, but it would appear as though the deviation from the transitional plan had found favour with Liverpool audiences and actors: when the architect Sir William Chambers came to design the Theatre Royal, opened on 5 June 1772, there was the same uncharacteristic treatment of the gallery— the playhouse, observed a contemporary, exhibited a 'peculiarity' in that this gallery extended towards the stage at the level commonly occupied by the upper boxes (plate 52).[32]

A 'peculiarity' it certainly was in this period, although one which was to become the commonplace during the years to come. All the active research which has recently been devoted to the study of provincial stages, with minute examination of already known pictorial material and, more importantly, with the unearthing of fresh

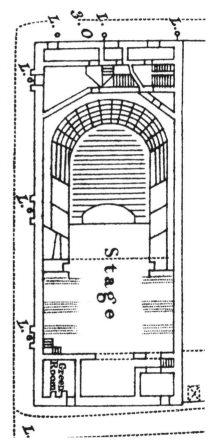

51
Ground-plan of
Queen's Theatre, Manchester.

52
Theatre Royal, Liverpool, front elevation.

sources of information and with detailed study of the few scattered relics of actual buildings still existing into our own century, amply proves the truth of this statement. While all of these cannot be dealt with here, at least a few examples may be selected.

Of the Frankfort Gate theatre at Plymouth, contrived in 1758 out of two older structures, James Winston has happily preserved a rough ground-plan, together with what seems to be a drawing of one side of its stage (plate 53).[33] A tiny house, it must have been representative of numerous other kindred playhouses of which all exact record has now been lost. Two boxes, one extending its edge over the side of the platform, are set parallel to the theatre's walls at each side; fronting the stage come three other boxes; and within this area the pit, with nine benches, is enclosed. The boxes themselves are of varying depths, the stage-box being only 6 feet 8 inches and the middle front-box, with its seven benches, no less than 14 feet 6 inches. If the associated drawing belongs to this house, then the stage-boxes at least had a certain amount of embellishment and were provided with a kind of open screen.

Interesting, too, are the few facts which remain concerning a theatre much closer to London—that at Richmond in Surrey—so near, indeed, that it might almost have claimed to belong to the

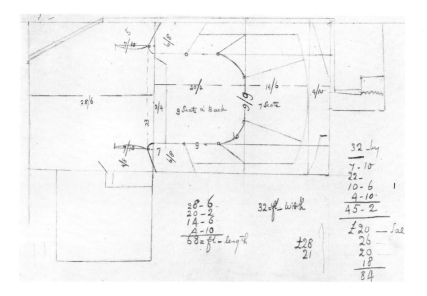

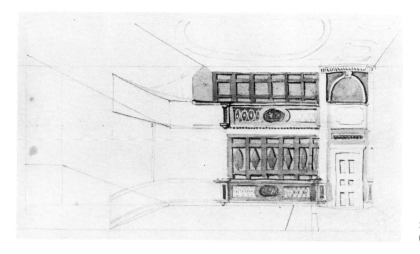

53
Frankfort Gate Theatre, Plymouth, 1758. (*Above*) ground-plan and (*below*) side of stage.

54
Richmond (Surrey), stage of the Theatre.

realm of the London stage. Not a great deal is known about the earlier playhouses on Richmond Hill though a drawing exists of the exterior of one of them and probably they were not of any great distinction;[34] but relics of the house built in 1765 were still preserved, neglected and forlorn, up to the time of its complete demolition in 1884 (plate 54).[35] In its general planning, it appears not dissimilar from the Plymouth theatre, with a tier of boxes surrounding the pit, and a second tier, consisting of boxes at the sides and an open gallery at the rear—a noteworthy feature of the structure being that the upper boxes were apparently set in such a manner that one was slightly higher than the next as they receded from the stage. Opened on 15 June 1765, with a prologue specially composed by

55
Richmond Theatre (Yorkshire): (*above left*) exterior; (*above right*) interior before recent restoration; and (*left*) model reconstruction.

David Garrick, it was described in glowing terms in a contemporary newspaper. 'In it,' we are informed, 'every imperfection in either of the Royal theatres of Drury Lane or Covent Garden is carefully avoided, and every advantage retained':

> the boxes form a kind of crescent, which renders them commodious; the lobby is as spacious as either of the above theatres; there is but one gallery, which, however, turns out to the advantage of the audience, as it prevents the necessity of having pillars which obstruct the view. The pitt is small, but that seems no inconveniency, as the principal part of the spectators occupy the boxes; a handsome space is allowed for the orchestra; and the panels, in place of being ornamented with a gingerbread stucco, are painted of a dark colour, which gives the stage an additional degree of light when the curtain is drawn up. The scenes are elegant, and by the connoisseurs the whole is reckoned for its size to be much the best constructed theatre in the British dominions.

Evidence relating to the theatre in a second Richmond—Richmond in Yorkshire—is of a different, and of a much more valuable,

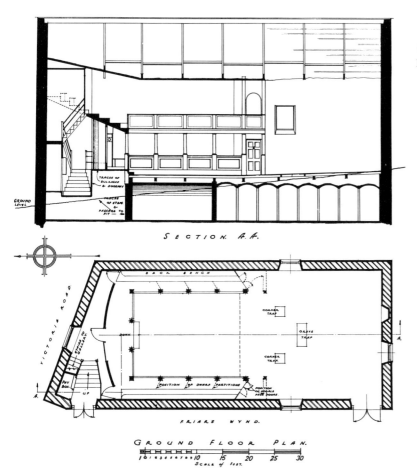

56
Richmond Theatre (Yorkshire):
(*above*) section and (*below*) ground plan.

sort, since its remains have braved the ravages of time and have yielded, therefore, a great deal of significant detail. Since, however, this house, built by the actor-manager Samuel Butler in 1788, strays by eight years outside the period 1740–80, only brief reference can be made to it here.[36] A model and reconstructed plans (plates 55 and 56) show that it was a simple building, with four side-boxes against each wall meeting an equally plain set of three front-boxes at the rear. Perhaps its chief importance for us at the moment is that, in association with the theatre at Bristol, it serves as a reminder that the basic model of the earlier houses of entertainment continued to dominate for many decades after newer models were being conceived.

Scattered relics, pictorial records and descriptions of numerous other theatres erected during this period add in various ways to our treasury of knowledge. A print dated 1813 depicting the interior of the Scarborough playhouse probably represents it much as it appeared when it was originally opened in the sixties of the century: of special interest here is the painted decoration, with Apollo once more acting as the patron god (plate 57).[37] Another picture, a print displaying the interior of the theatre at Sunderland (plate 58), indicates that, as in Covent Garden, painted representations of Tragedy and Comedy flanked and framed the wings. Until a few years ago

57
Theatre Royal, Scarborough, interior, 1813.

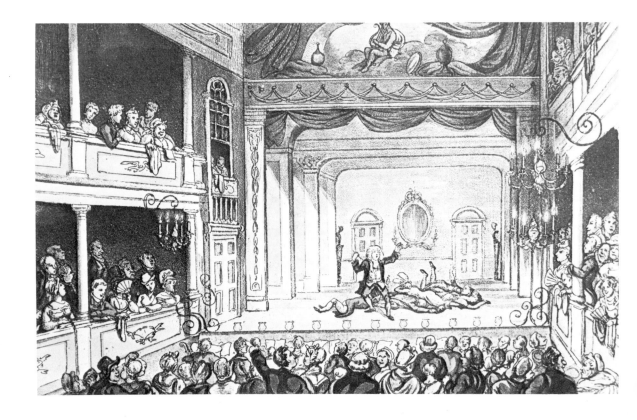

St George's Hall in King's Lynn preserved a fascinating relic of the playhouse constructed within its walls in the year 1766: this consists of a large framework—six pillars supporting a ceiling—placed over a front platform, 14 feet deep by 20 feet wide. It must, indeed, have been the surrounds and top of the main acting area, stemming in origin from the late seventeenth century and demonstrating effectively what continued to remain the true place for histrionic action.[38]

Strangely, and most unfortunately, little pictorial material relating to the early Dublin theatres has come down to us, although once these enjoyed a distinction almost rivalling that of London's stages. The Smock Alley playhouse, then called the playhouse in Orange Street, which arose originally in 1662, was reconstructed in 1671 and again in 1735, and on its stage many great actors, including Garrick himself, made their appearances; but not much can be said about its planning and interior arrangements. Another theatre in Aungier Street, built 'after the Form of that in *Drury Lane*', was opened in 1734; a third, in Crow Street, which, we are told, was 'as ample and magnificent as that of Drury-lane', arose in 1758 and, with the enthusiastic aid of Tommaso Giordani, helped to make operatic history: yet concerning these also little information exists to tell us about their appointments.[39] In view of the activities of all three playhouses and of the unquestioned interest which they

58
Theatre, Sunderland, stage, 1785.

stimulated, the absence of reliable exact evidence, particularly pictorial, is surprising; but maybe our surprise at the lack of similar evidence from Scotland need not be so great. In that northern land play-enthusiasts had a much harder time; they were fiercely denounced from the pulpits, and on more than one occasion rude mobs, excited to fury by bigoted leaders, deliberately set the theatres ablaze. Not until a group of Edinburgh citizens secured a patient for a Theatre Royal did anything approaching settled conditions begin to prevail: under the terms of this patent an older theatre which had succeeded in escaping the fires was opened under the 'Royal' title on 9 December 1767, with a prologue specially written for the occasion by James Boswell, and almost exactly two years later a new Theatre Royal took its place. Glasgow's progress was even tardier and more disturbed: its first barn-like playhouse was severely damaged during a riot, while its successor was set on fire just before its intended opening in 1762—and, as if this were not enough, when restorations had been completed, flames again consumed the fabric, levelling it to the ground. Under these circumstances, we need hardly express wonder that illustrative material relating to such ventures has not come down to us.[40]

Of one thing, however, we may be reasonably sure—that, even if we now possessed precise plans and pictures of all the theatres set up in the British Isles during the Garrick period, the general image which we have formed of the stage from 1740 to 1780 would not have to be seriously modified. What we actually do have, disappointingly meagre though it may be and sometimes tantalisingly elusive, is amply sufficient for our purposes. Taking all the records together, we can have no difficulty in forming an accurate opinion of the impression which might have been in the mind of a contemporary theatrical tourist in a pilgrimage from south to north and across the Irish Channel. Different although the various playhouses undoubtedly were in size and decoration, their plans, with one or two special exceptions, would have been found to be fundamentally the same, stemming back traditionally to the theatres constructed in the later part of the seventeenth century and, as we have seen, continually invoking the pattern of one of these houses in particular, the Theatre Royal in Drury Lane. The lines of the boxes might have deviated one from another, but almost every one of these playhouses had its benched pit, its rows of side- and front-boxes, its gallery, its platform and its stage-doors: each one was designed basically in tri-partite form.

From these records, indeed, we can even imaginatively reconstruct others about which virtually nothing is known. What, for example, did the Ipswich theatre look like in the summer of 1741 when the youthful actor who called himself Lyddall appeared there just before he proceeded to capture the attention of the London public? (plate 59). Almost all we know is that a brewer named Henry

Betts constructed this house in the year 1736 as a kind of appendage to the Tabard Inn, that its stage was only 12 feet deep, that it had side-boxes, a pit, a middle gallery and an upper gallery:[41] but do we really require more? All we have to do is to think of Plymouth and Richmond, and the interior of this vanished little house, in all its essentials, will come vividly into view.

NOTES TO CHAPTER THREE

[1] Arthur Murphy, *The Life of David Garrick* (1801), vol. ii, p. 201.

[2] Wren's sectional drawing, preserved at All Souls College, Oxford, was first brought to light by Hamilton Bell ('Contributions to the History of the English Playhouse: II—On Three Plans by Sir Christopher Wren', *Architectural Record*, xxxiii, 1913, pp. 359–68). Since then it has frequently been discussed: three articles in particular should be noted—'Wren's Drury Lane' by Richard Leacroft (*Architectural Review*, cx, 1951, pp. 43–6) and 'Wren's Restoration Playhouse' by Edward A. Langhans (*Theatre Notebook*, xvii, 1964, pp. 91–100) and his important study of 'Pictorial Material on the Bridges Street and Drury Lane Theatres' (*Theatre Survey*, vii, 1966, pp. 80–108), in which he surveys all the available evidence relating to the early building. The former argues for a magnet or horseshoe auditorium plan; the latter,

besides demonstrating that the association of the sectional drawing with Drury Lane has to be regarded with some caution, believes that the form of this playhouse assumed a U-shape. It may be noted that, while the site of the theatre built in 1674 (119 feet by about 59 feet) remained the same as that used for the existing Theatre Royal, which it replaced, an additional plot of land at its rear was rented for the erection of a 'scene-room' (Hotson, *The Commonwealth and Restoration Stage* (1928), p. 256).

[3] Modern estimates vary concerning this theatre's original capacity. From a careful examination of the Wren sectional drawing, E. A. Langhans believes that it could not have accommodated more than about five hundred to seven hundred spectators; but of course we cannot be absolutely certain that the drawing does in fact show the house as it was built in 1674. In *The London Stage*, I, pp. xlii–xliii, E. L. Avery and A. H.

Scouten suggest that the building might have provided seating for a higher total of about one thousand persons. For conjectures regarding the capacity of the theatre after its reconstructions see, especially, H. W. Pedicord, *The Theatrical Public in the Time of Garrick* (1954) and the commentaries by Avery, Scouten and G. W. Stone Jr. in *The London Stage*, II, i, pp. xxiv–xxvi, III, i, pp. xcv–xcvi and IV, i, p. xxxi.

[4] A full account of the alteration is given by Colley Cibber (*Apology*, ed. R. W. Lowe (1889), vol. ii, pp. 84–6).

[5] John Summerson, 'Theatre Royal Bristol' (*Architectural Review*, xciv, 1943, pp. 167–8); Kathleen Barker, 'The Theatre Royal Bristol, the First Seventy Years' (Bristol Historical Association, 1961) and *The Theatre Royal Bristol 1766–1966*, (1973); James Ross, 'An Eighteenth-Century Playhouse' (Royal Society of Literature, *Essays by Divers Hands*, n.s. xxii, 1945, pp. 61–85); J. Ralph

Edwards, 'The Theatre Royal, Bristol' (*Archaeological Journal*, xcix, 1943, pp. 123-6).

[6] On the Adam plan see Walter H. Godfrey, 'The Apron Stage of the Eighteenth Century as illustrated at Drury Lane', *Architectural Record*, xxxvii, 1915, pp. 31-55.

[7] These two theatres must be kept distinct from a third building, which was generally called the New Wells, located in Hooper's Square, Lemon Street, opened in 1739 in the same area. It was there that the Hallam family ran their seasons before their setting off for American shores. See C. B. Hogan, 'The New Wells, Goodman's Fields, 1739-1752', *Theatre Notebook*, iii, 1949, pp. 67-72.

[8] See particularly Robert Eddison, 'Capon and Goodman's Fields' (*Theatre Notebook*, xiv, 1960, pp. 127-32), Laetitia Kennedy-Skipton, 'Notes on a Copy of William Capon's Plan of Goodman's Fields Theatre, 1786 and 1802, and on a Copy of one of the Ceiling Paintings, in the Folger Library' (*Theatre Notebook*, xvii, 1963, pp. 86-9), and A. H. Scouten, *The London Stage*, III, i, pp. xxi-liv.

[9] Although a contemporary description speaks of it as 'made more than 50 Foot long' (*The Daily Advertiser*, 29 December 1733).

[10] *The Gazetteer and New Daily Advertiser*, 11 November 1784.

[11] This and another oval of Apollo and the Muses were noted in *The Daily Advertiser*, 12 September and 4 October, 1732. A reproduction of Apollo and the Muses stated to be based on a drawing by Wm Capon in the British Museum was included in *Londina Illustrata* II (1825), by Robert Wilkinson.

[12] The fortunes of this house are traced by Henry Saxe Wyndham, *Covent Garden Theatre* (1906), but much additional material concerning it has later come to light: see G. W. Stone Jr. in *The London Stage*, IV, i, pp. lxiv-lxvii. Desmond Shawe-Taylor has a useful short summary in his *Covent Garden* (1948).

[13] Sybil Rosenfeld and E. Croft-Murray, 'A Checklist of Scene Painters working in Great Britain and Ireland in the 18th Century' (*Theatre Notebook*, xix, 1, 1964, p. 8 and xix, 3, 1965, p. 104). This checklist is an invaluable survey of information on the various artists employed in theatre work from 1700 to 1800.

[14] See the 'Checklist' cited above, *Theatre Notebook*, xix, 1, 1964, pp. 18-19.

[15] *Parallèle de plans des plus Belles Salles de Spectacles d'Italie et de France* (1774), pl. 28.

[16] *A Treatise of Theatres* (1790), p. 83.

[17] For both of these see below.

[18] Vol. i, opposite p. 190.

[19] See Robert Eddison in *Theatre Notebook*, xiv, 1959, p. 20.

[20] The history of this house is fully and expertly narrated in *The Survey of London*, xxix, 1960, pp. 223-50. See also Daniel Nalbach, *The King's Theatre 1704-1867*, (1972).

[21] See the note by Richard Southern, quoting *The German Spy*, in *Theatre Notebook*, ii, 1948, p. 54.

[22] Useful and informative lists of places where performances are recorded appear in the various volumes of *The London Stage*. C. B. Hogan adds summary notes on many of these in his *Shakespeare in the Theatre 1750-1800* (1952-57), vol. i, pp. 462-5 and vol, ii. pp. 720-3.

[23] The standard study of theatrical activities at the fairs is Sybil Rosenfeld's *The Theatre of the London Fairs in the Eighteenth Century* (1960).

[24] Sybil Rosenfeld has an excellent study of *Strolling Players and Drama in the Provinces, 1660-1765* (1939). Much fresh information is being turned up in the several volumes which have recently been devoted to tracing the theatrical activities in various towns and 'circuit' areas: an important guide to these is Alfred Loewenberg's *The Theatre of the British Isles, excluding London: A Bibliography* (1950); numerous later articles and books on the subject have been printed or referred to in the relevant volumes of *Theatre Notebook*.

[25] Arnold Hare, *The Georgian Theatre in Wessex* (1958), pp. 32-5. Comparison may be made with a similar record given by Cecil Price in his *English Theatre in Wales* (1948), p. 165: a small company of five players at Abergavenny presented *The Beaux' Stratagem* and *The Parting Lovers* at one performance in 1741. Their expenses were 8d for music, 7d for candles, 2d for paper, 4d for ale, 3d for a drum, they took in 7s and shared out about 1s each.

[26] D. M. Little and G. M. Kahrl, *The Letters of David Garrick* (1963), vol. i, no. 297, p. 367, and vol. ii, no. 351, p. 446.

[27] John Bernard, *Retrospections of the Stage* (1830), vol. i, pp. 11-12. The second drop reminds us how long the essential principles of the Elizabethan stage endured.

[28] Id. vol. i, p. 160.

[29] Belville S. Penley, *The Bath Stage* (1892). S. Rosenfeld, *Strolling Players, op. cit.*, pp. 168-204. Richard Southern's *The Georgian Playhouse* (1948) deals with this and other provincial theatres of the period.

[30] *Norwich Gazette*, 28 January 1758, quoted by Sybil Rosenfeld in *Strolling Players and Drama in the Provinces, 1660-1765* (1939), p. 91. See also T. L. G. Burley, *Playhouses and Players of East Anglia* (1928).

[31] See *The Early Manchester Theatre* (1960) by J. L. Hodgkinson and Rex Pogson, particularly pp. 75-6, 107 and 128.

[32] R. J. Broadbent, *Annals of the Liverpool Stage* (1908).

[33] Richard Southern, 'The Winston MS. and Theatre Design' (*Theatre Notebook*, i, 1947, pp. 93-5); Richard Leacroft, *The Theatre* 1958), pp. 50-1. Henry Francis Whitfield, in his *Plymouth and Devonport* (1900), pp. 304-25, gives some information concerning this theatre.

[34] The activities of the Richmond seasons between 1700 and 1737 are recorded in parts II and III of *The London Stage*. See Rosenfeld, *Strolling Players and Drama in the Provinces, 1660-1765*, pp. 274-305.

[35] A brief memorial, entitled *A Celebrated Old Playhouse: The History of Richmond Theatre (in Surrey), from 1765 to 1884* (1886), was written by Frederick Bingham.

[36] See Richard Southern, 'The

Georgian Theatre at Richmond, Yorkshire' (*Architectural Review*, xcvii, 1945, pp. 23–6), and 'Progress at Richmond, Yorks.' (*Theatre Notebook*, iv, 1949, pp. 9–12); also his chapter in *The Revels History of Drama* ed. Clifford Leech and T. W. Craik, vol. VI, 1750–1880, pp. 79–81. Richard Leacroft, *Theatre* (1958), p. 43; Sybil Rosenfeld, 'The XVIII Century Theatre at Richmond, Yorkshire' (York Georgian Society Occasional Paper, no. 3, 1947).

[37] See *Theatre Notebook*, i, 1946, p. 60.

[38] Richard Southern, 'Concerning a Georgian Proscenium Ceiling' (*Theatre Notebook*, iii, 1948), Fig. 1

and his chapter in *The Revels History of Drama*, *op. cit.* vol. VI, pp. 61–81.

[39] See La Tourette Stockwell, *Dublin Theatres and Theatre Customs, 1637–1820* (1938).

[40] See John Jackson, *The History of the Scottish Stage* (1793); J. C. Dibdin, *The Annals of the Edinburgh Stage* (1888); Walter Baynham, *The Glasgow Stage* (1892). There is a fairly extensive pamphlet and other literature relating to the theatres in Scotland, although most of this concerns the period after 1780: reference may be made to Alfred Loewenberg's bibliography (1950).

[41] Sybil Rosenfeld, 'An Ipswich Theatre Book' (*Theatre Notebook*, xiii, 1959, pp. 129–33). The 'Book' in question is a manuscript volume of jottings prepared by H. R. Eyre, preserved in the Ipswich Public Library. Most of its material relates to the later history of this house (see an interesting article by Richard Southern in the *Architectural Review*, c, 1946, pp. 41–4). There is a valuable ground-plan showing the interior as it was in 1810, but, since this was made after a series of alterations, it is not illustrated in the present volume: a reproduction appears as fig. 20 in Richard Southern's *The Georgian Playhouse* (1948). See also Elizabeth Grice, *Rogues and Vagabonds* (1977), pp. 37–42.

Mixing with the audience   4

On Tuesday 4 May 1756 the Moroccan Ambassador, who was then paying a formal visit to the English court, witnessed his first theatrical performance. That he was coming to Drury Lane had been duly announced beforehand, and, as he entered his box, all eyes were upon him. Greeted by applause, he solemnly made his acknowledgment and then settled down in his seat. The spectators, watching him eagerly and curiously, observed with interest that the audience itself 'attracted his notice so much for some time, that he seem'd very well entertain'd before the drawing up of the curtain', and public interest increased still more when, even during the course of the play, Shakespeare's *Henry VIII*, he was seen constantly turning his gaze from the stage to the house.[1]

This Moor had travelled a far distance to be present in Garrick's theatre, and perhaps we, too, if we were suddenly to sweep over a corresponding distance in time into the unfamiliar eighteenth-century world, might well have behaved much as he did. The playhouse is a building designed for actors' performances, but these performances are given before a public; and since the public's attitudes and tastes to a large extent determine the styles of the productions, with them it is proper to start. Here, however, a difficulty arises. While several contemporary illustrations do give us glimpses of what Garrick's public looked like, obviously these cannot in themselves provide more than suggestions of the habits and behaviour of those seated in the auditorium; information on these matters must therefore be sought for in the written records of the time. The subject is of paramount importance, and yet in the present context it can receive only summary treatment; and it would seem that perhaps the most effective plan will be to begin with a single representative production, using that as a basis for a more extended, although still rapid, view of some of the conditions operative during the course of these forty years.

DAVID GARRICK'S FIRST PRODUCTION

The selection of such a representative production is not a difficult task. Garrick assumed the management of Drury Lane in 1747, and it is with Shakespeare's *The Merchant of Venice*, presented there on Tuesday 15 September, that we may appropriately step into the Theatre Royal.

Talk and speculation, we must suppose, had been active for some considerable time among London's playgoers, and without doubt many eyes scanned the announcement in *The General Advertiser* concerning the first offering of the season, or looked more carefully at the further particulars on the playbills posted outside the theatre and on the walls of coffee-houses.

Garrick himself was not acting that night, but the cast included a number of distinguished players. Charles Macklin, already famous for his interpretation of Shylock, headed the list (see plate 8): William Havard, a favourite of many, took Bassanio; and lively Kitty Clive took the role of Portia. Since this was an extraordinary occasion, a prologue had been specially composed by the young manager's friend, the redoubtable Dr Samuel Johnson, and this was to be spoken by Garrick himself. Lastly, and for the playgoers by no means least, another particular friend of Garrick's, the beautiful Peg Woffington, was to speak the epilogue. The bills stated that the play would begin at 6 o'clock, with choice of places at 5s in the boxes, 3s in the pit, 2s in the first gallery and 1s in the upper gallery. Those wishing to have box seats were advised to secure tickets in advance from Mr Hobson at the stage-door. And at the very foot of the bills came a bold statement, declaring that since 'the Admission of Persons behind the Scenes has occasioned a general Complaint on Account of the frequent Interruptions in the Performance, 'tis hop'd Gentlemen won't be offended, that no Money will be taken there in the future'.

With this final statement we may start. By an old-standing tradition, gentlemen who were willing to pay for the privilege had been accustomed to wander into the back-stage portion of the building, there to watch the action from the sides or to flirt with the actresses in the greenroom and elsewhere: for a long time, spectators seated in the pit and lower boxes had expressed annoyance at seeing some impertinent fellow strolling across the front of the platform in order to greet his friends on the other side or at having the sight of a brocaded coat and a powdered wig suddenly appearing round the edge of one of the wings, and, since the custom was equally annoying for those concerned with the performances, both managers and actors had recently been making attempts to control this nuisance. At the start of the 1740–41 season Covent Garden bills pointed out that their 'entertainment' of *Orpheus and Eurydice*, depending for its effect largely on its scenic devices, demanded an absolutely clear stage, and that therefore gentlemen must be 'refused Admission behind the Scenes'; during the following season Drury Lane's manager followed this lead and even declared that the ban was being imposed 'By His Majesty's Command'. It was easy enough to print the announcements, but the task of eliminating the abuse proved somewhat more difficult. Traditions in general are difficult to break, and this particular tradition had assumed the character of a social privilege. Fashionable gentlemen, therefore, were still prepared to push their way past the keeper of the stage-door, and, if sufficient guards were appointed to bar their entrance, then they were ready to go into the auditorium for the specific purpose of making their annoyance loudly apparent. A few months after the opening of Drury Lane under Garrick's management, for instance, a loud sound of hissing could be heard and an apple was aimed at Charles Macklin—all due to a party of gentlemen, headed by Lord Hubbard, whose main cause of anger, 'in spite of their Excuses, was their

60 left and opposite page
Side-boxes at the opera, 1785. Four pen and wash sketches by Thomas Rowlandson.

being refus'd admittance behind the Scenes'.[2] The ban, indeed, did
not become universally effective until several years later—and then
for a simple reason: spectacular pantomimic and related shows were
becoming more and more popular, and at last it dawned on the dull
brains of Lord Hubbard and his minions that a cluttered stage was
bound to spoil their enjoyment.

Maybe this tradition and the difficulties which the managers experienced in their attempt to eradicate it provide a suitable introduction to what playgoers found when they entered the theatres.
Those who were fashionable and wealthy enough to take their seats
in the boxes had a reasonably easy time—the ladies in glittering
array and their escorts wearing full dress, not even doffing their up-

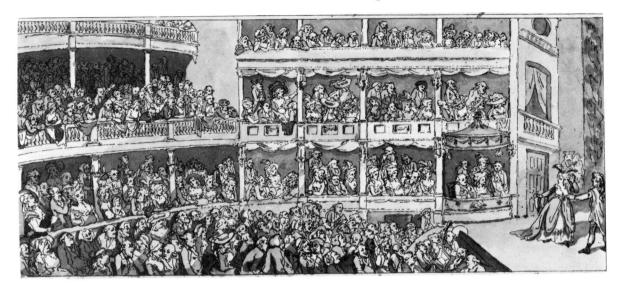

to-date hats;[3] (plates 60 and 61) but the playgoers in the pit (generally a mixture of minor gentlemen and intellectuals), in the middle gallery (mostly tradesmen and their wives) (plates 62 and 63) and in the upper gallery (a motley assemblage embracing all ranks from servants to impecunious professionals) could literally risk life and limb in their attempts to gain admission to the show (plate 64). On some nights, of course, there was plenty of room, but when any special attractions were announced it was necessary to reach the playhouse doors at least an hour and a half before the scheduled time of the performance, and Englishmen in those days were not accustomed to forming decorous queues: when the doors were opened, there was a wild rush, sometimes resulting in injuries, even deaths, and among those lucky enough to force their way in, many

61
Covent Garden audience in 1786. Coloured aquatint by Thomas Rowlandson.

62 *left*
'The Weeping Audience.' Anonymous water colour.

63 *opposite page*
'The Laughing Audience', after William Hogarth.

might be compelled to stand throughout the performance. We need glance only at the entries in a single diary, that of Sylas Neville,[4] to get a vivid concept of what efforts had to be made and what trials endured. Sometimes this enthusiast came to the theatre at a quarter past four and still was unable to find a seat; from bitter experience he discovered that the corner of the orchestra was the best place to stand in; on one occasion, in trying to reach the pit, he was swept up by the crowd into the two-shilling gallery passage and, 'after being squeezed abominably for an hour', managed to wriggle and force his way down to the street again; on another occasion he scurried frantically from one entrance door to another and, at last, although he could find no seat and was 'dreadfully squeezed', he was 'rewarded by seeing Garrick play Hamlet.'

That last statement implies a great deal. There were numerous playgoers in London so keenly anxious to witness the performances that they were willing to suffer not inconsiderably for the privilege; and their willingness no doubt explains why the methods of entering the playhouses remained for so long awkward, cumbersome and inefficient. Box seats, for example, could be purchased beforehand, but there were no numbered places; and even although a correspondent suggested to Garrick a simple system of reserved seats, no action was taken. Not until 1768 did some members of the public who normally sought accommodation in the pit and galleries come to realise that the waste of time and effort occasioned by the early opening of the doors might be remedied: on 5 October of that year the Drury Lane prompter noted in his diary that 'This morning a printed Paper was handed about requesting the Lovers of theatrical Performances to meet this Evening at the Theatre to insist upon the Doors not being opened till five o'clock.—As soon as the Curtain was up, they called for Mr Garrick, and would not suffer the play to begin' until the actor Thomas King, as spokesman for the management, promised that such procedure would be adopted.[5]

The initial difficulties involved in entering the theatre, then, prepare us, at least partially, for what is to be found inside. We have scrambled and pushed our way into the pit, and when we have recovered our breath the first thing to strike us is the intimacy of the audience, intimacy in a double sense. With the spectators in their places, the interior of the house seems to be more compact than it had appeared when empty, and, in particular, we realise more forcibly than we did before how the ladies and gentlemen in the stage-boxes serve to connect the audience with the acting platform. We are struck, too, by observing how many members of this audience are personally known to each other. Elaborately dressed men and women in the boxes greet each other with bows or else engage in animated conversation, fans constantly a-flutter and shirt lace flicking formally; the playgoers in the pit chat among themselves, and from time to time some man rises from his seat in order

64 *opposite page*
'The Overflowing of the Pitt', after S. H. Grimm, 1771.

to speak to friends whom he has espied in the lower boxes. Those in the middle gallery are more subdued, but there also a feeling of compactness is evident, with acquaintances recognising one another and with a buzz of talk. All of this, indeed, as the Moroccan Ambassador discovered, was a lively entertainment in itself (see plate 16).

The sounds of chatting and laughter, however, soon become drowned by sounds different and less genteel, and the formal movements in pit and boxes are supplanted by ruder and more disturbing actions. Already we have become conscious of noise and clamour in the upper gallery, but this has been nothing to what we hear when the musicians start to file into the orchestra well: shouts and yells resound, jeering and oafish laughter, and sometimes there is behaviour more disturbing and apt to be dangerous. This experience is a new one for us, and it will be repeated wherever we visit a theatre during our eighteenth-century wanderings. Each time it comes to us afresh, and always it raises a puzzling question. Almost all foreign visitors to London noted and objected to the deafening tumult—although it is true that some of them charitably, and even half-admiringly, took it as a manifestation of the Englishman's typical love of liberty. 'The uproar of the common people in the theatre before the curtain rises,' one visitor confides to his diary, 'is simply frightful', and he takes due note of the fact that the pockets of the galleryites are often filled with oranges designed to serve 'the double purpose of refreshment and entertainment', the peels being hurled down onto the stage, often becoming so heaped up that before the curtain is raised a servant has to enter with a broom in order to sweep them up.[6] And often it was not only the stage at which the gallery public aimed. Another visitor speaks feelingly of his mortifying experience when, seated in the pit, he wanted to look round at the architecture of the house: immediately 'a heap of orange-peels, striking me with considerable force in the face, robbed me of all curiosity'. The best plan, he discovered, was 'to keep your face turned towards the stage and thus quietly submit to the hail of oranges on your back'. Orange-peelings are reasonably soft, but on occasion other things not quite so innocent had to be endured. The German visitor's hat was once 'so saturated (I really do not know with what watery ingredients) that I was compelled to have it cleaned next day at the hatter's', and such 'watery ingredients' of unknown origin were sometimes accompanied by weightier objects—yet even these appeared in general to be taken in their stride by hardy London playgoers; mugs and bottles they accepted with reasonable equanimity; it took something much heavier to excite them to action. In 1755 'a hard piece of cheese, of near half a Pound Weight ... greatly hurt a young Lady in the Pit', and Garrick was constrained to offer a ten guineas reward to anyone who could identify the culprit. Some ten years later, in 1776, a malefactor was actually arrested, but the account of the affair in *Lloyd's Even-*

ing Post suggests that many of the spectators were amused rather than alarmed: this was a time when fashionable ladies heaped up their heads with miniature mountains of hair and fantastic ornaments, and, when a drunken man threw down a keg full of liquor, it luckily fell on a woman attired in the latest mode, so that, as the paper announced, her head-gear prevented 'the mischief that otherwise might have been occasioned'.[7]

Drunkenness, no doubt, was usually responsible for the more serious misdemeanours, but high spirits, stupidity and a clinging to tradition were the forces most potently at work. The gods behaved in this way largely because their forerunners had done so, and many of their stock cries, borrowed from their predecessors, became meaningless with the passage of time. An excellent instance of this may be introduced by a passage in a book published as late as 1876: therein Lord William Pitt Lennox[8] recalls how, as a boy, he went to see a play at Chichester. 'The house was crowded to the roof,' he says, 'and the discordant sounds that were carried on in the gallery nearly deafened me'; most of these were made up of a medley of 'yelling, shouting, hallooing, cat-calling' intermingled with 'the roaring of lions, mewing of cats, and hooting of screech owls, with an admixture of howling of dogs'. One cry, however, puzzled the boy—something that seemed to apply 'to the nasal organ of the band'. On reading this record, a memory at once comes to our mind of an account by Tate Wilkinson in 1790 describing the way in which at York the rowdies in the gallery were accustomed to shout 'Nosey' at the chief musician;[9] and that account, in turn, carries us back to the year 1753, when Garrick engaged a not undistinguished cello player named James Cervetti, a gentleman who was afflicted by the possession of a nose of extraordinary proportions and whom the gods immediately named 'Nosey' (plate 65). The cry first was heard at Drury Lane towards the start of Garrick's management; although Cervetti had never visited York and had long since retired, it was being echoed there thirty-six years later; and at Chichester it was still being meaninglessly parroted long after that date.[10]

65
James Cervetti, the cellist, after 'Zofini'.

RIOTS AND OTHER DISTURBANCES

The discordant sounds from the upper gallery, however, appear normally to have been stilled as soon as the play began, and we may believe that, with four occasional exceptions, the public listened attentively to what the actors had to say and permitted the action to proceed without interruption. The exceptions may be classed as (*a*) minor demonstrations by groups of spectators when they felt that their supposed 'rights' were being infringed upon, (*b*) temporary exhibitions of disapproval directed either at individual performers or new plays, (*c*) very occasional major upheavals usually fanned into flame by trouble-makers, and (*d*) the confused conditions, quite distinct in kind, associated with the 'benefit' performances.

Eighteenth-century audiences were prepared to speak up firmly and loudly when they imagined that in any way the performers were not giving them of their best. If, for example, they believed that a player had absented himself or herself from the theatre on some inadequate pretence, they did not hesitate to demand an apology— although, in making this observation, we ought also to note that once the apology had been made all became quiet again. Illustrative of this is an account by a German visitor of a performance in 1784 when Mrs Siddons had been billed to appear. Evidently, he remarks, she had been deemed guilty of some offence, and

> when she was on the point of speaking, she was greeted with such mighty hissing and whistling and other signs of displeasure that she could not make herself heard. Many voices cried, 'She ought to apologise on her knees!' and 'She ought to justify her conduct!' At length, after she had been kept for some time in a state of confusion, quiet ensued. Then someone again urged her to 'justify her conduct', whereupon she made a little speech in which she did not altogether deny the affair, but excused herself as well as she could, concluding with the words: 'After all, if everything were precisely as has been charged against me, I believe every Briton will pardon me when I confess publicly, I am a weak woman'. This apology was accepted, the audience applauded and shouted 'Very well!', and she proceeded in the performance of her role without the slightest interference.[11]

The combined appeal to sentiment and patriotism had done the trick: it was almost as though this were part of the show.

Similarly, the audience held jealously to another 'right', that of showing their open disapproval of new plays which they did not like. It was the custom, towards the close of such pieces, to announce their next performances, or, in eighteenth-century parlance, to 'give them out'; and there are numerous records telling us how the audience made their wishes clear. Again, one example will suffice. On 8 December 1772, a play called *The Duel*, by William O'Brien, was presented for the first time: evidently the audience found it boringly disagreeable and several groans and hisses were to be heard during the course of the action; then, as it was being announced for a second showing, these groans and hisses turned into clamorous objections; both Garrick and King sought to argue with the spectators but at length, by the author's consent, the piece was withdrawn.[12] Usually, on such occasions, there was nothing more than verbal debate, but sometimes words threatened to become transformed into actions. Even at the very close of Garrick's professional career, when everyone knew that he would shortly be giving his farewell performance, he was involved in trouble over a new farce entitled *The Blackamoor Washed White*, by Henry Bate.

Apparently the row was started by a certain Captain Roper and his boon companion who, very drunk, started hissing: some folk in the gallery determined to join in, while at the same time a few gentlemen in the pit took issue with the inebriated couple—and, within a few moments, all was confusion: several spectators clambered onto the stage and came to blows, and a full half-hour passed by before order was restored. Two days later, hissing greeted the second presentation of the play; King appeared several times in an attempt to pacify the crowd, but Garrick was imperiously called for; when he appeared, he was hardly allowed a hearing. He managed, however, to draw the audience's attention to the fact that his theatrical life was shortly nearing its end and that he would be glad to close it in peace—to which a man in the pit loudly cried out: 'If you have a mind to die in peace, don't let this farce be played

66
'The Theatrical Dispute.' This engraving depicts the riot at Drury Lane on 5 February 1776, over the performance of Henry Bate's *The Blackamoor Washed White*.

again.' Eventually quiet was restored only when King reappeared to announce that the author had taken the prompt copy of the play and left the theatre with it (plate 66).[13]

This trouble over *The Blackamoor Washed White* seems to have been started by two men whose actions had been inspired by no more than drunkenness and perhaps boredom; but on several occasions the initial impetus was the deliberately planned result of personal or political animosity towards unfortunate authors. Even James Boswell, who ought to have known better, thus made one of a party who sat in the pit on the first night of David Mallet's *Elvira*—a play which many believed might have concealed political connotations—with oaken cudgels in their hands and 'shrill sounding catcalls' in their pockets, they tried their best to get it damned without a hearing.[14] Needless to say, whenever a playwright and *his* friends suspected that anything of such a sort might happen, they were tempted to make up an opposing claque of their own, still further exciting confusion in the house.

From episodes of this kind it is easy to pass to the happily few deplorable occasions when minor skirmishes expanded into pitched battles and riots. Two violent outbursts, in both of which Garrick was involved, may serve as examples, and, since these have frequently been described, they may be summarily dealt with here. The first again illustrates both the determination of the spectators to stand up for their presumed 'rights' and the way in which a small body of discontents might easily transform a theatrical audience into a mob. The 'right' in question was that of entry, at half-price, at the conclusion of the main play, so that an individual might have the pleasure of seeing such afterpieces as the management had included in the evening's entertainment. Clearly, this was a messy and annoying custom, and no surprise can be felt that Garrick, no doubt after consultation with the authorities of Covent Garden, attempted to get rid of it. On Tuesday 25 January 1763, *The Two Gentlemen of Verona*, together with a pantomime, was announced, and at the foot of the bills appeared a stern declaration that 'nothing under Full Price will be taken'. Immediately a gang was organised by a certain Thaddeus Fitzpatrick: a rush was made on the stage, woodwork was smashed and chandeliers shattered; so much damage, indeed, was caused that, when a second riot was threatened the following night, Garrick capitulated.[15] Then came the turn of Covent Garden. Undeterred by what had happened at the other house, its management, on Thursday 24 February, announced the opera of *Artaxerxes*, and the bills even more emphatically informed playgoers that 'Nothing under FULL PRICE can be taken'. Along came Fitzpatrick and his loutish myrmidons, with the result that the entire inner fabric of the playhouse was wantonly destroyed. We may believe that the Covent Garden management had originally intended to be firmer than Garrick had been, but this was too much for them and they, too, had to climb down, uttering placatory cries.

The second example gives a slightly variant picture, when mob fury was stirred by supposedly 'patriotic' sentiment. In the year 1755 Garrick had been busily engaged in organising a particularly elaborate performance, to be called *The Chinese Festival*, the whole show being conceived and directed by that dancer who is now widely acclaimed as the founder of modern ballet, Jean-Georges Noverre,[16] and at last, in November, final arrangements had been made for a great company to present their lavish production. Unfortunately for the actor-manager, however, the Seven Years War was already throwing its ominous shadows over the horizon, and rabid patriotic sentiment was being stirred up against the French: all things from across the Channel were being vilified, and the dancers who had been invited to Drury Lane were being spoken

of by some demagogues in such terms as suggested they were the
advance guard of an invading army. Some rumblings were heard
in the playhouse on the evening before the première, Saturday 8
November and, in order to disarm criticism, a statement was hurriedly inserted in *The Public Advertiser* declaring that Noverre was
Swiss, that he had an international reputation, that out of the fifty-
odd persons making up the company only a few came from France,
and that, in any event, the whole show had been planned more than
a year before. The King's presence at the opening performance had
the effect of limiting disturbance to a fair amount of hissing and
a few opprobrious cries; but at later performances, when royalty
was absent, confusion reigned. The gentlemen in the boxes, swords
drawn, sought to defend the management, but they were out-
numbered by the dissentients. For several nights pandemonium
raged and serious damage was done to the theatre's structure and
scenery, so that in the end Garrick was forced to bow to the will
of the misled bullies.

Such inflammatory episodes were by no means confined to London. In 1747 Thomas Sheridan had to suffer the great 'Kelly' riot
at the Smock Alley theatre in Dublin when, among other things,
he tried to prevent spectators from going behind the scenes;[17] and
the much-tried John Jackson has a lively account of a riot, twenty
years later, when the interior of the Edinburgh playhouse 'was
demolished, the moveables ransacked, and the fixtures destroyed'.[18]
All these records tell a sorry story; yet, even so, a balance must be
maintained. Although on various occasions performances were
interrupted, we may believe that for the most part audiences were
intent upon the productions set before them and that usually silence
reigned. Perhaps, indeed, we may come near the truth if we regard
most of the disturbances as arising from that very quality which
gave to Garrick's stage its characteristic atmosphere—the close
association of actors and spectators. There, in the middle of the
house, they symbolically became one; the cries from pit or gallery,
the direct addresses made from the stage to the auditorium, resulted
from an unconscious feeling that this was a kind of family party.
When we find Samuel Foote starting to invite his 'friends' to 'tea'
or 'chocolate' at the Haymarket, of course we realise that his main
object was to devise a plan for getting round the provisions of the
Licensing Act; but in his selection of this particular method, he was
also instinctively acknowledging his awareness of the current social
relationship between performers and playgoers.

THE BENEFITS

And thus we arrive at what was one of the most peculiar and
typical theatrical customs of the eighteenth century, the benefit performances. Although there were no uproars or riots on these

occasions, unquestionably they carried the family party atmosphere to its ultimate conclusion. During the course of each season many were the nights given over to them—benefits for authors of new plays, benefits for actors and other members of the theatre staff, benefits in aid of charities, benefits for the assistance of individuals in distress. In so far as the players were concerned, these perform-ances were not gratuities; stipulated in their contracts, the receipts provided an important part of their incomes; and, this being so, the actors naturally sought to reap as rich harvests as they could, employing several means towards such an end. After selecting the play or plays to be presented and after persuading some of their popular colleagues to grace the event, they set out on the task of securing the support of their 'friends' in the audience: the actor or actress concerned would then insert an advertisement in the papers, giving his or her private address, so that interested members of the public might there purchase tickets directly—and, if the player was one esteemed by the 'quality', there was the additional hope that, over and above the stipulated prices for the seats, some golden guineas might be slipped in as a present. In the provinces the poor performers had to demean themselves most abjectly by going the rounds begging for assistance; there, indeed, it was not uncommon for the 'manager' to set forth, even for ordinary performances, attended by a drummer, in an attempt to secure public support (see plate 48). Tate Wilkinson feelingly describes this 'horrid custom', whereby it was necessary for 'the performer, whether man or woman, to attend the playbill-man round the town, knock humbly at every door honoured with or without a rapper, and supinely and obediently stop at every shop and stall to leave a playbill, and request the favour of Mr and Mrs Griskin's company at the benefit. The heroine (if unmarried) was equally responsible for steering her steps—no matter whether the Juliet, the Cleopatra, the Lady Townly, or the Queen Elizabeth: no dignity of any kind allowed for such an omission, without being construed a violation of duty.' The 'severe law of custom then in force', he declares, had to 'be complied with, or looked on as an infringement of rules and re-spect': if an actor or actress refused to comply with the convention, he or she was regarded as tinged with undue 'pride, impudence, in-solence, and want of reverence ... No matter how severe the weather, if frost, snow, rain, or hail, Jane Shore and the proud Lady Macbeth were expected equally to pay the same homage'.[19] Cer-tainly the members of the Drury Lane and Covent Garden com-panies did not have to sink so low, yet in essence their behaviour was somewhat similar. Once more a single example will serve. Dur-ing the season of 1760–61 John Beard was given 23 March as the night of his benefit, but, on discovering that this would prove an inconvenient date for some of his principal patrons, he succeeded in getting the date altered to Saturday the 14th, and the following advertisement was inserted in the press:

> Several of Mr Beard's Friends being pre-engaged for Monday 23
> March, advertised for his benefit, and Mr Rich having kindly given
> him Saturday the 14th, he humbly hopes (the shortness of the Time
> not permitting him to wait on his Friends as usual) those Ladies and
> Gentlemen who desire to favour him with their presence, will be
> pleased to send for their tickets and places, to his House next Old
> Slaughter's Coffee House in St Martin's Lane.[20]

Nothing could be more adroit, or more representative of the spirit
of the age—the combination of discreet humility and the free
assumption of amicable familiarity.

And at the benefit performances themselves all the arrangements
were made in the spirit of a large social party. Since obviously the
actor or actress could gain most profit from the higher-priced seats,
special provisions were made for offering as many of these as possible: not only were additional seats set up before the ordinary stage-
boxes (as they are depicted in Hogarth's early painting of *The
Beggar's Opera* and in Philip Dawes' satirical picture of 1765 (plate
67 and see frontispiece); the entire acting area was often built up
with further accommodation for the spectators. During that 1747–
48 season with which we started, for example, Kitty Clive's benefit
came on Monday 7 March: for this she chose Thomas Otway's
Venice Preserv'd, and the bills announced that 'the Stage (for the
better accommodation of the Ladies)' was being 'form'd into Front
and Side Boxes'—which meant that two sets of spectators faced each
other, the one in the house proper and the other in the 'scene'. The
actors were thus restricted to a small space on the platform, with
members of the public in an 'amphitheatre' behind them, others in
the special 'boxes' fitted up to their left and right, quite apart from
those in a crowded 'house' in which the pit and lower boxes had
been 'laid together' so that every seat might be charged at the full
box price.

On numerous occasions the area left available for the performers
was miserably small, and John Jackson's account of a benefit at
Edinburgh may be accepted as typical: 'the wings and stage,' he
records, 'were so crowded that when I came on in the character
of *Hotspur*, to encounter the *Prince of Wales*, we had not room
enough to stand at sword's length'.[21] The players were thus actually
brushing against the playgoers in a manner which might well have
been a replica of the conditions operative in the presentation of an
early sixteenth-century interlude within a baronial hall. When
Charles Holland, at his benefit on Tuesday 20 April 1756, essayed
the part of Hamlet for the first time, he adopted the business of
letting his hat fall off as he started back from the Ghost, but one
'ignorant man', not realising that the trick was deliberate, promptly
picked it up and 'clapt it upon his head'.[22]

'My kind reader,' says Tate Wilkinson in his *Memoirs*,[23] 'suppose an audience behind the curtain up to the clouds, with persons of a menial cast on the ground, beaux and no beaux crowding the only entrance, what a play it must have been whenever Romeo was breaking open the supposed tomb, which was no more than a screen on those nights set up, and Mrs Cibber prostrating herself on an old couch, covered with black cloth, as the tomb of the Capulets, with at least (on a great benefit night) two hundred persons behind her, which formed the back ground, as an unfrequented hallowed place of *chapless* skulls, which was to convey the idea of where the heads of all her buried ancestors were packed ... The stage spectators,' he continues, 'were not content with piling on raised seats, till their heads reached the theatrical cloudings; which seats were closed in with dirty worn out scenery, to inclose the painted round

67
The stage audience, 1728–29. Oil painting by William Hogarth showing a performance of *The Beggar's Opera* in 1728 or 1729.

from the first wing, the main *entrance* being up steps from the middle of the *back scene*, but when that amphitheatre was filled, there would be a group of ill-dressed lads and persons sitting on the stage in front, three or four rows deep, otherwise those who sat behind them could not have seen, and a riot would have ensued: So in fact a performer on a popular night could not step his foot with safety, least he either should thereby hurt or offend, or be thrown down amongst scores of idle tipsey apprentices.'

This is theatre-in-the-round with a vengeance; or perhaps it would be more correct to describe it as theatre-in-two-ovals; one oval curving round the players on the stage and the other large oval sweeping in from the gallery. In the acceptance of these conditions of performance is a symbol of the spirit animating Garrick's stage. Nevertheless, we must not forget that the theatre during these forty years was slowly taking steps towards a different goal. In 1762 Garrick made such alterations at Drury Lane as to add considerably to its capacity, and in consequence he secured the company's consent to do without the cluttering of the platform and the scene: at the beginning of the 1762–63 benefit season, *The Public Advertiser* carried an announcement that 'the Performers will have no building on the stage, nor take any money behind the scenes being willing to forgo that advantage, for the sake of rendering the representations more agreeable to the Publick'.[24]

AUDIENCES ATTITUDES

Before we leave the audience, one or two further observations may be made. In the first place, it seems to be certain that, in general, the English public came to the playhouse with the desire to be entertained. Thomas Davies was right in drawing a distinction between audience tastes in Paris and in London: French spectators, he observed, delighted in the long speeches provided for them by a Racine, a Crebillon and a Voltaire, savouring 'the beauty of sentiment and energy of language' and deriving pleasure from being given the opportunity of shedding tears at scenes of distress; whereas the Englishman 'looks upon the theatre as a place of amusement; he does not expect to be alarmed with terror, or wrought upon by scenes of commiseration; but he is surprised into the feelings of these passions, and sheds tears because he cannot avoid it. The theatre, to most Englishmen, becomes a place of instruction by chance, not by choice.'[25]

In condemning a few plays, the spectators may sometimes have been motivated by political sentiments or by 'moral' objections to the subject-matter (as when they protested against the 'low' scenes which Oliver Goldsmith originally included in *The Good-Natur'd Man*), but usually their hissing meant that they were bored. At the same time, it must not be assumed that all audiences were the same.

Garrick himself noted that the typical Covent Garden house differed from, and was less severely critical than, a typical gathering at Drury Lane; and there were other contemporaries who drew attention to still wider variations. When Lichtenberg went to see a show at Sadler's Wells, he immediately sensed that, amid this 'less brilliant' audience, 'the sum total of the pleasure enjoyed is greater than that of all the other houses together. One's amusement is more spontaneous, since less people are led thither by the dictates of the mode than is the case in the other theatres.' And Sadler's Wells was packed: when he arrived, he says, 'it was so full that I could only obtain a seat by taking a nice little maiden of six years old on my lap'.[26]

Outside of London, habit, custom and taste in one playhouse were not necessarily akin to what might be found in another. Tate Wilkinson, speaking from long and diversified experience, thus stresses the 'difference of audiences', describing it as truly 'amazing':

> A farce, if it possesses true humour, in London will be greatly relished and applauded: In the country very possibly the same (even decently acted) shall be termed vile, low, vulgar, and indelicate. The Love for Love of Congreve, the Trip to Scarborough, the Way of the World, the Confederacy, and others, are in London attended to as plays of wit and merit ... but in the country not permitted, or if permitted to appear, not upon any account fashionable, which is just as bad.[27]

The dictates of society ruled everywhere, but were not identical:

> a Lady in London will go to a known bad opera on the Saturday, and though she professes being an amateur in music will not go on the Tuesday, though a good opera, because it *is* Tuesday. A Lady will go to the theatre at Edinburgh, Bath, and York, though to the most indifferent play, and as indifferently acted, on the Saturday *because* it is Saturday; yet the best acted comedy shall be offered to the public, at either of those three theatres, on any other night, and be totally neglected, unless it is hinted that the night is fashionable, which alters the case. At Hull, the house would not even be a decent one, to whatever play might be performed, if it *was* a Saturday, unless the fashion.[28]

Out of such diverse records must an imaginative picture of the audiences be wrought, all allowance being made for local deviations and for the impress of fashionable foibles. Probably we shall be near the truth in believing that, taken as a whole, the spectators, had mixed reasons for attending the playhouses, buying their tickets partly for the purpose of seeing their friends and of being seen, partly for the purposes of being able to enjoy the performances; that, despite their occasional uproarious aberrations, they were usually good-natured, just as eager to greet Garrick with loud shouts and huzzas after his return from a European tour as they were to express their criticisms in a loudly vocal manner; that they took almost equal joy in witnessing a Shakespearian performance, because they

became involved in its characters, and in watching some pantomimic show, because of its surprising tricks and bustling movements. Not a sedate audience, maybe, but assuredly a lively one.

THE PLAY BEGINS

With some such image in our minds, it may be wise to return
to that from which we started—Drury Lane at the very beginning
of Garrick's assumption of its management.

We have listened to the clamour from the gallery, but now it is
coming close to the hour of six o'clock, the third music is being
played, and the noise from above is becoming noticeably more
subdued. Throughout the whole of the house there is an air of ex-
pectancy; all eyes are turning towards the stage. As we look there,
we see, somewhat to our surprise, that two grenadiers, armed with
muskets, have taken up sentinel posts close to the stage-doors—
and once more we discover something strange and characteristic
of the theatre this time (see plate 19).

The presence of these two soldiers has been so constant in the
playhouses for so many years that, as it were, nobody notices them
at all, nor can anyone say with assurance when and why they were
originally put upon this duty. One man declares that they were first
introduced after a theatre riot in 1721; another claims that this
explanation cannot be correct since Richard Steele, in his *Town
Talk*, refers to them in 1715; a third asserts that King George II
ordered their attendance after some 'bloods' had publicly insulted
the actor James Quin on the stage. Nothing seems certain, save that
for decades they have always been at their appointed positions,
remaining there throughout the entire course of the performance,
unobserved save when some untoward accident occurs. During a
presentation of *Twelfth Night* at Drury Lane on 28 October 1763,
for example, such an incident occurred: in the duel scene of the
fourth act, when Viola draws her sword, the actor taking the part
of Aguecheek bumped backwards against the sentry at the
prompter's side of the platform; possibly the poor fellow, tired with
standing, had been half-dozing on his feet; at any rate he was sufficiently startled to exhibit extreme terror and fall flat on the stage.[29]
Apparently the sole attempt to draw them into the action was that
made by Aaron Hill; at the time when excited rumours about the
'45 rising in the north were circulating in London, he wrote a prologue intended to be spoken by Peg Woffington before a production
of *Henry V*; dressed 'in the new Blue uniform, with Firelock (and
fixed Bayonet) in her Hand', she was bidden to go up to, and to
shake hands with, 'one of the Stage Grenadiers'. Precisely when they
were relieved of their duties cannot be said with certainty; all we
know for certain is that Drury Lane still retained them as late as
1765 and that Tate Wilkinson in 1790 speaks of their disappearance

'within the last twenty years'.[30]

We return once more to the stage. The grenadiers having taken their places, two other persons step onto the platform—liveried servants this time, armed with candle-lighters. As they enter, the great hoops or rings above the platform are seen to descend; the candles are deftly kindled, and at a signal the chandeliers are raised up. Almost at the same moment, a batten of lamps is hoisted from below stage into a footlight trough. The platform is now fully illuminated, and the audience, stifling its chattering and clamour, is all attentive.

Suddenly one of the stage-doors is thrust open, and in strides a finely-clad, light-footed and dapper figure. It is David Garrick. Applause echoes from all parts of the house. He bows, and, as the clapping subsides, he begins to speak in lively and expressive tones:

> When learning's triumph o'er her barb'rous foes
> First rear'd the stage, immortal Shakespeare rose.

Epigrammatically the couplets proceed to tell of Jonson's 'studious patience and laborious art', of the Restoration playwrights for whom

> Intrigue was plot, obscenity was wit.

Then comes the age when

> crush'd by rules, and weaken'd, as refin'd,
> For years the pow'r of tragedy declin'd;
> From bard to bard the frigid caution crept,
> Till declamation roar'd, while passion slept—

followed by the then present period when 'pantomime and song' is tending to supplant the efforts of the serious stage. What, Garrick asks, can the future hold? Perhaps, he says, new follies may come, but, if that is to be the fate of the theatre, one thing must be accepted:

> The drama's laws the drama's patrons give,
> For we that live to please, must please to live.

At these words, Garrick's voice, which has been satirically sharpened as he recounted the stage's errors, suddenly deepens:

> Then prompt no more the follies you decry,
> As tyrants doom their tools of guilt to die;
> 'Tis yours, this night, to bid the reign commence
> Of rescued nature and reviving sense;
> To chase the charms of sound, the pomp of show,
> For useful mirth and salutary woe;
> Bid scenick virtue form the rising age,
> And truth diffuse her radiance from the stage.

The acclamation, as Garrick gracefully steps back to the stage-door, is almost deafening; and, listening to it, we fully appreciate the force exerted by prologues and epilogues during this era. The

68
Garrick in the character of a Countryman, speaking the prologue to Brown's *Barbarossa*, 1754.

69
Thomas King as Fame, delivering the prologue to John Burgoyne's *The Maid of the Oaks*, 1774.

prologue, constantly assuming new forms and diversified in appeal, is accepted by the audience as an entertainment in itself—and properly so, since it is wholly in accord with the spirit animating the entire theatre (plates 68, 69, 70 and 71). The host of this family party, or else one of his fellow hosts, is speaking directly to the guests, and we realise why, if a particular prologue proves unsuccessful, it may prejudice the reception of the play which follows it, and why, when it is truly appealing, the guests should demand its repetition night after night. Thomas Campbell presents us with an excellent example of what could happen. On 4 March 1775, he went to see a performance of Richard Jephson's *Braganza*. It was the tenth presentation of this tragedy, and usually prologues and epilogues for new plays were discontinued after the ninth night; but evidently these particular addresses had mightily appealed to the audiences, so that on this occasion, as Campbell reports, 'a scene ensued which strongly marked the English character'. At the very start the prologue was called for, and obediently the actors acquiesced. Later, however, came confusion:

70
John Palmer as Christmas, delivering the prologue to Garrick's *The Christmas Tale*, 1775.

> When the overture for the farce began to be played the Epilogue was called for—the musick ceased for it could not be heard—a long interval ensued—the players came on—they stood their ground for a long time—but were hissed at length off—Mr. Vernon attempted to speak, but he would not be heared—still the cry was, off, off, the epilogue, &c—after a long pause the bell rang for the musick—this set the house in an uproar—the women however who were singers came on in hopes of charming these savage breasts—but they were a second time pelted off—then Weston—a mighty favourite of the town came on—he was pelted (with) oranges—however he stuck to the stage as if he had vegetated on the spot, & only looked at the gallery & pointed up at it when the orange fell, as if to say I knew you threw that—Once he took up an orange & put it in his pocket—this & a thousand other humorous tricks he played yet all to no purpose—John Bull roared on—and poor Weston could not prevail. The Players came again & again & Vernon after a third effort was allowed to tell the pit that Mrs. Yates was sent for & begged leave that the farce might go on till she came—But this was denied—the house grew more & more clamourous calling for Garrick or Mrs. Yates—at length Mr. Yates comes on & tho' he declared in the most solemn manner that his wife was gone sick to bed, yet this would not tame the savages of the gallery.—The players were twice hissed off after this till a promise of Mrs. Yates's appearance on Monday &c somewhat abated their madness.

'But what to me seemed most expressing of Angloism,' continues this Irish visitor,

71
Charles Macklin delivering his farewell epilogue to Colley Cibber's *The Refusal*.

> was the conduct of some in the pit beside me—some were more moderate & asked others why they made such a noise—one before asked another behind, how he dared make such a noise & told him—after

some altercation—that he deserved to be turned out of the pit—This produced no other effect but to make my friend behind me more vociferous.—The smallest fraction of such language would have produced a duel in the Dublin Theatres—And the millioneth part of the submissions made by these poor players would have appeased an Irish audience—yea if they (had) murdered their fathers.[31]

No such expression of 'Angloism', however, occurs on this occasion we are attending. Garrick has pleased and delighted his guests, and all ears and eyes are attentive as the great green curtain slowly ascends.

NOTES TO CHAPTER FOUR

[1] Frances Brooke, in *The Old Maid*, 8 May 1756, quoted in *The London Stage*, IV, ii, p. 543. If Philip Dawes' picture used as frontispiece in the present volume was painted a few years before its exhibiting and final dating in 1765, then we may see this Moroccan Ambassador with one of his companions in a stage-box.

[2] The comment is by Cross, the Drury Lane prompter, on 22 February 1748: quoted in *The London Stage*, IV, i, p. 31.

[3] On the wearing of hats see *Dr. Campbell's Diary of a Visit to England in 1775*, edited by J. L. Clifford (1947) p. 58.

[4] For these entries see *The London Stage*, IV, ii, especially pp. 1244, 1252, 1295 and 1379.

[5] Dougald MacMillan, *Drury Lane Calendar* (1938), p. 134. Since the primitive and cumbersome systems of admission to the playhouses cannot be pictorially illustrated (except perhaps by reproductions of the tokens or coins used for the purpose) that subject is deliberately omitted here. The methods employed are dealt with in W. J. Lawrence's *The Elizabethan Playhouse and Other Studies* (2nd series, 1913), pp. 95–118 and *Old Theatre Days and Ways* (1935), pp. 42–3 and 117–86; see also the introductions to parts III and IV of *The London Stage*. The standard works on the audience, its tastes and behaviour, are Harry W. Pedicord's *The Theatrical Public in the Time of Garrick* (1954) and James J. Lynch's *Box Pit and Gallery: Stage and Society in Johnson's London* (1953).

[6] J. A. Kelly, *German Visitors to English Theatres in the Eighteenth Century* (1936), p. 54: the reference immediately following appears on pp. 150–1.

[7] Numerous allusions to episodes of a similar kind are recorded in part IV of *The London Stage*: for the above examples see vol. i, pp. 468–9 and vol. iii, p. 1955.

[8] Lord William Pitt Lennox, *Celebrities I Have Known* (1876), vol. i, pp. 269–82: quoted by A. Hare in *The Georgian Theatre in Wessex* (1958), pp. 210–11.

[9] *Memoirs* (1790), vol. i, p. 28.

[10] As might have been expected, of course, the cry of 'Nosey', once established, was readily applied to any member of an orchestra who happened to have a nose somewhat larger than the normal. So it was at York, and Frederick Reynolds records, on the authority of the actor Thomas King in 1799, that the leader of the Covent Garden orchestra, a Mr Baumgarten by name, was 'better known by the undesired cognomen attached to him by the gods of the theatre—"Nosey"' (*Life and Times*, (1826), vol. i, p. 288).

[11] J. A. Kelly, *op. cit.* pp. 100–1. She had, in fact, been accused, falsely, of having taken money for acting at a benefit.

[12] *The London Stage*, IV, iii, p. 1678, quoting from the diary of Hopkins, the Drury Lane prompter.

[13] *The London Stage*, IV, iii, p. 1950, quoting from the prompter's diary.

[14] *The London Stage*, IV, ii, p. 973.

[15] The full story has often been told, with particulars taken mainly from an account in *The Gentleman's Magazine* and from such pamphlets as *Theatrical Disquisitions; or a Review of the late Riot at Drury Lane Theatre* (1763) and *An Appeal to the Publick in behalf of the Manager* (1763). For a general account of outbursts of this sort and for an attempt to classify their causes, see Sir St. Vincent Troubridge's interesting essay 'Theatre Riots in London' in *Studies in English Theatrical History* (Society for Theatre Research, 1952), pp. 84–97.

[16] See M. Delaistre, *The Chevalier Noverre* (1950), especially pp. 26–40; Deryck Lynham, *The Chevalier Noverre* (1972 reprint), pp. 35–9.

[17] Esther K. Sheldon gives an excellent account of this affair in her article 'Thomas Sheridan: Gentleman or Actor?' (*Theatre Survey*, ii, 1961, pp. 3–14) and her *Thomas Sheridan of Smock Alley* (1967), pp. 82–9.

[18] John Jackson, *The History of the Scottish Stage* (1793), pp. 65–8.

[19] *Memoirs* (1790), vol. iii, pp. 127–8.

[20] *The London Stage*, IV, ii, p. 850.

[21] John Jackson, *History of the Scottish Stage* (1793), p. 24.

[22] *The London Stage*, IV, ii, p. 539, quoting the prompter's diary. Another example of the way in which theatrical anecdotes become embellished is provided by Tate Wilkinson's account of this event. According to him Holland, on seeing the Ghost, 'was much frightened, and felt the sensation and terror usual on

that thrilling occasion, and his hat flew *a-la-mode* off his head. An inoffensive woman in a red cloak, (a friend of Holland's) hearing Hamlet complain the air bit shrewdly, and was very cold, with infinite composure crossed the stage, took up the hat, and with the greatest care placed it fast on Hamlet's head, who on the occasion was as much alarmed in *reality* as he had just then been feigning. But the audience burst out into such incessant peals of laughter, that the Ghost moved off without any ceremony, and Hamlet, scorning to be outdone in courtesy, immediately followed with roars of applause: The poor woman stood astonished, which increased the roar, &c. It was some time before the laughter subsided; and

they could not resist a repetition (that merry tragedy night) on the re-appearance of the Ghost and Hamlet' (*Memoirs* (1790), vol. iv, pp. 114–15).

[23] Vol. iv, pp. 110–11, 114.

[24] *The London Stage*, IV, ii, p. 979. For crowded audiences and Garrick's efforts to keep them off the stage in 1748 see Cecil Price, *Theatre in the Age of Garrick* (1973), pp. 84–5, 95.

[25] Thomas Davies, *The Life of David Garrick* (new edition 1808), vol. i, p. 178.

[26] *Lichtenberg's Visits to England*, edited and translated by M. L. Mare and W. M. Quarrell (1938), p. 54: letter dated 8 October 1774.

[27] *Memoirs* (1790), vol. iii, p. 119.

[28] *Memoirs* (1790), vol. i, pp. 183–4.

[29] *The London Stage*, IV, ii, p. 1016. Later this story got attached to Garrick and, as is the way with stories, became much embellished.

[30] A sum of 14*s* for 'Soldiers' appears in a daily pay-list of 1765 printed by H. H. Furness in *Notes and Queries*, 6th series, 1885, pp. 461–2. Later records of payments for guards would seem to apply not to stage sentinels but to men stationed elsewhere on special duty. The grenadiers should not be confused with the Beefeaters who for a long time were officially placed close to the royal box when the King attended the playhouses.

[31] *Dr. Campbell's Diary of a Visit to England in 1775*, edited by J. L. Clifford (1947), pp. 44–5.

Lights and scenes 5

The great green curtain rises, then, to reveal the scene and to give a signal for the commencement of the play. Here, however, we need no longer imagine ourselves seated at Drury Lane playhouse on the one particular night when Garrick inaugurated his management of that theatre in 1747. Only a wider view can prove effective, and before we can profitably seek to gain such a view it is necessary to pause for a moment in order to consider the nature of the evidence which is available for us.

PAINTINGS, DRAWINGS AND PRINTS

An approach towards this can best be made by observing that, while of course the total amount of illustrative material relating to performances and to individual players far surpasses whatever is to be found relating to theatre plans and interiors, this total amount must appear meagre indeed when it is compared with the vast stores of similar information concerning the playhouses of Italy, France and even of lesser countries during the same period. If we turn to the Continent, we can still see theatres which have continued to exist from the time of the Renaissance onwards, some of them altered during the passage of the years although preserving their main features, and some of them remaining almost totally untouched: even when we pass from Italy, richest in such structural relics, we can find in Sweden, in Yugoslavia and in Czechoslovakia extant playhouses which enable us to move round their auditoria and stages as though we were contemporaries, and in some of them we are privileged to see the original scenes and machines employed by their long-gone actors. The Georgian theatre at Bristol is a precious relic in England, but the fact that this building is the only one of its kind erected before 1780 sharply marks the contrast between this country and many others.

The contrast, too, is further emphasised when we set the iconographic evidence relating to the theatre in Garrick's time against the corresponding evidence relating to contemporary playhouses in Italy and elsewhere. In national libraries abroad and in special collections there is an opportunity of examining hundreds, perhaps thousands, of original scenic designs: if it had not been for the lucky chance that about a dozen of De Loutherbourg's maquettes were fortunately secured, a few years ago, by the Victoria and Albert Museum, we should have had to confess that practically nothing remained of the work done by the dozens of artists, both English and foreign, who applied themselves to the stage during the years when Garrick reigned. The contrast is perhaps most strikingly indicated when we think of the numbers of Italian scene-designers who were engaged at the opera-house in the Haymarket; we have many records of their activities, but not a single theatrical sketch by any one of them has come down to us; and, if it were not for one small engraving which recently has come to light, Francesco Bigari's setting for the last act of *L'Olimpiade* in 1769 (plate 72), there would not even be a solitary print to place against the numerous engravings of operatic scenes to be found elsewhere.

In considering this, a further interesting fact comes to our attention. Comparing and contrasting the illustrative material available for the English stage from 1740 to 1780 with that which is available for the Italian stage during the same period, we must be somewhat

72 left
The final scene in *L'Olimpiade* by F. Bigari, Kings Theatre, 1769.

73 right
A scene in Milton's *Comus*, *c.* 1772.

surprised to discover that, relatively meagre though the former is, it paradoxically gives more information concerning Garrick and his fellow-actors than has been preserved concerning the continental performers. This cannot be simply a matter of chance, and perhaps Henry Angelo was correctly pointing to the true cause when he declared that

> Of all civilized nations, ancient or modern, England perhaps has manifested the greatest fondness for portraiture, whether the human character was to be depicted with the pencil, the chisel, or the pen. . . . Chaucer drew portraits with his pen; Holbein was destined to record them with his pencil; and Shakespeare is admired, not so much for the *beau-ideal* of his wondrous fancy, as for the resemblance which his magnificent portraits bear to their prototypes in nature.[1]

If we accept this generalising statement, then maybe we shall have an explanation for the relative scarcity in England of pictures and prints illustrating scenery and the surprising number of portraits of actors in costume. Although it is true that scores of English plays were published from about 1730 onwards with scenic frontispieces,

74 *left*
William Thomas Lewis as Hippolytus in Edmund Smith's *Phaedra and Hippolytus*, 1776.

75 *right*
A scene in John Burgoyne's *The Heiress*, 1786.

the men who were responsible for the dozens of volumes of *The New English Theatre* and *The British Theatre* during the seventies of the century seem to have correctly gauged what the public wanted—series of prints in which single performers appeared in their appropriate roles.

These illustrations of individual players raise problems of their own, but at the moment we must concern ourselves only with those which essay to depict 'scenes'. Such illustrations vary very considerably, and for convenience they may be classified into major groups. (1) First come the very few pictures and prints which, so to say, present the theatrical settings 'realistically', showing the wings and shutters by means of which the designs were transposed into practical stage forms. So few are these that they hardly number more than a dozen in all. 'The Downfall of Shakespeare' by Philip Dawes (frontispiece), the small painting of *Macbeth* as performed at Covent Garden (see plate 19) and John Nixon's water colour of the Bath playhouse (plate 49) are almost unique among the original pictures of those forty years; and among the prints the engraving prepared for *Comus* in 1777 (plate 73, cf. 74 note) is paralleled by hardly anything until the print of 1786 which illustrates a scene in *The Heiress* (plate 75). (2) By far the majority delineate actors in front of what seems to be a 'natural' background, as, for example, in Zoffany's two paintings of *Lethe* (plates 76 and 77). Naturally, such illustrations are of diverse kinds: Zoffany's canvases clearly show the actors realistically, but there are many others in which the entire picture seems to be of a fanciful kind. In fact, it is certain that numbers of them must have been so. When, for example, we look at a print illustrating a Shakespearian play which was either in the repertory or was revived during the period we may well start speculating as to what elements, if any, were taken by the artist from some actual performance in the theatre; but when we turn from such a work to another which we know was never acted at that time we can say with certainty that the scene depicted was one that emanated from his mind. Nevertheless, even in this area, there is the necessity of remaining alert, since there is always the possibility that some such prints may incorporate features similar to those familiar in stage representations. A convenient example may be found in the series of frontispieces used to embellish the 1774 edition of Bell's *Shakespeare*. Unlike the majority of the eighteenth-century 'Shakespeares', this edition prints the texts of at least a large number of the plays as they were currently performed in adapted form, thus literally complying with the statement on the title-page—*Bell's Edition of Shakespeare's Plays, As they are now performed at the Theatres Royal in London; Regulated from the Prompt Books of each House*.[2] Instead of designing a set of frontispieces clearly based on theatrical productions, however, the artist, E. Edwards, has allowed himself considerable freedom—yet the fact that he has put most of his characters

in 'Elizabethan' dress indicates that his imagination was working in harmony with the trend of the times, and it is still possible that some elements in the backgrounds against which he has set these characters may have a direct connection with the stage. (3) From these illustrations we may move on to a third category, those which are manifestly the result of a free exercise of the imagination. The sketch executed by Johann Heinrich Füssli or Fuseli of the dagger scene in *Macbeth* after he had first seen Garrick's performance (plate 78) unquestionably remains closely tied to the reality of the playhouse representation, but a later sketch, dated 1774 (plate 79) is, without any doubt, an emanation of his brain. Similarly, Francesco Zuccarelli's 'Macbeth, Banquo and the Witches' (plate 80) has nothing directly to do with the stage: while it is possible that the artist may have been inspired and excited by his having witnessed a production of the play, the entire concept of his painting derives from the emotions aroused within his artistic consciousness by con-

76 and 77 opposite page
Scenes in Garrick's *Lethe*, 1766.
Oil paintings by J. Zoffany.

sideration of Shakespeare's text. And, of course, there are dozens
of eighteenth-century pictures of a kindred sort.

When our chief object of attention is the playhouse of this period,
it is very tempting to confine our attention solely to those prints
and pictures which fall into the first category or to any in the second
category which might be thought to include features of a possibly
theatrical kind; and this temptation can lead us so far as to find
expression in a statement that, since such illustrations are so rare,
the vast mass of the pictorial evidence is of little or no service to
us. Here, however, a very important consideration must be kept in
mind. Many years ago the philosopher Kant declared that 'The eye
brings with it what it sees', and the truth of this observation is two-
fold. In ordinary life we are accustomed both to ignore many things
of a familiar sort—things which, although our eyes may scan them,
are not consciously registered on our minds precisely because of
their familiarity—and at the same time our perception of other

78 above
The dagger scene in *Macbeth*, with Garrick and Mrs Pritchard by Henry Fuseli.

79 left
The dagger scene in *Macbeth*, a later version by Fuseli dated 'Roma July 74'.

80
Macbeth and Banquo meeting the Witches, F. Zuccarelli.

things is conditioned either by the circumstances amid which we live or by our particular emotional and other attitudes. Now, this truth needs constantly to be remembered by anyone who essays to explore any form of artistic expression, and perhaps it has such special significance in connection with the effort to re-evoke the theatre of the past as to demand further examination here.

Without any doubt, our first task is to seek for evidence which may enable us to reconstruct in our imagination the playhouse structures of the period and at the same time to examine minutely the means employed for the performance of the plays presented within these structures; and, although we certainly could wish for more, the evidence available for us is happily sufficient to yield us the information we require. So far as the scenic spectacle is concerned, much of this evidence for the period 1740–80 is of a 'literary' nature, and naturally, when we turn to pictorial sources, we are inclined to seize avidly upon those few paintings and prints which may confirm or add to the conclusions reached after scrutiny of newspaper paragraphs, autobiographical reminiscences, stage-directions in prompt-books and the like. Yet in fact this is not enough.

The theatre historian needs to preserve, or try to preserve, a double vision. His first objective must be to determine what might be called factual or physical truth—the shape of the theatres, the methods used in translating scenic designs into actual sets, the mechanics of the stage, the prevailing trends in histrionic style, the playhouse habits and customs. But, in addition, and even more importantly, it should be his task to try to see these things as they were seen by contemporaries, and it is here that Kant's statement becomes of paramount significance. Obviously, for example, the painters and engravers frequently refrained from depicting certain things so familiar as to remain almost unseen. The stage-doors, for example, were permanent features of all playhouses, but on occasion an engraver could omit them entirely (as in the frontispiece and plate 44) while hardly any illustration shows us performers making their exits or entrances by their means. This leads us to suppose that, although the doors would have been close objects of attention for us if we had been able to attend one of Garrick's performances, they were practically invisible for the spectators of Garrick's own time. Another example of this is provided by consideration of the sentries on the stage. That they were stationed on the platform we know from many sources, and yet only once do they appear in any picture—and this picture, characteristically, is one clearly painted by a somewhat amateurish artist painfully intent upon reproducing to the best of his ability the actual objects in front of him (see plate 19). We may be quite sure that those who witnessed that scene of Macbeth and Banquo being greeted by the Witches on the platform of Covent Garden unconsciously invested the grenadiers with cloaks of invisibility.

This application of Kant's statement, however, is less important than another. In examining contemporary paintings and engravings we are generally inclined to concentrate attention upon those in which the artists have set the actors against backgrounds delineated in a 'theatrical' manner, with indications of wings and shutters and free-standing pieces; and concurrently we often dismiss other pictures painted in a different manner, showing interiors that look like real interiors or boscage that looks like real trees and shrubs. Thus, for instance, we tend to give particular attention to such a print as that showing the tomb scene in *Romeo and Juliet* (plate 81) as it might have appeared on the stage, while we dismiss other prints of the kind wherein the backgrounds to the players are manifestly far removed from the playhouse reality. What has to be remembered, however, is that while the first print has value because of its confirmation of what we have learned from other sources, the value of the others may be greater and deeper precisely because they reveal what eighteenth-century audiences *thought* they saw. The probability is that the spectators did not really notice the wings—except of course when some accident drew direct attention to their presence—because only by means of these wings and their accompaniments were the stage pictures of the time created. Thus a set of painted tree-wings with a suitable pair of shutters no doubt appeared to their eyes as a real forest, and the relatively meagre stage decorations put before them in a revival of *Romeo and Juliet* assumed a richness and grandeur which they did not possess. The truth of Kant's statement, too, is demonstrated if we turn to consider scenes purporting to be interiors. If we are correctly to place ourselves among the spectators of, let us say, 1740 or 1750, we have to banish from our minds all the box-sets with which we are so familiar: at that period nobody had seen anything like a box-set, and therefore the entry or exit of an actor between two wall-wings not only did not seem an absurdity, it was not even noticed. In effect, the interior created by these wall-wings was seen as though it were a box-set; and the eyes of the spectators became conscious of the

81
Monument scene in *Romeo and Juliet*, after B. Wilson.

wings, and hence of their 'absurdity', only in later years when a
few innovators began to draw attention to them. What the eye saw
when Garrick first appeared as Richard III was not that which it
saw when he was giving his farewell performances.

Even beyond this we may go. Many of these illustrations are significant in a double manner. Some of them help us towards seeing
the settings as contemporary audiences saw them, while others more
distantly removed from the stage may be regarded as having had
a formative influence in their own period. Zuccarelli's vast,
extended landscape in his painting of Macbeth's meeting with the
Witches (see plate 80) obviously goes far beyond the dimly-seen
back-drop of mountain and moor vaguely delineated in the little

82
Scene in *Cymbeline*, 1770. Oil
painting by Edward Penny.

83 *left*
Joseph Wright of Derby, 'The Cave of Salerno'.

84 *below*
'Prospero's Cell with a Vision', after Joseph Wright.

painting of the *Macbeth* performance at Covent Garden (see plate 19), yet there are two suggestions which may be made. The first is that, however far it departs from the playhouse, Zuccarelli's painting and others like it were in fact conditioning the eyes of the audiences so that they saw, or thought they saw, much more than was placed before them on the stage; and the second suggestion is that such pictures gradually led towards a desire to see more. Encouragement, therefore, was being given to the managers and their machinists to devise new means whereby the settings might approach nearer to the audiences' desires. A canvas such as that by Joseph Wright showing a grotto near Salerno, with dark rocks in the foreground and bright sunlight beyond (plate 83) has abso- lutely nothing to do with the theatre; but paintings of this kind soon were brought within the playhouse sphere, as in Edward Penny's 'Discovery of Imogen in the Cave' (plate 82) and Wright's 'Pros- pero's Cell with a Vision' for Boydell (plate 84) and scenic-artists began to aim at similar effects in their designs for example in the cavern scene in *The Grecian Daughter* (1772): no doubt, despite contemporary praise, such settings were only rough approximations of what the easel-painters were exhibiting, but the spectators' eyes saw them in the light of the pictures being exhibited at the Royal Academy and by the Society of Artists.

The essential truth, then, is that, if we tend to confine our interest to the limited number of paintings and prints of a purely 'theatrical' kind, we shall be travelling along a wrong road: virtually nothing within this pictorial sphere can be regarded as alien to our purposes, and often what may appear to be least informative may prove of greatest value.

TRADITION AND INNOVATION

In turning to the stage and its scenery during these forty years, three confident propositions confront us. One investigator assures us that conditions were primitive until De Loutherbourg created a revolution in the seventies of the century. A second asserts that a definite break-away from the past was effected by several artists in the years before that master was engaged by Garrick to take charge of Drury Lane's spectacles. And a third argues that everything, or almost everything, to be seen in the playhouses from 1740 to 1780 can be traced back directly for a period of more than a hundred years—through the earlier part of the eighteenth century, then to the Restoration age, eventually finding its source in the masques presented by Inigo Jones for the delight of James I and Charles I. For all of these propositions suitable evidence can be discovered, and the third in particular would seem to be fully justified by the fact, already sufficiently stressed, that a single stable theatrical form was accepted during the four decades of the 'Garrick' era, a form which ensured that the platform remained the principal location of the dramatic action, with the scenery placed well to its rear. Nevertheless, not any one of the assertions, when taken alone, seems adequate to account for the evidence before us.

Maybe our best plan will be to take a slightly different approach by suggesting that, while certainly the theatrical form remained stable and while most, if not all, the scenic methods can be traced back to the seventeenth century, several things happened during the sixties of the eighteenth century which prophesied a change in theatrical practice. Although at first seeming to be entirely unrelated to each other, these innovations reveal themselves on closer examination as inspired by one central idea.

In 1763, as has been seen, Garrick did away with the conditions previously pertaining to benefit performances: no doubt his action was motivated largely by a selfish desire to rid himself of the inconveniences attendant upon productions of this kind, but, when we look closer, we realise that it reflected a new spirit at work in the playhouses, an instinctive and only partly conscious breaking away from the family party atmosphere which had hitherto prevailed. At the benefits appeared a prime and indeed extreme manifestation of the union of audience and actors: the new spirit was tending towards their separation. Many decades, of course, were to pass by before this separation became complete and up to the time of Garrick's retirement he continued to act as host to his friends; yet the signs of the future were being written on the theatre's walls.

Almost at the same time contemporary evidence begins to accumulate to indicate that the curtain was starting to be used in a new way and that a novel device, the 'act-drop', was coming into service. And, finally, in 1765 Garrick established a wholly new method of lighting the stage.

All these three innovations, deriving essentially—although separately—from a single source, combined to alter the balance in stage productions and to give the 'scene' a significance such as it had not possessed in the past. We must not assume that there was a complete change either in attitude or in practice, yet the groundwork was being laid for a theatre based on a different plan and exhibiting conventions of a new kind.

THE ILLUMINATION OF THE STAGE

Obviously actors can, if necessity demands, dispense with all but one extraneous aid: they can do without a stage, without a scenic background, without props, without appropriate costumes, but they cannot do without light. They must be seen, whether in the sunshine beating down on a Greek open-air structure or in the artificial illumination of an indoor house. With Garrick's alteration of the Drury Lane lighting in 1765, therefore, we may begin—and of course we realise that, in considering the illumination provided in eighteenth-century theatres, whether before 1765 or later, Kant's observation concerning the exercise of the eye has very particular application.

Today, with our universal electric lighting, it need hardly be said that in our ordinary lives we are habituated to ample illumination even when night comes. We go to an hotel, entering a brilliantly lit reception hall, passing along equally bright corridors and eventually being ushered into a bedroom glittering with lamps overhead and on the tables. An eighteenth-century gentleman, if he were staying at an inn, would walk into a lobby provided with perhaps only a candle or two, a candle would be used to guide him along the corridors, and with the candle's tiny flame he would be left in his room. This means that, if we were suddenly enabled to be present at a performance in Garrick's Drury Lane, our eyes would certainly be continually conscious of and oppressed by its dim outlines. It may, on the other hand, be justifiable to suggest that the contemporary public, on entering the playhouse, must paradoxically have been impressed, and even afflicted, by its glare. After leaving their own inadequately lit houses and walking through the streets in winter's blackness, the sight greeting their eyes must have proved both welcome and attractive—and yet, despite their conditioning, it must be assumed that their eyes also would have been unable to see clearly all parts of the interior: some areas would have appeared to be bright and others obscure.

For the performance itself, as has been noted, the heavily counter-weighted hoops or rings and the batten of lamps (or of wicks floating in oil) provided light for the platform, and naturally that area was further illuminated by the scores of glittering candles set in double sconces below or at the sides of the boxes. Lighting in the 'scene' was provided by another three or four rings, each with a dozen candles, and also by vertical battens or 'ladders' which could be placed behind the wings: as early as 1743 Covent Garden possessed at least twelve pairs of these 'Scene ladders fixt with ropes', 192 'tinn candlesticks' and twenty-four 'blinds';[3] no doubt Drury Lane was equally well stocked. In spite of such lighting fixtures, however, it has to be repeated that the scenic area must always have been rather dim and difficult to see—dim, because the candles cannot have illuminated it sufficiently, and difficult to see, because of the distracting glare of the rings above. The main platform, on the other hand, must have been the brightest spot in the playhouse, with its candles overhead, and in the side sconces, with its footlight lamps augmented by radiance from the auditorium. Again we may look at the little painting of Covent Garden (see plate 19): noting how the artist has striven to demonstrate this on his canvas: Macbeth, Banquo and the Witches, standing on the platform, are fully visible, whereas the scenery beyond remains little more than a darkened shadow.

The various sconces, rings, footlights and scene-ladders used in the English theatres of the time differed in no essential way, and indeed may well have originally been borrowed, from the similar fixtures with which French theatres were equipped in the seventeenth century; but it must be observed that during the early part of the eighteenth century Parisian managers had become conscious of the very serious disadvantages attendant upon the use of the hanging chandeliers—no matter where a spectator might sit, a constant glare of light was certain to catch his eyes. As a result, most of the playhouses in the French capital gradually abandoned the hoops and rings, thus restricting the stage lighting to the footlights in front and the rows of candles or lamps behind the wings.

When, in 1763, Garrick visited the Comédie Française his first impression was that the house seemed to be 'dark and dirty',[4] yet it was not long before he came to realise that considerable benefit accrued from the absence of the unshielded overhead lighting fixtures; and his return to London found him fully determined to effect a change—almost a revolution—at Drury Lane. What he actually did is certain, and there would seem to be but small doubt concerning the way he did it. The certainty is that he removed the chandeliers, while at the same time he sought such means as might compensate for their loss. To achieve his end, he evidently did three things. First, he increased the number of candles set in concealed positions, and probably he insisted that these candles should be of the best quality: whereas his annual lighting costs in 1747 had amounted to a little more than £400, in 1766 they had risen sharply to £1,200 and during the season of his retirement they soared to nearly £2,000.[5] In 1765 *The Public Advertiser*, commenting on his innovations, was right in declaring that now the public was being given 'a perfect Meridian of Wax'.[6] Secondly, there is reason to believe that he both improved the lamps in the footlights and supplied them with reflectors: at any rate he was at this time showing considerable interest in instruments of such a kind; on June 15, 1765, his friend Jean Monnet, obviously in answer to an enquiry, wrote to say that he would send him 'a reflector and two different samples of the lamp you want for the footlights at your theatre'.[7] Thirdly, there is further reason to guess that he equipped the scene-ladders behind the wings with similar reflectors, thus causing *The Annual Register* to note particularly the 'lights behind the scenes, which cast a reflection forwards'.[8]

Although the ultimate consequences of these improvements may not at first have been fully appreciated by their inventor, two fundamental changes in theatrical attitude developed from this source. It is almost needless to say that the disposal of nearly all the lighting instruments in concealed positions offered better opportunities for controlling both the strength and the colour of the illumination, while at the same time a new significance came to be attached to the scenic area. When, during the following season, the King's Theatre in the Haymarket followed 'Mr Garrick's example, in removing the pendant lustres' and in lighting the playhouse 'after the foreign manner', *The Public Advertiser* drew special attention to the fact that now 'you have a full view of the whole stage'.[9]

'You have a full view of the whole stage'—these words aptly describe the true nature of the revolutionary change: the platform was no longer the brightest part of the area reserved for the actors. As a result, the actors gradually were prepared to move back from the front position which previously they had tended to occupy and they were prepared to make at least some of their entrances and exits from within the space behind the frontispiece. Nevertheless, the movement was slow, and many years were to pass by before the stage-doors were abolished, before the platform was cut down and before the players, forced to accept the conditions and conventions of a new age, came habitually to perform their dramatic movements within settings framed like pictures.

The second consequence of the alteration in lighting methods ran a similar course. Assuredly, after 1765, we can trace increasing activity among the scene-designers, and in a sense it might be said that De Loutherbourg's appointment as scenic director of Drury Lane was the inevitable corollary to Garrick's transformation of its lighting system. Here, however, in order to undertstand aright what was happening, it may be wise to anticipate and, instead of considering what this artist actually accomplished, to look at what occurred after a few years. No doubt he enjoyed himself at the Theatre Royal, but the surprising thing is that after a comparatively short time he left the playhouse for the purpose of devoting much of his time to the so-called 'Eidophusikon'.[10] For the title which he gave to this one-man exhibition, the painter had probably applied to one of his learned friends, who concocted a single word from three Greek roots meaning 'sight', 'nature' and 'image', the whole conveying the idea of an image of representation of natural visual effects. Renting a room in Lisle Street, now Leicester Square, he first opened its doors on 26 February 1781, and later, on 31 January 1786, he presented a second series in the Strand. In effect, this Eidophusikon consisted of miniature scenic manifestations on a stage no larger than six feet by eight. While it is impossible to call the performances 'theatrical' in the full meaning of that word, a glance at the interior of the exhibition room (plate 85) immediately indicates why De Loutherbourg abandoned the playhouses for this toy, and it also properly places the scenic and lighting innovations of Garrick's time in their proper perspective. Those innovations were important, certainly, but they were anticipations rather than a fulfilment: we might indeed relate them to the 'flying coaches' by means of which, during

85
The 'Eidophusikon' of P. J.
De Loutherbourg, c. 1782.

the very same years, the eighteenth century suddenly felt impelled
to abandon the simple tenor of its slow-moving existence in favour
of speed—a speed which, even if it anticipated the future, could not
be attained until the establishment of the railways several decades
later. In the playhouses, De Loutherbourg had more control over
the instruments of his craft than earlier scene-designers had
possessed, yet his scope, however expanded, was still strictly limited
by the fact that the source of his lighting effects was restricted to
candles and lamps; even although he could play with those which
were set in concealed positions behind the wings, the house itself
could not be dimmed. The significance of his tiny show-place lies
in the fact that it is a kind of microscopic prophecy of the nineteenth-
century theatre to come when gas and electric illumination allowed
an absolute control to the technician. Here is a framed picture
which, being small, could be brightly and colourfully lit; here is an
auditorium in which the spectators, being few in number, could
easily be seated in semi-darkness.

SCENIC METHODS: WINGS AND THEIR MANIPULATION

It has already been said that a third innovation made its appearance during the seventeen-sixties, involving the use of the curtain;
but in order to appreciate what this change meant we must first
turn to consider the typical resources available to the scenic artists
for the securing of their effects. Since, however, this is a subject
which has recently been widely explored, no more is required here
than a general survey.[11]

Everyone knows that the basic, and usual, setting presented to

86
Slanting wings in Arthur Murphy's
The Citizen, 1769.

the theatre public at the beginning of the period was composed of
some three pairs of side-wings, a corresponding number of upper
borders and a back-flat—all placed within the area of the 'scene'.
Besides this 'scene', there was the possibility of utilising a stage area
in the rear, so that when more elaborate effects were desired the
flats could be shaped as cut-outs, thus offering to the spectators an
extended view of further wings and flats beyond. Normally the
wings were arranged neatly and symmetrically on lines parallel to
the stage front, although occasionally they may have been set up
obliquely in the manner suggested by Andrea Pozzo in the first
volume of his *Perspectiva pictorum et architectorum* (1693); for an
understanding of the methods he advised, English theatre-men did
not need a knowledge of either Italian or Latin, since a Mr John
James of Greenwich had obligingly prepared a translation nobly
printed in folio as *Rules and Examples of Perspective proper for
Painters and Architects* (1707). Whether Aaron Hill's reference to
'slanted scenes' in 1750[12] should be interpreted as implying the use
of obliquely set wings remains uncertain, although it would appear
as though this is what he intended, but there is clear evidence of
their employment some twenty years later (plate 86).[13]

We are thus presented with two certainties and one uncertainty:
the normal setting was that which was created by means of parallel
pairs of wings and a back-flat, and the use of obliquely placed wings
was not unknown, but, at the same time, we cannot tell how frequently the latter may have been put to use. And precisely a similar
pattern of certainty and uncertainty appears when we consider the
means which were employed to move these basic scenic elements.
Wings and back-flats had been the invention of the Italian theatre,
a simple device whereby settings might be quickly changed, and in

all probability they were originally made to slide along narrow run-
ways affixed to the stage floor: under the names of 'guida', 'gar-
game' and 'strada' such 'grooves' no doubt came into service towards the close of the sixteenth century, and, although they tended
to be ousted by the introduction of various kinds of scene-changing
mechanism, they remained known in the country of their origin until the nineteenth century. All the evidence seems to prove that, in
general, the English playhouses adopted the simple system as their
normal standard equipment; the wings were shoved on and pulled
back by the scene-shifters, while the flats at the rear were traditionally constructed as two 'shutters' so that they might easily be
handled in a similar manner: at Drury Lane the back-scene was 23
feet wide and 12 feet 6 inches high.[14] Arrangements were also made
so that, if desired, similar shutters could be run in at wing positions,
and by this means a deeper set might be prepared behind a front
one, or, alternatively, a deep set might be closed by shutters run
in before it. The device was simple, but, provided that the convention was accepted, perfectly satisfactory.

The principles and methods, thus firmly set at an early date,
endured for many generations. Even when a new kind of stage developed during the nineteenth century, they still held their own in
numerous theatres, and, carried across the Atlantic, a few of their
relics endured in the United States almost into our own times. Up
to the close of the Second World War, for instance, there could
still be seen at East Haddam in Connecticut the untouched grooves
and flats which had originally been installed in the Goodspeed
Opera House about the year 1880 (plate 87).[15]

87
The Goodspeed Opera House, East
Haddam, Connecticut, 1938. (*left*)
wings and flats or back-drop, (*right*)
overhead grooves.

While all of this is true, however, it is also certain that other scene-changing devices were known and utilised in London and elsewhere, although we cannot be sure from existing evidence just how extensively these were employed. Despite the known fact that the wings were commonly changed by the hands of the scene-men, the Drury Lane prompter's diary suddenly records, on 12 October 1763, a mishap that occurred in the final part of the afterpiece, when 'the Wings did not change on Account of the Barrel being broke'.[16] Now the word 'barrel' was regularly used as a variant of 'drum', and 'drum' was a direct translation of the French *tambour*, an essential part of the elaborate scene-shifting mechanism used in France. Obviously one defect in the simple manual system was that, while absolutely perfect timing was demanded for its effective operation, contemporary records indicate that often the various members of the

88 left
Machinery for moving wings in French theatres, 1772.

89 right
Plan of stage and machines in the theatre of the Seminary of the Collège Romain, 1774.

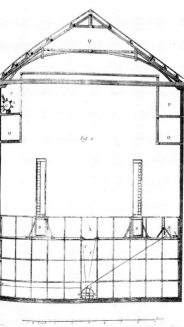

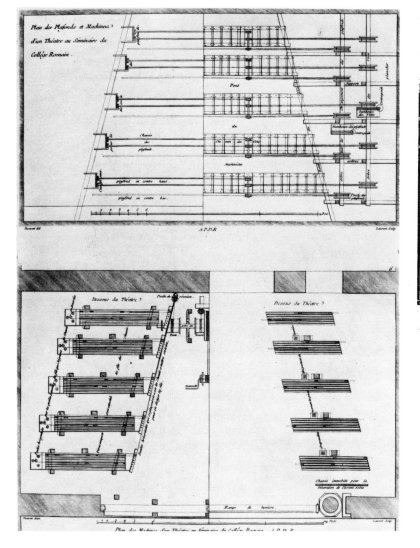

scene-shifting crew failed to work in unison. Hence during the early baroque period in Europe much time and effort were devoted to the devising of mechanical means for moving the various frames smoothly and simultaneously. In order to accommodate such machines, theatre-buildings were heightened and deepened; space was provided above for instruments which raised and lowered the sky-borders, while, below, in the space underneath the stage, the cellars were opened up to give room for extensive mechanical devices.

90
A French stage being set, 1774.

Since Paris was the European capital most easily accessible from London, and therefore the city most likely to have had a theatrical influence on the English metropolis, the practice of its playhouses may best serve to illustrate the chief method employed. For the side-wings the stage floor was cut into slits; through each of these slits projected a long narrow piece of wood, attached at its lowest end to an under-stage carriage with wheels running on rails and at its upper end, above-stage, bearing an open frame to which a wing might be affixed (plates 88, 89 and 90). All the carriages belonging to one set of wings were attached by ropes to a *tambour* or drum, so that when this was turned by means of a winch all these wings moved simultaneously forwards or backwards as required. By a similar use of drums the back-flats were controlled from below stage and, in the flies, the sky-borders were made to descend and ascend in unison.

The broken barrel referred to at Drury Lane in 1763 quite definitely was employed for the manipulation of the wings, and this reminds us of the fact that various 'barrels' were listed in a Covent Garden inventory just twenty years previously. Unfortunately, however, their presence at Covent Garden in 1743 does not aid us in determining precisely when scene-shifting by mechanical means was introduced to the English stage: the barrels certainly were part of the theatrical equipment, but they might have been employed only for the controlling of flying chariots or for the manipulating of such things as 'Banquo's trap' by means of which the bloodstained ghost was made to rise silently onto the boards. And when we turn elsewhere puzzlements and perplexities confront us. W. R. Chetwood, for instance, informs us that when he went to Ireland in 1741 he engaged, at the Smock Alley theatre, 'an experienc'd *Machinist*, who alter'd the Stage after the Manner of the Theatres in *France* and *England*, and formed a Machine to move the Scenes regularly all together'.[17] Now, Chetwood was a man who knew what he was talking about: he had previously been prompter at Drury Lane; he seems to have been aware that such machines were in service in Parisian playhouses, and due weight must be given to his assertion that the device was also employed on the London stage. Our puzzlement, however, increases when we note his further comment that the machine was soon 'laid aside' at the Smock Alley house and when we find that Robert Hitchcock, writing apparently some time before the year 1774,[18] after alluding to Chetwood's machinist as the man 'who first worked the wings by means of a barrel underneath' the stage, declares that the method was later 'well understood and constantly practised'.

All we can say with certainty is that a scene-shifting machine of some kind was known in London and Dublin by the year 1741 and that Chetwood's mention of France suggests the utilisation of the Parisian chariot system. Yet at the same time it is necessary to remember, first, that allusions to the man-handling of wings are fairly frequent throughout the entire course of these forty years and, secondly, that there was at least one other and simpler under-stage barrel device known at the time—one by which the wings were placed on small wheeled carriages moving along stage grooves, these carriages being drawn back and forth by ropes carried down to a drum below the floor.[19] Maybe it was this less elaborate device which was occasionally operated on the English and Irish stages during the Garrick period.

CURTAINS AND DROPS

Normally, with the use of the wing and back-shutter equipment, the main front curtain rose at the beginning of the main play, fell at its close, rose again for the afterpiece and finally descended when that was finished. Throughout the action, therefore, the 'scene' was left open to the view of the spectators: all that happened at the close of an act was the tinkling of a little bell, which warned the orchestra to be ready for the intermission music.[20] This main curtain was generally called the green curtain, and, although attempts have been made to suggest that it was drawn up in folds, it appears to have been quite flat and raised on a roller. True, many prints of this time are bordered at the top by what look like looped curtains, but almost certainly they were modified representations of the painting of a curtain which formed the upper part of the frontispiece: in the small picture of the Covent Garden interior (see plate 19) such a curtain border, coloured russet-brown, is unquestionably part of the proscenium frame, and in the Cipriani design for its successor (see plate 43) it again appears in slightly altered form. This, then, was simply a flat, fixed canvas or wooden piece serving the double purpose of decoration and practical utility. Apparently the true green curtain is represented in one solitary contemporary print (see plate 66) which shows actors, during a minor riot, standing in front of it as the galleryites pelt them with oranges, small sticks and other missiles.

The curtain did not have to descend within the course of a play for three reasons. First, the audiences were accustomed to the wings-and-shutter convention, using their imaginations to translate the formal painted frames into something richer; secondly, the frames themselves could be changed swiftly from one scenic picture into another; and, thirdly, whenever the necessity arose, part of the scenic area could with ease be shut off by forward shutters, thus enabling furniture and other properties to be set in position while the actors carried on their business.

With this general picture in our minds of familiar stage practice we may now turn to consider the use of 'drops'. In 1764, Tate Wilkinson informs us, he paid a visit to the theatre at Plymouth, and there, to his surprise, he found that the 'flat scenes' moved on a principle he had never seen before: they pushed up and down a groove in one straight frame like a window-sash, which must be a good plan, as they, so worked, must be always steady, and the canvas not wrinkled as when on rollers.[21] The significance of this statement rests less in its reference to the 'window-sash' device than to the implied assumption that by 1764 flats on rollers were common substitutes for the frames shoved in from the sides of the stage. To these Tate Wilkinson returns in his later volumes of reminiscences, published in 1795. In the provincial theatres which were under his control, he tells us, the flats were 'chiefly on rollers', apparently because there was inadequate space at the sides for the manipulation of sliding frames—'my stages', he explains, 'are too confined, and not having room for many sliding scenes, the drop ones' had to be 'let down from their fixtures'.[22]

Although other contemporary evidence leaves us without all the information we might desire, sufficient remains to corroborate the wandering patentee's observations and, further, to indicate that painted scenes on rollers, while already in use at the beginning of the Garrick period, became increasingly commoner as we reach the seventeen-sixties.

Many of them were probably back-cloths, or, more properly, backing cloths, lowered at the very rear of the scene to close a prospective opened up through profiled shutters: it seems probable that, in general, the utilisation of a cloth backing in such a position would have been easier to manipulate than any painted frames requiring their upper and lower groove equipment. Perhaps, in scrutinising the Covent Garden inventory of 1743, it is reasonable to assume that the 'open country cloth', the 'sea back cloth' and the 'King's Arms curtain' belonged to this category, and it is possible that most of the other items listed there under the heading of 'Back Flats' may also have been of the same kind—'Harvey's palace', the 'Bishop's garden', a 'waterfall', a 'long village', a 'long wood', a 'canal', a 'seaport' and the like.

In addition, however, there were drops used in a front position, and since it would seem that the earliest references to these come immediately after the year 1750 the guess may be hazarded that they were introduced, or at least first freely employed, about that time. The earliest record so far discovered is in an account, printed in *The London Magazine* for February 1752, of Lewis Theobald's pantomimic *Harlequin Sorcerer* at Covent Garden: there, we are told, 'a scene drops, and gives us a prospect of ruinous rugged cliffs, with two trees hanging over them, beautifully executed'; and it is interesting to observe that within a few months Drury Lane, deliberately vying with the spendours of its rival's pantomime, used the same device in its *Genii*, produced on 26 December. There, too, a scene dropped with 'a rural prospect' and this later was made to rise.[23]

Quite possibly these two competing pantomimes, both ecstatically praised by contemporaries, may have set the fashion for drops which were scenes in themselves; and later references to 'landskips' and 'streets' lead us to conjecture that, in the main, they tended to assume two conventional patterns, one showing a rural prospect and the other introducing perspectively painted rows of houses (plates 91 and 92).[24]

91
A scene in Ben Jonson's *Every Man in his Humour*, 1751. (*Left*) anonymous engraving and (*right*) anonymous drawing of the same scene.

Very soon it must have been realised that front drops could be put to excellent service both for introductory and concluding action, as well as for the concealing of the 'scene' when a deep setting had to be prepared. It has thus been noted that in a *Macbeth* prompt-book of uncertain date but probably recording Drury Lane practice during Garrick's regime a 'street' is dropped so that the scene-men could remove the banquet paraphernalia—and here the very unsuit-ability of the word 'street' suggests that it had become a technical term.[25] Similarly, although no mention is made of a drop two inter-ior scenes in the fifth act of Hugh Kelly's *School for Wives* (1773), are separated by a short scene of a *'street'*; *'two chairs cross the stage knock at a door and set down BELVILLE and a Lady'* almost immediately we move from outside into Belville's *'Apartment'*. Tate Wilkinson provides us with an interesting example of an opposite

Mr. Garrick in the Charecter of the Roman Father.

92
Scene in William Whitehead's *The Roman Father*. (*Above*) anonymous engraving and (*left*) original drawing.

procedure: at a benefit for Mrs Abington, he tells us, the actress had specially prepared a little sketch designed to be performed between the main play and a concluding farce; this started with a conversation conducted by two gentlemen 'in the street', and as soon as this was finished 'the scene was drawn up, and discovered several well-dressed ladies and gentlemen at supper'.[26] No great inventive genius was required to see that such drops could also be employed very effectively at the conclusion of acts: the prompt-book of the 1773 production of *Alfred*, a play originally written by David Mallet and James Thomson, thus orders, at the close of Act I, 'as the Fryer is going up to his cell *Drop Landskip*'.[27]

This last instance is the most important of all, since it suggests that a new system was coming into practice. It has frequently been observed that, when Oliver Goldsmith in 1760 made his fictional Chinese visitor tell the story of a tragic play which he had seen performed in London, specific mention is made of the lowering of the curtain after each of the acts.[28] With reasonable assurance we may say, first, that Goldsmith could not have been mistaken in this account since he was well acquainted with theatrical affairs, and, secondly, that the curtain in question could not have been the great green curtain. What he describes was almost certainly the front drop which, assuming a fresh function, had turned into the act-drop.[29] In view of the date of this record, interest attaches to the fact that the first specific reference to an act-drop made to replace or to supplement the green curtain comes in Benjamin Victor's *History of the Theatres of London and Dublin*, published just nine years later, in 1769: there he states that about 1750 John Lewis painted one such for the Smock Alley theatre.[30]

Materially, of course, the act-drop did not differ at all from any of the other 'cloths' on rollers, but it was distinguished from them by being painted with a distinctly different purpose. At the start, no doubt, it was designed as an 'atmospheric' curtain to be employed within the scope of a particular spectacular production. That seems to have been the objective of Robert Carver when in 1762 he won praise in Dublin for his 'Astonishing Effect of the Representation of the Waterfall at Powerscourt' made for *A Trip to the Dargle*; six years later he painted a 'new prospect' of this waterfall, and, after he moved to London, he was commissioned to repeat his triumphs by preparing 'a representation of a storm on a coast'.[31] Similarly, Philip De Loutherbourg in 1779 designed his great rocky landscape painting specifically for act-drop use in his spectacular *The Wonders of Derbyshire*. Very soon, however, the special ceded place to the general, so that a painter might be instructed to equip an individual playhouse with a characteristic drop suitable for use in all its performances, while later still he might have assigned to him the task of supplying a drop painted with a simulated curtain all in rich red folds and golden tassels.

It need hardly be said that the development of this device between 1750 and 1770 not only harmonised with the other new conventions which began to shape themselves during those years but also materially encouraged the scenic artists to attempt bolder and more splendid effects than those familiar in the past. When once they knew that a scene could be set, with ample time to spare, out of the audience's vision, obviously they could consider the freer use of ground-rows and 'pieces'; they could even begin to think of such novelties as partially built-up sets with practicable stairways and bridges which the actors might really step upon and cross.

THE SCENIC TRADITIONS

In turning from a consideration of the equipment available to an estimate of the effects produced by that equipment, therefore, it is essential to make a distinction between an earlier tradition dominant up to about the year 1765 and a new style which began to rule the stage after that date. This generalisation, of course, should not be interpreted with stern exactitude, since even in the fifties we begin to see anticipations of the later style and since, correspondingly, we still find relics of the old enduring well into the nineteenth century. Nevertheless, the distinction between the two must be maintained.

A second generalisation may also be made. There were three main categories of scenic effects—one was the kind of setting normally used for the main stock tragedies and comedies which formed the staple of the theatres' repertory; one belonged to the pantomimic pieces which, largely popularised by John Rich at Covent Garden, soon were eagerly exploited at Drury Lane as well; and one may be defined as a series of sporadic exceptions when, for one reason or another, attempts were made to provide specially painted settings for some new play or for an important revival.

Obviously it will be well to examine the earlier tradition first, and a start may be made with the assertion that, in so far as stock plays were concerned, it was the general practice of the managers to make use of correspondingly stock wings and flats taken from the playhouse store-room. Here, once more, we must be careful to take fully into account the typical audience attitude towards the backgrounds provided for the players. In a small country theatre, as we have seen, the manager of an itinerant company could present all his plays with the use of merely a couple of back-drops, one an interior and one an exterior, the spectators being expected to adapt these in their imagination to whatever play might be in the evening's bill. While these two scenes formed but miserable theatre equipment when compared with the fairly well-stocked scene-rooms at Drury Lane or Covent Garden, in effect the same principle was operative both for the country manager and for David Garrick: in looking at the ordinary plays in the repertory, neither the provincial nor the metropolitan audience expected more than token visual background for the actors. These token backgrounds, whether simple 'cloths' or sets presented by means of side-wings and shutters, were invested by the spectators' fancies with a richness and appropriateness they certainly did not possess in themselves; and, the eye thus bringing to them what it saw, the public remained for long quite content to accept, indeed to remain unconscious of, the inadequacies of the settings. Thoroughly typical is the advice given to the Dublin managers by an anonymous writer in 1758, when he remarks that a well-run theatre ought to 'be furnished with a competent number of painted scenes to answer the purposes of all the plays in the stock'; these scenes, he adds, could 'easily' be 'reduced to the following classes'—Temples, Tombs, City Walls and Gates, Outsides and Insides of Palaces, Streets, Chambers, Prisons, Gardens and 'Rural prospects of groves, forests, desarts'.[32] A collection almost precisely the same is listed in the 1743 Covent Garden inventory, and more than thirty years later Dublin's Crow Street theatre was similarly equipped.[33]

Since these were only token backgrounds, not only did conventionalism rule, but the audiences were even prepared to overlook various unintentional discrepancies. A few examples will serve to make this clear. As late as 1790 Tate Wilkinson observed that Covent Garden was then still using a setting, originally constructed in 1747, which had 'Spanish figures at full length' painted upon the wings and shutter[34]—and we know from various other records that the inclusion of such full-length figures was by no means uncommon. Even an enthusiastic innovator like Aaron Hill was prepared to accept the convention: when he wrote to Garrick in 1750 urging him to have a 'magnificent' set specially prepared for the last scene in his *Meropé*, he specifically asked that the scene-painter should depict on wings and shutter 'significantly busied groupes of interested people', extending 'the prospect with scarce a sensible distinction, from the *real* life' of the performers standing on the stage.[35] If Hill could thus find nothing wrong with this procedure, it is not surprising that ordinary playgoers were prepared without question to admit almost anything. William Ireland, in telling us that the first drama he ever saw 'was Henry the Fourth, when Quin performed Falstaff' at Covent Garden in 1753, recalled that on this occasion, instead of the tree-stump on which Sir John seats himself during the battle-scene, the actor was provided with 'a crimson velvet arm chair, with gilt claw feet and blue fringe'. The boy, precisely because he was seeing his first play, noted and remembered this, but it is almost certain that most of the adult spectators, accustomed to the conventions, would have taken no particular exception to that incongruous chair.[36]

In the same manner, early audiences took little notice of discrepancies within the sets, whether these were caused by the exigencies to be encountered in smaller provincial theatres or, in the larger Theatres Royal, caused by the carelessness of the scene-shifters. In 1795, Tate Wilkinson, speaking of the York and Hull playhouses, admitted that 'Palace-wings to prisons and plain chambers are no doubt a great and glaring absurdity', but, he adds, 'not to be prevented'; he had such restricted working space round and above the scenic area as to make 'it an absolute and unavoidable necessity to drop a handsome apartment down occasionally to cover in, which should with propriety very likely be a farmer's house'.[37] From necessity we may turn to incompetence. In *The Gentleman's Magazine* for May 1789 a long letter is given space: the editor explains that this had been penned some thirty years before but he regarded its strictures as still being pertinent. Basically, the writer's main complaint concerned a 'want of due order and regulation in the lower department of scene-shifters' who not infrequently left 'clouds hanging in a lady's dressing-room', tree-wings 'intermixed with disunited portions of the peristyle; vaulted roofs unsupported'; sometimes, he remarked, when a general was supposed to be giving his commands on a field of battle, prison-wings might remain unaltered while the shutter or back-drop showed a distant prospect; and in indoor scenes 'it is equally ridiculous to behold the actors making their *entrées* and *exits* through plastered walls and wainscot pannels'. Naturally, it is but seldom that contemporary illustrations show examples of what is here criticised, but there are occasional exceptions—the sketch of the Sunderland theatre during a performance of *Hamlet* (plate 58) manifestly has wings which disagree with the distant 'prospect'; Philip Dawes, no doubt with satirical intent, has a back-drop with a windmill accompanied by what seems to be a free-standing pyramid (frontispiece); and in one engraving it looks as though a pair of wings has carelessly been left out of series. Such aberrations in performance must have been fairly common, but nobody except the super-critical grumbled.

The presentation of pantomimes and kindred shows, however, was a vastly different matter. These depended for their effect upon rapid action, upon spectacular scenery and often upon trick stage devices; and it was to their preparation that the machinist-scene-painters mostly devoted their time and effort (plate 93). On many occasions, indeed, so much work was put into the making of these scenes that the best of them were carefully stored and, after a lapse of years and possibly after a certain amount of refurbishing, were utilised in later productions alongside freshly made sets.

Thoroughly typical is the record of work carried out by N. T. Dall, Covent Garden's scene-painter, during the season 1768–69.[38] Only one or two of the flats he constructed and designed were for plays; several were made for George Colman's 'entertainment' of

93
Garrick and his mechanicals, 1772.

Man and Wife, a concoction hurriedly composed for the purpose of
rivalling Garrick's *Jubilee*; the 'Farm House that changes to Hedge
& Gate' and the 'loaded Cart & Hayrick that changes with five
Cows' were clearly of the trick variety; while 'Four pieces of Rock
for the Flys in Pluto's Palace' were almost certainly intended to
accompany the settings used in the pantomime of *The Rape of
Proserpine*—settings which had originally been painted by J. N.
Servandoni some thirty years previously, carefully prepared and,
when brought out of storage, received with 'due Praise' by the
'judicious Public'.[39] It was, therefore, within this sphere that the
scene-painters gained most of their experience and proved most
inventive: here they spread themselves in spectacular display; here
they devised enormous serpents which moved about the stage on
specially constructed grooves,[40] as well as such devices as that
introduced into Richard Bentley's *The Wishes* (1760) when, in the
last scene, Harlequin tells his mistress he '*wished he might be
hanged*' and 'a Gibbet instantly rose from behind the Couch, which
drew him up by the Neck into the Air, where he hung, dangling, a
very wretched, dismal Spectacle.'[41]

THE NEW MOVEMENT

After Garrick's changes in the lighting of his theatre, associated
with other alterations in stage practice, a definite shifting in public
attitudes and an equally definite elaboration in scenic methods is
to be traced.[42] Much of this was still largely concerned with shows

particularly designed for scenic display and naturally those theatre historians who in recent times have attempted to discuss the visual aspects of stage production during the seventies have devoted most of their attention to entertainments of such a kind: yet perhaps the most significant development within this period was that associated with the preparation of new plays and of special revivals.

Up to the time when Garrick, returning from France, introduced his new lighting at Drury Lane references to new scenery provided for the main dramas, whether contemporary works or works of the past, are rare indeed, and when we look at the meagre list we are usually able to guess that special circumstances induced the management to give them preferential treatment. The first significant exception, for example, seems to have been Dr Johnson's *Irene* in February 1749: this was embellished by several exotic sets, 'splendid and gay', exhibiting 'the inside of a Turkish seraglio' and 'a view of the gardens'—all 'in the taste of Eastern elegance'.[43] Why was this singled out? Presumably for two reasons: Johnson was Garrick's mentor and friend, and no doubt he wished to do him signal honour; while, apart from that, it was probably realised that, in a time when the orient was attracting public interest, the possession of these scenes could later be put to profitable use in other plays. In the following year the bills announced that 'Proper Decorations' had been made for *Merope*, and here we may be assured that the author, Aaron Hill, was largely responsible: he had scenic ideas considerably in advance of his age. We know that he had been in correspondence with Garrick about these 'decorations', and, although unfortunately we cannot tell whether he succeeded in persuading the theatre to supply the elaborate setting which he wanted for his final tableau,[44] we can be sure that his influence and persevering persistence lay behind the production as a whole.

The next exception was Garrick's ill-fated revival of *Antony and Cleopatra* in 1759, and again there may be reasonable assurance as to why it was given some 'fine scenes'. Shakespeare's play was utterly unknown to the stage, and the manager realised that the only hope of making it appeal to the audience was the provision of some spectacular display. That in fact he was deluded of this hope does not matter: he had at least gone out of his way to aim at attracting the interest of the public.[45] A few months later came Arthur Murphy's *The Orphan of China* with 'a most magnificent set of Chinese scenes'.[46] That this was another special case seems proved by a remark by the author's biographer, Jessé Foot: the play, he reports, 'was brought out with great splendour; to which what remained of the scenes of the Chinese Festival contributed, and were applied to a nobler purpose'.[47] What happened is obvious: since the notorious riots of 1755, four years previously, the remnants of the decorations prepared for *The Chinese Festival* had lain unused in the Drury Lane scene-room; and now, when Murphy brought

94
Scene in Murphy's *The Desert Island* (*opposite page, left*) and (*below*) its French model.

forward his tragedy, the canny manager realised that he could get
at least a little return for his losses by pulling them out and repairing
any damage they had received.

For an entire decade, then, from 1749 to 1759, there seem to be
records of only four productions of this kind—and in each instance
a particular incentive explains their exceptions to the general rule.
Gradually, however, as we pass into the sixties we begin to see signs
which indicate the start of a new movement. Murphy's tragedy had
been received with 'universal applause', and it is significant that this
author's next two plays, *The Desert Island* and *The Way to Keep
Him*, both acted together on the night of 24 January 1760, were
adorned with 'new Scenes, Cloaths, and other Decorations': perhaps the facts that he was now high in fame and that the Chinese

95 right
Scene in Murphy's *The Way to
Keep Him*, 1760.

sets had proved popular combined to induce Garrick thus to favour him. The former piece was based on Pietro Metastasio's short opera, *L'Isola disabitata*, first performed at Vienna in 1752, and on *L'Isle déserte* (1758) by Collet de Messine; and interestingly, in his text, Murphy has introduced stage-directions so phrased as to suggest that they describe what was shown to the spectators, while the first edition of the piece provides an engraving which illustrates the opening scene of '*a vale in the Desert Island, surrounded by rocks, caverns, grottos, flowring shrubs, exotic trees, and plants growing wild. On one side is a cavern in a rock over the entrance of which appears in large characters an unfinished inscription. CONSTANTIA is discovered at work on this inscription in a romantic habit of skins, leaves and flowers; in her hand she holds a broken sword and stands in act to finish the imperfect inscription.*' In connection with this a problem arises: the inscription declares that it was designed and engraved by A. Walker, but if we turn to look at the rather rare print by N. le Mire after C. Cochin which appears as the frontispiece to the French *L'Isle désert* (plate 94) we recognise at once that the former was inspired by if not directly copied from the latter: nevertheless, before setting it aside as uninformative, perhaps we might give thought to the possibility that what the London audience saw was a set based on Parisian example. Whatever our final judgment concerning this, unquestioned interest attaches to Murphy's later descriptions—towards the end of the first act '*The sun is seen to rise at a distance, as it were out of the sea*'; the second act displays '*Another view of the island, with an opening to the sea between several hills and rocks*'; later '*The back scene closes, and presents a thick wood*'; and finally the audience is brought back to the initial prospect of rocks and caverns.

The stage-directions in the first edition of *The Way to Keep Him* are equally interesting. A 'Hall in Lovemore's House', possibly a front-drop, changes in the middle of the first act to 'another Apartment'; the second act opens with 'a Room at the Widow Bellmour's, *in which are disposed up and down*, several Chairs, a Toilette, a Bookcase, and a Harpsichord'. This scene was repeated for act III and fortunately a frontispiece by Walker gives us a partial picture of it (plate 95). Probably the artist has reproduced its main features: if so, of particular interest is the way in which he has shown what seem to be painted 'reflections' in the two mirrors hanging on the rear wall—the first record of careful attention being given to scenes, not Turkish or Chinese, but contemporary and familiar.

Shortly before Garrick set off on his continental tour he ordered 'New Scenes and Habits' for a revival of *Cymbeline* on 28 November 1761, and these won critical praise; possibly, too, he left instructions behind him for the 'grand and elegant' scenes which enriched a revival of Nathaniel Lee's *The Rival Queens*, produced during his absence abroad. Perhaps, when he visited the theatres of Paris, his imagination was already planning further displays of a like kind; perhaps the French lighting methods brought no sudden revelation but simply an answer to what he had been seeking; the particular manner in which the Comédie Française used its candles and lamps appeared to him to be wrong, but almost immediately he realised how the basic principles could be adapted for what he had in mind.

The real movement forwards, then, even although it was heralded by these earlier exceptions, came only after his return, when both Drury Lane and Covent Garden started effectively to illuminate the 'scene'. Now we come to the period when the words 'New Scenes' appear on the bills with increasing frequency, and public appreciation is shown by the way in which the two Theatres Royal found it profitable to advertise the merits of their resident designers. Covent Garden could take pride in the work of John Inigo Richards and Nicholas Thomas Dall, while Drury Lane correspondingly drew attention to the creations of its Robert Carver. The efforts of all these men seem to have been significant; no doubt all of them spent most of their time, as their predecessors had done, on spectacular shows rather than upon comedies and tragedies; but their combined endeavours laid the basis for what was to come. Already audiences had been thrilled by the drop-scene painted by Carver for Drury Lane—'a representation of a storm on a coast, with a fine piece of water dashing against some rocks, and forming a sheet of foam truly terrific; this with the barren appearance of the surrounding country, and an old leafless tree or two, were the materials that composed a picture which would have done honour to the first artist, and will be remembered as the finest painting that ever decorated a theatre'[48]; already they had looked with admiring wonder at his two scenes showing two aspects of Mount Vesuvius, one with the volcano in the distance, its flames reflected in the waters of the Bay of Naples, and the second a nearer view of the eruption, depicting 'the torrents of the lava, like a river of liquid fire, falling into a cascade from a rock'; already they had been made familiar, not only with such pictorial essays in the romantic style, but also with scenes exotic, realistic and even with pretensions towards archaeological exactitude.

PHILIP JAMES DE LOUTHERBOURG

All of this reached a culmination in the work of De Loutherbourg, a native of Alsace who, after having won some distinction as an artist in France, arrived on English shores in 1771. He brought with him a letter of introduction to Garrick, and a few months later he had been engaged, on an annual salary, at Drury Lane. For some ten years he remained as the theatre's scenic master, taking charge of many productions from *Alfred*, a show concocted by Garrick himself, in 1773 on to Richard Tickell's *The Carnival of Venice* in

1781. After his withdrawal from Drury Lane at the close of the latter year, he seems to have amused himself chiefly with his 'Eidophusikon', although in 1785 he was responsible for one last spectacular production—the *Omai* which John O'Keeffe composed for Covent Garden.[49]

In considering this man's achievements, it is very easy to fall into one of two traps: reading the ecstatic praise extended to him and not having any earlier designs by others which may be compared with his extant maquettes, we may readily be tempted into assuming that he was a complete innovator, a theatre artist unique in his position, in his style and in his use of technical resource, that when he came to Drury Lane he found the stage in primitive gloom and left it gloriously bright; on the other hand, looking backwards, we may equally well be tempted to argue that almost all that he accomplished had already been achieved by others. The truth, of course, must lie between these two opposed and partial attitudes: we should be able to recognise from contemporary praise that his designs were graced with a quality beyond the reach of his companions, for he was indeed an accomplished artist; at the same time we should not ignore what others had done to make his position possible and secure.

Especially important is it to adopt this wider view when we explore those new means of illumination without which he could

96
Prison scene by P. J.
De Loutherbourg, probably for
Robinson Crusoe, 1781.

97 opposite page
Sea coast scene by P. J.
De Loutherbourg. Water-colour
designs for wings, pieces, groundrows
and back-drop. Set may have been
intended for *Robinson Crusoe*.

not have achieved his effects. In 1826 John O'Keeffe declared that Loutherbourg 'invented transparent scenery—moonshine, sunshine, fire, volcanoes &c.'[50] Now, without doubt, we must accept the fact that Garrick's artistic director was particularly noted in his

own time for the skill with which he planned such displays—the gradual approach of dawn, the stealing in of twilight, the wonder of sunsettings. Nevertheless, two things have to be duly observed—first, that others before him had achieved similar effects and, secondly, that there is some evidence to indicate that he was not the inventor of the devices used to produce these lighting changes. Quite apart from the fact that, having lived on the Continent before his coming to London, he must have known the methods used by machinists and designers abroad, he seemingly was not the first to

98
'The First Scene of The Maid of the Mill', 1765.

introduce these, or associated, methods to England. In this con-nection, the younger Henry Angelo gives us an interesting record concerning a revival at Drury Lane, as far back as 1768, of *Harle-quin's Invasion*. According to him, his father, during a visit to Venice, had been attracted by a kind of puppet-show in which card-board figures were moved across a lighted 'transparency'. On returning to London, he built a similar little stage for himself and demonstrated it to a number of admiring artists, including no less a person than Gainsborough. Later, at the end of a dinner party at Angelo's house, Garrick and he, 'sitting over the wine', discussed the possibility of enlarging the device so that it might be used in the revival of the pantomime. For this John French, who since about 1763, had been engaged at Drury Lane, 'produced a very fine composition' with ordinary side-wings and a transparency at the rear.[51] In itself, the transparency was no novelty: not only had these been in regular service for a long time in Italian and French playhouses, they can also be traced back on the English stage to the period of Inigo Jones. The younger Angelo explains that 'what rendered this scene apparently the work of enchantment ... was a contrivance, which originated in the inventive faculties' of his father. The contrivance consisted of a set of screens 'covered with scarlet, crimson, and bright blue moreen' placed diagonally on the stage; when 'a powerful light' was put before them, the various colours were reflected on to the set. 'The success of this novel experiment,' he adds, 'gave rise to other scenes, in which transparent paintings were adopted.'[52]

99
Scene in Bickerstaffe's *The Maid of the Mill*.

When we survey all the available records and place them together, we must, then, be forced to look upon De Loutherbourg, not as the inventor he has sometimes been made out to be, but as one who brought highest fulfilment to the inventions of others. And such an attitude towards his work probably must be extended so as to apply to his technical methods in setting the stage as well as to his manipulation of the lights. He certainly was able, by his artistry, to produce effects more impressive than those executed by the majority of his fellows (plates 96 and 97) and no doubt O'Keeffe was right in drawing special attention to the way in which he broke up the setting and created an illusion of miles of distance: at the same time, it appears likely that all the means he employed had been in the possession of the stage for some considerable period before he was engaged by Garrick. The act-drop which he designed for *The Wonders of Derbyshire* in 1779 was assuredly not the first of the act-drops, as has several times been asserted. The cavern or grotto effect which, he, in common with numbers of contemporary landscape artists, loved so much was no novelty in the playhouse. Nor was he responsible, in the planning of interiors, either for the putting of practicable doors in the flats or for introducing similarly practicable stairways.

A scrutiny of the designs by De Loutherbourg convinces us that he had a masterly style, but if we turn to the engravings which illustrate *The Maid of the Mill* (plates 98 and 99) in 1765 we are equally convinced that these sets painted by Inigo Richards could not have been realised without the employment of scenic methods often attributed to the ingenuity of his successor.[53]

NOTES TO CHAPTER FIVE

[1] *Reminiscences* (1830), vol. i, preface pp. v and vi.

[2] On the illustrated 'Shakespeares' see T. S. R. Boase, 'Illustrations of Shakespeare's Plays in the Seventeenth and Eighteenth Centuries' (*Journal of the Warburg and Courtauld Institutes*, 1947, pp. 83–108).

[3] Covent Garden inventory, 1743, recorded by H. Saxe Wyndham in *The Annals of Covent Garden* (1906), vol. ii, pp. 309–14.

[4] G. W. Stone Jr., *The Journal of David Garrick* (1939).

[5] *The London Stage*, IV, i, pp. ccxxxiv–ccxxxv.

[6] 25 September 1765, quoted by Dougald MacMillan in *Drury Lane Calendar* (1938), p. xvii.

[7] F. A. Hedgcock, *David Garrick and His French Friends* (n.d.) pp. 391–2.

[8] September 1765.

[9] 30 October 1766.

[10] See Sybil Rosenfeld, 'The Eidophusikon Illustrated' (*Theatre Notebook*, xviii, 1964, pp. 52–4). Cotemporary notices appeared in *The Morning Herald* for 28 February and 1 March 1781 and in *The European Magazine*, March 1782, pp. 181–2, and W. H. Pyne has an informative account in *Wine and Walnuts* (1823), vol. i, p. 284.

[11] See particularly Richard Southern's excellent and detailed *Changeable Scenery* (1952).

[12] Aaron Hill, Works (1753), vol. ii, p. 376.

[13] See Kalman A. Burnim, 'Some Notes on Aaron Hill and Stage Scenery' (*Theatre Notebook*, xii, 1957, pp. 29–33).

[14] Letter from David Garrick to Sir William Young, 3 August 1758 *Letters of David Garrick*, ed. David Little and George M. Kahrl (1963), vol. i, pp. 284–5.

[15] This theatre has recently been refashioned and is now being used for summer productions.

[16] See *The London Stage*, IV, ii, p. 1012.

[17] *A General History of the Stage* (1749), p. 73.

[18] *An Historical View of the Irish Stage* (1788), vol. i, p. 116. A preliminary note in this volume draws attention to the fact that, although the 'original proposal' for this work aimed at dealing with the subject up to 1788, the account 'closes with the year 1774'.

[19] This second machine is described and illustrated in a manuscript by Jacopo Fabris dated 1760 and entitled *Instruction in der Teatralischen Architectur und Mechanique*; the manuscript, with an introduction, has been reproduced by Thorben Krogh (1933).

[20] Kalman A. Burnim in *David Garrick, Director* (1961), p. 94 quotes a pertinent reference to this from Pierre J. Grosley, *A Tour to London*, translated by Thomas Nugent (1772), vol. i, p. 178. Burnim's study presents a wide-ranging survey of scenic methods employed during this period and is a valuable supplement to the work of Richard Southern.

[21] Tate Wilkinson, *Memoirs* (1790), vol. iii, pp. 257–8.

[22] *The Wandering Patentee* (1795), vol. iv, pp. 42 and 119.

[23] Quotation from *The Ladies Magazine* for 6 January 1753, in Kalman A. Burnim, *David Garrick, Director* (1961), p. 92. Much earlier material relating to cloths and rollers appears in Richard Southern's *Changeable Scenery* (1952), but here we are concerned not with the origins of drop scenes but with their employment in the mid-eighteenth-century playhouses.

[24] Unfortunately, there does not seem to be any painting or print which can positively be said to represent a front-drop. The notes to plates 91 and 92 indicate that we cannot safely assume the illustrations for the 1751 *Every Man in his Humour* or the 1750 *Roman Father* to be of this kind.

[25] Kalman A. Burnim, *David Garrick, Director* (1961), pp. 92 and 120.

[26] *Memoirs* (1790), vol. iii, p. 88.

[27] Kalman A. Burnim, *David Garrick, Director* (1961), p. 94.

[28] *The Citizen of the World* (1762), I, p. 79.

[29] W. Telbin has a useful essay on this theme, 'Art in the Theatre: Act-drops' (*Magazine of Art*, 1895, pp. 335–40).

[30] Vol. i, p. 214.

[31] See, for references, Sybil Rosenfeld and Edward Croft-Murray, 'Checklist', *Theatre Notebook*, xix, 1, 1964, pp. 15–16.

[32] *The Case of the Stage in Ireland* (1758), quoted by G. C. D. Odell, *Shakespeare from Betterton to Irving* (1921), vol. 1, pp. 417–18.

[33] The last-mentioned inventory is given by James Boaden in his *Memoirs of the Life of John Philip Kemble* (1825), vol. i, pp. 469–77.

[34] *Memoirs* (1790), vol. iv, p. 92.

[35] *Works* (1753), vol. ii, p. 376.

[36] *Letters and Poems by the late Mr. John Henderson* (1786), pp. 179–180.

[37] *The Wandering Patentee* (1795), vol. iv, pp. 42, 119.

[38] Philip H. Highfill, Jr. 'Some Covent Garden Scenes' (*Theatre Notebook*, xv, 1961, p. 88). 'Spectacular Scenic Effects of the Eighteenth-century Pantomime' (*Philological Quarterly*, xvii, 1938), are discussed by M. Wells.

[39] B. Victor, *The History of the Theatres of London and Dublin* (1771), vol. iii, pp. 165–6.

[40] John O'Keeffe, *Recollections* (1826), pp. 94–5.

[41] B. Victor, *The History of the Theatres of London and Dublin* (1771), vol. iii, p. 35.

[42] This subject has not as yet been fully examined, although various contributions have been made to it during the past few years. Unfortunately Russell Thomas' essay on 'Contemporary Taste in the Stage Decorations of London Theatre, 1770–1800' (*Modern Philology*, xlii, 1944, pp. 65–78) is concerned chiefly with the period after 1780.

[43] T. Davies, *Life of David Garrick* (new edition 1808), vol. i, p. 156.

[44] See p. 131.

[45] G. W. Stone, Jr. 'Garrick's Presentation of *Antony and Cleopatra*' (*Review of English Studies*,

xiii, 1937, pp. 20–38).

[46] Arthur Murphy, *The Life of David Garrick* (1801), vol. i, p. 338.

[47] Jessé Foot, *The Life of Arthur Murphy* (1811), p. 151.

[48] Edward Dayes, *Works* (n.d.), p. 323.

[49] Ralph G. Allen has an unpublished thesis on 'The Stage Spectacles of Philip James de Loutherbourg' (Yale University, 1960). On his accomplishments compared and contrasted with those of his predecessors and contemporaries see two articles in *The Magazine of Art*, 1895, by W. J. Lawrence—'Stage Scenery in the Eighteenth Century' (pp. 385–8) and 'The Pioneers of Modern English Stage Mounting: Phillipe Jacques de Loutherbourg' (pp. 172–7). R. G. Allen suggests that his first production at Drury Lane was *The Pigmy Revels* in December 1772, but for this there is no contemporary evidence. R. Joppien, *Die Szenenbilder Philippe Jacques de Loutherbourg*, printed dissertation, Cologne, 1972. See also his catalogue of the exhibition at Kenwood: *Phillipe Jacques de Loutherbourg.*

[50] *Recollections* (1826), vol. ii, p. 114.

[51] It should, of course, be noted that the term 'transparency' had two distinct meanings: it could indicate a painting on thin material through which light from the rear might shine; but it could also be used for a cut-out revealing another scene beyond.

[52] *Reminiscences* (1828–1830), vol. i, pp. 10–15.

[53] This is the judgment of that astute theatre historian W. J. Lawrence (see 'Stage Scenery in the Eighteenth Century', *Magazine of Art*, 1895, p. 187).

Costumes old and new

If the pictorial evidence relating to stage settings during this period is far less rich than we might have desired, a wide range of pictures and prints confronts us as we turn to consider the costumes worn by the actors. Henry Angelo, as we have seen, observed that among 'all civilized nations, ancient or modern, England perhaps has manifested the greatest fondness for portraiture';[1] the eighteenth century saw the growth and development of a characteristic school of painters and, although many of these did devote very considerable attention to landscape subjects, portraiture and 'conversation pieces' fascinated and delighted both the artists and their patrons, while at the same time technical improvements in the various kinds of engraving offered opportunities for the distribution of such material among the general public. And for artists and public alike what better subjects could be found within the field of portraiture than the actors, what conversation pieces could be more lively than groups of performers in selected scenes?[2]

William Hogarth and Francis Hayman were both actively interested in the playhouse. The tentative experiments of Richard van Bleeck found expansion in the work of his son Pieter, and Benjamin Wilson definitely associated himself with the actors, especially with David Garrick. Indeed, it has been suggested with some justification that the basic interest in the painting of theatrical scenes may have been considerably extended by this performer's astute realisation of the publicity value inherent in pictorial efforts within the playhouse orbit: certainly he was responsible for giving encouragement and artistic support to the most important member of the group, Johann Zoffany or Zauffelij, who, arriving in England in 1760, soon became an acknowledged master.

Paradoxically, therefore, whereas the study of the settings put before the public between 1740 and 1780 is hindered by the rarity of original designs and of reliable representations of the scenes, the study of costuming is made complex by what might almost be described as an embarrassment of iconographic riches. Numerous paintings of actors, singly and in groups, have been preserved; there are scores of pen and wash sketches, large and small; engravings of players in their stage habits abound. At first it would appear as though we possessed all that we might require for a thorough treatment of the subject; yet before we proceed further a number of serious questions and even doubts must be examined.

In particular, it is essential to consider three main general aspects of the theme—the validity of the material presented to us, the general interest in costuming and the attitude of the actors towards their stage appearance.

THE ICONOGRAPHICAL EVIDENCE

At first, when we look at these representations as a whole, we may be tempted to take them all at face value, especially when we find that many of them, and, in particular, those which purport to represent this or that performer in such and such a part, are accompanied by the statement that the original drawing or picture had been made '*ad vivam*'. Nevertheless, care and caution are demanded.

(*1*)   At the very start, we must beware of deliberate fabrications

100
Mezzotint by W. J. Ward, 1829, purporting to be of 'Garrick in the Greenroom' by Hogarth.

or at least of erroneous ascriptions. To illustrate this, one interesting example will serve. More than one book published within the past few years has given pride of place to the reproduction of a mezzotint entitled 'Garrick in the Greenroom' (plate 100). The mezzotint in question was executed by W. J. Ward and issued on 1 January 1829, with an inscription declaring that it had been made from an original painting by William Hogarth, then in the possession of the publisher, J. W. Southgate: it was accompanied by a 'key' purporting to identify the various persons in the group—the most famous players of the time, seated and standing, all attentive as David Garrick, lounging on a chair, recites a part or gives instructions. Obviously, this seems to be a work of basic significance, and yet it must now be deemed to have nothing whatsoever to do either with Garrick or with the English stage.

The original from which the mezzotint was made is now in the Lady Lever Art Gallery at Port Sunlight, and it was reproduced in colour, as by Hogarth, in 1933.[3] By a somewhat strange coincidence, the same year saw the publication of a drawing preserved at the Museo Correr, Venice, with a firm ascription to Alessandro Longhi;[4] and this was, without doubt, the original sketch for the painting, which in turn is seen to be the work, not of Hogarth, but

101 left
Mrs Massey as Christina in Henry Brook's *Gustavus Vasa*, 1778.

102 right
Anne Crawford (Barry) as Sophonisba.

of Longhi.[5] Presumably it represents some dramatic poet reading his verses before a group of friends in a palazzo on the Gran Canale: certainly we are far enough away from Drury Lane's greenroom.

With this warning exhibit set up before us, we may take two other examples from the well-known *Bell's British Theatre*. In the 1778 edition of that work appears an engraving, based on a drawing by J. Roberts, purporting to show Mrs Massey as Christina in Henry Brooke's *Gustavus Vasa* (plate 101), but this tragedy, after having been banned by the Lord Chamberlain in 1739, was never acted in London during the period 1740–80, and, although it was presented in Dublin in 1744, there is no record of Mrs Massey's appearing as Christina. With reasonable assurance, therefore, we may regard this print as a fabrication. And, in treating it as such, we immediately realise that numerous other engravings are similarly suspect. Of these, the print executed by J. Thornthwaite from a drawing by J. Roberts which pretends to show Mrs Barry as the title-heroine in James Thomson's *Sophonisba* (plate 102) may serve as the second general example. This tragedy was never acted during the period, and that fact has been sufficiently attested, by implication at least, in the list of '*Dramatis Personae*' preceding the text. Usually, these lists are accompanied by the names of performers who appeared in the plays at Drury Lane and Covent Garden, but here all is a blank save that Mrs Barry's name has been inserted after the character of Sophonisba. No doubt it is possible that this actress might have come to Roberts' studio with such an attire as she considered proper to the part, but, even so, the obvious suggestion that she had appeared thus attired on the stage must be deemed a complete falsification.

(2) Deliberate deceptions of this sort may not be very numerous, but there are many others over which we may easily trip. In 1780, for instance, the publishing firm of Fielding and Walker issued a set of prints, mostly engraved by T. Cook after drawings by D. Dodd, showing various actors and actresses reciting prologues and epilogues (see plates 68–71). The first of these claims to be a representation of Nell Gwyn, and of course we immediately dismiss this as pure invention because well over a century had passed by since King Charles' lady friend had delighted Restoration gallants with her racy reading of the lines. Although no real difficulty arises here, the presence of this engraving raises doubts concerning other prints in this series. We may assume that all the original drawings by Dodd were commissioned by the publishers, and as soon as we examine them with the Nell Gwyn picture in mind we begin to wonder whether all, or at least some, of the set were not equally imaginary. The artist might have had an opportunity of seeing Thomas King when he spoke the prologue to John Burgoyne's *The Maid of the Oaks* in 1774 (see plate 69), but it is impossible that he could have attended the performance of Colley Cibber's *The Refusal* at Drury

Lane on 20 December 1753, when Charles Macklin delivered his farewell epilogue (see plate 71). It would seem, therefore, that this particular collection of engravings must be regarded as suspect; and, immediately we reach that conclusion, other suspicions enter into our minds.

(3)   Suppose we turn to the engravings prepared for *Bell's Shakespeare* in 1776, for which some of the original drawings are preserved in the Burney collection at the British Museum. Here, for instance, is a little picture by Robert Dighton said to represent Thomas Weston as Costard (plate 103)—very interesting, until we recall that *Love's Labour's Lost* was never put upon the stage throughout the entire course of the eighteenth century. This, therefore, can have no immediate theatrical validity. At the same time, it is impossible simply to lay it aside as worthless: the sketch has a liveliness about it which suggests that maybe it did not derive entirely from the artist's fancy, that Weston may have come to his studio and served as a model. If that were so, then the costume he is wearing might have at least some value as indicating how he would have attired himself had he actually been called upon to take the role—but obviously we cannot be sure.

The picture of Weston, then, serves as an example of not a few illustrations of performers described as appearing in plays which, in fact, were never produced at this period. With these it is not difficult to deal: we simply note that no contemporary audiences could have seen the actors in their assigned roles and consequently we recognise that the drawings are either imaginary or else made from the life in the seclusion of a studio. Others, however, pose slightly different, and often worrying, problems. Take, for instance, the drawing by Roberts which essays to show Garrick in the part of Demetrius: this, engraved by J. Thornthwaite (plate 104), appeared as a frontispiece to the tragedy, Edward Young's *The Brothers*, in *Bell's British Theatre*, 1777. The engraving is dated precisely 6 September of that year: almost exactly at the same time, 11 October, another engraving of Garrick in this part, executed by J. Collyer after an entirely different drawing by D. Dodd, was published in *The New English Theatre* (plate 105). Both of these prints have been reproduced on various occasions as authentic records—but are they? The plain fact is that *The Brothers* was produced on 3 March 1753 and that, after a very short run, was never revived. Thus the drawings by Roberts and Dodd were made a full quarter-century after the event, and, since Garrick had already gone into retirement, there would seem to be no possibility that he took the trouble of coming to the studio, donning the Roman 'shape' he so much disliked and sitting for his portrait.

The statement has been made that Roberts' sketches for the *Shakespeare* and *British Theatre* issued by John Bell provide us with reliable evidence concerning the manner in which the characters

103
Thomas Weston as Costard.

were dressed on stage, but, when we consider the sketch of Weston as Costard (a part this actor certainly never took) and of Garrick as Demetrius (a performance which probably the artist had not had an opportunity of seeing), the quite contrary judgment might be deemed valid—that, while no doubt some of these illustrations correctly reproduce the theatrical reality, each single drawing or print requires to be carefully considered in the light of available information before it can be accepted.

Such a judgment becomes strengthened when we proceed to examine a variant set of problems. What, for instance, are we to say about Roberts' coloured sketch of Jane Lessingham as Ophelia (plate 106)? This actress did take the role in London—but, so far as we can tell, only on one solitary occasion, at her Covent Garden benefit on 21 April 1772. Why, we are forced to enquire, did the

104 left
Garrick as Demetrius in Edward Young's *The Brothers*, 1753, (*left*) engraving by Thornthwaite, 1777.

105 right
David Garrick as Demetrius, engraving dated 11 October 1777.

artist select Jane Lessingham from among the several well-known
Ophelias of the period? As soon as that question is raised, our attention is caught by the fact that a fair number of Roberts' drawings
are of a similar kind, either showing performers in roles which they
had taken only for single displays at their benefits or else, as in the
representation of Miss Barsanti as Helena in *A Midsummer Night's
Dream* (plate 107), in which there is no record of their having
appeared in London. There is, of course, the possibility that the
actors and actresses thus delineated had performed their parts in
the provinces or in Dublin, but even if this were so the question
would remain as to why they were selected instead of others more
widely known. Is it possible, we ask ourselves, that the artist,
commissioned by the publishing house to prepare a set of frontispieces for the plays, was swayed either by his friendship with particular players or by the gift of a few guineas to grant them some
publicity? And if so, what value do we assign to the costumes they
are wearing? Were these simply taken from the theatres' store-
rooms, or were they invented by the painter, or were they newly
prepared for use on the stage?

106 left
Jane Lessingham as Ophelia, 1775.

107 right
Miss Barsanti as Helena in
Midsummer Night's Dream, 1776.

(4)   These questions associate themselves with others relating to the accuracy of the drawings and prints. These obviously must have varied considerably. In writing to a friend, Lichtenberg describes a performance of *The Beaux' Stratagem* which he attended in 1775, and to one episode in particular he gives special praise: then he proceeds: 'I have found the scene described above among the small pictures that are made of actors here. Only Garrick has not got a red feather, and Weston is wearing a different wig and coat. It's as like Weston as his image in a mirror; but not at all like Garrick.' (Plate 109.) In another letter written to a different correspondent a few months later he makes further reference to this, specifically naming the 'small pictures' which he has in mind. 'An engraving has been made of this part of the scene,' he says, 'and Sayer has included a copy of it among his well-known little pictures. But it is not particularly like either Weston or Garrick, and of the latter, in especial, it is an abominable caricature.' Evidently in the interim he had somewhat changed his mind about the Weston likeness, but his view of the Garrick figure is even more emphatic. On the other hand he draws attention to the fact that the picture of Abel Drugger (plate 108) in the same series 'is Garrick to the life', while the two sketches of this actor 'in character as Sir John Brute, showing him sitting down and drunk, are good likenesses, and that in which he is fighting with the Bow Street runners tolerable'.[6]

While we, of course, have no means of knowing which illustrations are reasonably accurate and which are not, Lichtenberg's remarks clearly have to be borne steadily in mind when we are engaged in trying to draw conclusions from the available iconographical evidence. The fact that commonly the engravers reversed the pictures they were engaged in copying perhaps rarely has significance if our concern is directed exclusively towards the actors' costumes, although it need hardly be said that if we are considering the gestures of individual players or the groupings of a number of

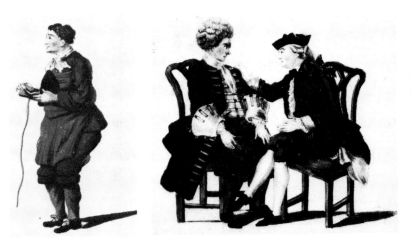

108 left
Garrick as Abel Drugger.

109 right
Thomas Weston as Scrub and Garrick as Archer in *The Beaux' Stratagem*, 1771.

performers on the stage this becomes of very considerable importance. What calls for prime attention here is the question of how far the artists delineated with reasonable exactitude the habits these performers actually wore, and here we are often left at a loss. Lichtenberg, as we have seen, declares that Weston's wig and coat on the stage were different from those shown in the Sayer print, but can we be absolutely sure that the actor always wore the same costume at every performance? Here we have to observe that for some prominent actors in favourite parts we are sometimes offered series of prints executed by different engravers and issued at different times, and that careful comparison occasionally reveals major or minor variations. A good instance of this is the set of illustrations showing Garrick in the part of the hero in James Thomson's *Tancred and Sigismunda*, a tragedy originally presented at Drury

110
Garrick as Tancred in Thomson's *Tancred and Sigismunda*, 18 March 1745.

Lane on 3 March 1745 and later performed on many occasions. Somehow or other Garrick seems to have acquired a Hungarian huzzar's uniform, more likely to have been imported from abroad than specially made in England, and this he donned for the interpretation of the role (plate 110). The earliest engraving was issued in 1752, but when we compare this with those which appeared during the sixties and seventies we see that there are several deviations: the bars fastening the jacket are present in all of them, but some show the breeches, instead of being plain, with ornamentation down the sides, while a falling lace collar is sometimes substituted for the upstanding military neckband. No doubt the variations here are not of any great significance, but they do raise a general question: did they result from the fancies of different artists, one 'improving' on another, or were all these artists being faithful to the reality confronting them? After all, theatrical costumes inevitably wear out, and it is quite possible that Garrick, after his first Hungarian model became dilapitated, caused it to be refashioned—maybe more than once; if so, in these refashionings theatrical changes might have been introduced which in the end drew it away from the original design.

(5)   This example of the huzzar uniform can be carried further still. In various collections there are to be found a few coloured sketches of Garrick in the Tancred role, and it might be thought that these could most readily give us an answer to our question. The difficulty here is to determine precisely whether such drawings were made from already published prints or whether they were executed independently. Undoubtedly, the set of little pictures made by James Roberts in or about 1776 were the sources from which the engravings in *Bell's British Theatre* and *Bell's Shakespeare* were executed, and, this being so, their evidence takes precedence; but many of the small sketches which can be found in extra-illustrated volumes and elsewhere look as though they may have been copied from already existing prints. In such instances, any deviations are likely to have come from the fancies of the draughtsmen.

Not even the colourings can be accepted as being necessarily true to the reality. This thought, in turn, raises another query. Obviously, a black-and-white engraving of a theatrical costume is unsatisfactory, since the total effect of a dress worn on the stage comes perhaps as much from its hues as from its cut. Now, we can find scores of prints which have been coloured, and at first we may be tempted to assume that the publishers commonly issued their illustrations in two forms, the cheaper black-and-white and the more expensive with washes of colour; and this assumption leads us towards an acceptance of these colours as being authentic. Sometimes it seems evident that they were so. Thus, for instance, the existing coloured specimens of the print showing Garrick in his foppishly elaborate suit as the Duke of Gloucester concur in giving him a dress made up of delicately tinted material, light pinks and yellows and blues predominating. We may, therefore, believe that here we are close, at least, to the stage reality.

Unfortunately, however, examination of other sets of prints immediately demonstrates that concurrence of this kind is by no means universal. If, for instance, we turn back to coloured copies of the engravings showing Garrick as Tancred, we find in one that his tunic is yellow trimmed with red and that his cloak is red, while in another the tunic is green faced with yellow and the cloak is black. No simple answer to this puzzle can be discovered: it may be that on occasion there was no uniformity of colouring in the publishers' offices; it may be that the colourings on some of the prints may have been made, not before their sale, but by those who purchased them, the greens and the reds and the yellows dictated by the whims of their possessors; it may be that for others the tints were resultant upon actual alterations in the suits themselves as worn-out costumes were resewn with fresh pieces of cloth. In any event, it is wise to tread carefully: all that can be said with assurance is that the colourings serve to reflect in general the diverse and often startling hues displayed on the stage: the ordinary civil dress of the period was rich

111
The Weird Sisters in *Macbeth* by J. H. Fuseli.

112
Shakespeare as seen by S. H.
Grimm. Water-colours, 1769 to 1782
(*above left*) *Merchant of Venice*, act 3
scene 2, and (*above right*) act 4 scene 2,
(*below left and right*) *As You Like It*,
act 1 scene 6, and (*above*) *Hamlet*, act
3 scene 6.

in tone, and the costumes worn by the actors are likely to have outdone the bright variety to be seen among the spectators in the house.
Beyond that we cannot go.

(6)   Almost all the remarks made above have been concerned
either with engravings or with small sketches associated with these,
but we have also to consider the more ambitious paintings of theatrical subjects. In this sphere questions arise similar to those already
discussed in relation to the scenes or backgrounds against which
the actors have been placed. The objectives of the artists, as we have
seen, might be of varying kinds. There is no difficulty in determining
that Zoffany's picture of Garrick and his companions in *Lethe* (see
plates 76 and 77) belongs in a totally different realm to that which
inspired Fusseli's painting of the Witches in *Macbeth*: in the former,
although the background against which the players stand has been
freely treated, Zoffany has manifestly tried to show these players

as they actually appeared, whereas Fuseli's picture is throughout an exercise of the imagination (plate 111). There is, of course, again the temptation to say that only pictures of the first sort are of interest to us as we attempt to explore the stage costumes of the period, but, just as in our examination of the settings, two considerations must make us pause. No doubt an imaginative painting can have no value as a direct piece of evidence; on the other hand, it may, on closer scrutiny, be found to derive its inspiration from a scene witnessed by the artist, revealing not what was present as a reality upon the stage, but the impression made upon the spectators by what they saw and heard. And, even if this quality is not present, the picture may have value in another way, since still further scrutiny may indicate that the particular artist's fancy itself influenced the costuming of later productions.

The problem of determining the categories into which the paintings are to be placed is, naturally, a very difficult one. The sharp contrast in approach exemplified by Zoffany and Fuseli is seldom applicable: many of the extant paintings come in between, and, as with the designs executed by Francis Hayman and by S. H. Grimm (plate 112), it is almost impossible to say what parts of them are pertinent for our present purpose and what are not. At the same time, there is hardly any contemporary picture connected with plays or players which we can safely ignore.

AUDIENCE ATTITUDES AND ACTORS' PRACTICE

All these pictures and prints need to be set against two things— public taste and the methods used by the players in their performances. So far as the first is concerned, it may be asserted with assurance that at the beginning of the century very few spectators knew anything in detail about historical costume and hardly a single playgoer was at all anxious to see on the stage reproductions of habits proper to particular times and countries. As a matter of fact, even those few who might have been interested in the subject of dress outside of their own milieu could have found little to enlighten them except within the classical period. Gradually, however, as decade followed decade and as antiquarian activities increased, this subject began to attract the attention of at least restricted groups, and those who sought for information were provided with studies which, if not always of deep scholarly value, revealed things hitherto unknown. In 1605 Richard Rowlands, writing about Saxon times in his peculiarly named *A Restitution of Decayed Intelligence* under the pseudonym of 'R. Verstegan', was an almost solitary enthusiast: during the third quarter of the eighteenth century there was a backing of interested readers for Thomas Jefferys' *Recueil des Habillements de Différentes Nations* (1757–72) (plate 113), Thomas Percy's *Northern Antiquities* (1770) and Joseph Strutt's *Angel-cynnan: A*

Compleat View of the Manners, Customs, Arms, Habits, &c of the Inhabitants of England, from the Arrival of the Saxons till the Reign of Henry VIII (1775–76). During these same years, moreover, English merchants were bringing back from distant parts specimens of native attire, so that from practical demonstration London society was being made aware of what the people of China, of India and of other far-off places actually wore.

Quite understandably, therefore, a new attitude towards stage costuming slowly came into being. Those who had become acquainted with ancient attires suddenly started to find the stock theatrical dresses inappropriate, and those who had actually handled a real mandarin gown wanted to see Chinese characters clad in the manner which they knew to be appropriate. This desire, which we may call the historical, coincided with another. Audiences always have liked novelty and show, and these eighteenth-century spectators discovered that, quite apart from the correctness, costumes of these kinds had a colourful gloss which bred delight. As we look at the theatrical records of the Garrick era, we must ever keep in mind this changing attitude on the part of the public.

And with this we must associate changing procedures within the theatres themselves. Fundamentally, it may be said, the actors at the beginning of the century behaved as individuals working to certain common patterns, the tragedians seeking to excite applause by an artificial delivery—'an elevation of the voice, with a sudden mechanical depression of its tones'—and the comedians tending to lose themselves in farcical tricks. For some years before 1740, a few critics had been pleading for a change, and then, as we have seen, a sudden transformation was wrought through the quite unrelated actions of Charles Macklin and David Garrick—and perhaps to these names ought to be added that of Thomas Sheridan, since both he and Macklin were of very considerable influence because of the 'schools' which they set up for the training of young actors. Thus the new 'natural' style was established.

In the older days, when conventionalism ruled, it is almost certain that, except for the preparation of pantomimes which depended upon concerted action and accurate timing, rehearsals were very perfunctory affairs and certainly there was no single person in the theatre who even vaguely resembled the modern director or producer. With the advent of the later histrionic style, however, more care was required in the co-ordination of the acting team, and enough evidence exists to warrant the conclusion that, while rehearsing hours remained inadequate even up to the close of Garrick's reign, more pains than before were being taken in the preparation of fresh productions. True, as late as the year 1775 a critic-chronicler could aver that 'everyone acquainted with modern rehearsals, must know how losely, and how much under the par of their abilities the generality of performers go through their parts,

113
'Habit of Comus, in the Masque of Comus.' Anonymous engraving.

and except it is a capital actor, or actress, that has a new one to get studied in, the rest are little better than a *theatrical muster*, who are called together to be in readiness for the night's review, without little more preparation than their bare appearances'.[8] True also are the facts that, according to a contemporary, such a distinguished actress as Mrs Pritchard, the noted Lady Macbeth of her time, 'read no more of the play ... than her own part, as written out and delivered to her by the prompter'—that Garrick had to plead with the equally distinguished Mrs Cibber when the first version of Arthur Murphy's *The Way to Keep Him* was in preparation, telling her that 'the Comedy will require four or five regular Rehearsals at least, and tho *You* may be able to appear with two, Yet I am afraid the rest of the Dramatis Personae will be perplex'd and disjointed if they have not the advantage of your Character to Rehearse with them.'[10]

Nevertheless, despite all this, signs of a new dispensation are plentiful. At Covent Garden in 1748, we are informed by Tate Wilkinson, rehearsals were 'very regular' under the aegis of James Quin: there, 'all was awful silence'; 'Quin was sole monarch, and had a manner most terrible to the under performers, carpenters, &c; if he spied me within two yards of the wings—"Get away, boy!"— and struck his cane with such violence as made me tremble'.[11] And such pleadings as Garrick had addressed to Mrs Cibber in 1760 were being supplanted fifteen years later by peremptory commands: his letter had closed with a declaration that both he and the author were convinced that 'something (in our Circumstances) must be determin'd directly', yet he is forced to add 'that determination I leave wholly to You'; vastly different was the tone of the formal letter addressed to Ann Brown by the Covent Garden management in 1775:

> Miss Ann Brown,
>   Madam,
>   The Proprietors of the Covent Garden Theatre require you to be on their Stage at 12 o'Clock, on Monday next, to rehearse your Songs in the new Comic Opera of the Duenna.
>   I am,
>   Yours very humble serv[t].
>   Tho[s]. Hull
> Dec[r]: 27th: 1775.—

This is endorsed by Hull, who was determined to make doubly sure: 'Sent the above by Ledger, who brought me Word the next day at Noon, that he had delivered it safe into the hands of M[r]. Saltpetro, who had engaged to deliver it to Miss Brown.'[12]

Along with the greater attention paid to rehearsals goes an increasingly greater attention devoted by the leaders of the new movement to the general planning of their productions: there is plentiful

evidence to show that both Garrick and Macklin were intent not
only on the casting and the general planning of plays with which
they were concerned but also on individual interpretations and the
minutiae of business. Thus was the ground being laid for the
appointment at Drury Lane of De Loutherbourg as a theatrical
officer given full authority over both the scenery and the costumes.
As yet the overall 'director' had not been established, but by the
seventies his future arrival was being heralded.

THE OLDER WARDROBES

In trying to make a wide survey of theatrical costuming during
the period 1740–80, clearly the first thing to do is to determine, so
far as we can, the types of dress familiar on the stage at the time
when Garrick first made his appearance as Richard III.[13]

Two or three generalisations can safely be made, although some
qualifications for each are essential. The first is that the choice of
dresses for all the members of the company was a kind of free-for-
all controlled by privilege, protocol and convention. Without doubt,
the principal players decided for themselves what they wished to
wear; they had the run of the wardrobe or, on occasion, had their
own attire made up specially for them: certainly there were struggles
among them over the problem of who was to secure which suit,
but as a rule they got what they wanted. On the other hand, it is
obvious that younger members of the company were denied such
liberty: it would have been absurd if an attendant in a tragedy were
to single out a royal suit indistinguishable from that majestically
worn by his hero-monarch. Presumably, therefore, by custom rather
than by regulation, the dressing of each stock play and even of most
new plays was determined by the chief members of the company;
they wanted to shine as resplendently as they could and they were
prepared to allow the others to obtain from the wardrobe almost
any costumes, whether fitting for the play or not, which would not
vie with theirs. Even they, however, were governed to a certain
extent by convention. While there were but few attempts to present
the dramatic characters in authentic dress appropriate to their
climes or times, it was recognised that some attention had to be
paid to established theatrical usage: several particular characters
had to be dressed in traditional garments, and a few plays set in
distant ages or in far-off countries required that their heroes should
appear in costumes selected from within fixed categories familiar
to spectators and performers alike.

The privilege and protocol, moreover, worked in two ways.
Partly they were determined by the fictional ranks of the drama's
characters, but sometimes the court procedure was conditioned by
the positions which the actors had within the company. Usually the
most prominent actor, when appearing in a tragedy, had the part

of a king, and in a comedy he was a man of fashion: in such circumstances the two systems of rank coincided. There were, however,
some tragedies in which the monarch was not the chief person and
some comedies in which a servant's role was fatter than that of his
master; and here trouble often arose. For the most part it would seem
that the actors were more amenable to reason than their female companions: for the sake of their parts the men were willing to come
on stage less shiningly attired than players of lesser importance who
happened to be cast as gentlemen of higher social cast; but the ladies
had different views. If a Mrs Woffington or a Mrs Clive interpreted
the role of a serving-maid, then she wanted to seem as fine as her
lady.

In the theatre thus ruled by individualism, established custom and
convention the wardrobes contained a variety of dresses which
tended to sort themselves out into some half a dozen kinds.[14]

(*1*)   For comedies and even for certain tragedies 'modern' costumes predominated, although it is to be observed that the word
'modern' is not always to be construed either as ordinary civil attire
or as strictly contemporary. Many records from the years before
1740 tell us of royal or courtly dresses being handed over to the
players or being bought by the managements: even coronation robes
and princesses' 'birthday suits' thus found their way onto the stage.
And, in addition to this, we have many other records to show that,
since clothes in those times were expensive, the garments worn by
the actors and actresses, although 'modern' in a general sense, were
frequently very different from those of the spectators. Civil fashions
might change, but on the stage out-of-date suits often continued
in use for many years. Precisely how far individual performers tried
to fit these costumes to their parts remains uncertain, but, before
any broad assumptions are accepted, we should perhaps steadily
bear in mind the account of how Thomas Doggett, who died in 1721,
made himself up for the part of Moneytrap in Sir John Vanbrugh's
The Confederacy: in this, we are told, 'he wore an old threadbare
black coat, to which he had put new cuffs, pocket-lids, and buttons,
on purpose to make its rustiness more conspicuous; the neck was
stuffed so as to make him appear round-shouldered and give his
head the greater prominency; his square-toed shoes were large
enough to buckle over those he wore in common, which made his
legs appear much smaller than usual.[15]

(*2*)   After the contemporary costumes, the commonest dress was
the Roman, largely because of the numbers of plays, early and late,
set in Roman and Grecian times which were popular on the stage,
and partly because everyone knew that men in those periods had
characteristic kinds of attire: few persons could have said what King
John wore, but all were familiar with the appearance of Julius Caesar.
'Roman shapes', then, were expected when classical military heroes
appeared on the stage, while an actor appearing as a Roman civilian

in ordinary dress, even if he wore contemporary breeches and waist-coat, was similarly expected to don some kind of gown which might be transformed by the imagination into a toga.

(3)   A third group of costumes was commonly designated, in a vague manner, as 'Persian'—a term probably employed to describe diverse kind of dresses more or less oriental in style, donned by actors representing characters whose supposed habitat might well have been lands far removed from that of the Shah. A long dressing-gown, baggy breeches, perhaps a turban and a scimitar, a pair of peculiarly cut boots, sufficed to carry the audience into the realms of the mysterious East. In all probability attempts to be more specific were rare, although it is noteworthy that a theatrical inventory made about the year 1714, besides mentioning 'Persian Vests', includes a number of 'Turkish Guard Coats'.[16]

(4)   A fourth general category of conventional form seems to have been the 'Spanish', with rather tight breeches, closely-cut tunic and, usually a falling lace collar—a type of dress which, like the others, continued familiar on the stage for many years.

(5)   It would appear as though, besides these basic groups, there existed certain particular character costumes, some of them at least handed down from the seventeenth century. As an example may be taken the person of Sir John Falstaff. Already in the time of Inigo Jones his flopping 'Elizabethan' clothes, with the huge doublet, soft-leather boots and feathered hat had assumed a theatrical quality; and this dress can be traced down not only to the year of Garrick's advent upon the stage but for decades thereafter.

(6)   And finally, of course, it is necessary to remember that the wardrobes of both Drury Lane and Covent Garden were stocked with scores of habits which had been specially made for spectacular productions or which belonged to current pantomimic entertainments. Even in the 1714 inventory there were shepherds' dresses, 'Feather Shapes', dresses for Scaramouch, Harlequin, Aesop, and Furies, attires for Baccanals and for Watermen.

Much more could be said about the costuming of plays before 1740, but the above account gives what is a fairly accurate brief general picture of the prevailing conditions and of the wardrobes' resources.

THE NEW LOOK

An understanding of what happened during the following forty years demands perhaps even more balancing of conflicting evidence than is necessary in the consideration of scenic methods. It is easy to accept at face value what Thomas Jefferys wrote in 1772: praise is given to Garrick because the costumes used in his Drury Lane productions were 'no longer the heterogeneous and absurd Mixtures of foreign and Antient Modes, which formerly debased our Tragedies, by representing a Roman General in a full bottomed Peruke, and the Sovereign of an Eastern Empire in Trunk Hose'.[17] It is equally easy to contrast a Garrick production of, let us say, 1775 with one under the direction of Macready or Charles Kean and to discern in the first a series of those 'absurdities' which Jefferys declared had been by that period utterly banished. Neither procedure is likely to lead us towards the truth. What we must do is to take the various confusing and often seemingly contradictory pieces of the jig-saw puzzle in an endeavour to work them into a general design.

The old categories of costumes, as the extant pictorial evidence fully attests, remained in use during all this later period, but continually the scope of the wardrobe's resources was being extended, and we may believe that this extension was largely inspired by the new attitudes within the auditorium. If once more reference is made to Kant's dictum about the eye bringing with it what it sees, we may say that, as a whole, the spectators in the earlier years of the century accepted uncritically a set of conventions, giving to these traditional elements an imaginative 'reality' which in fact they did not possess, whereas the spectators during the period 1740–80 gradually came to question the conventions and to look upon the dresses of the performers in a new way.

Perhaps this can best be illustrated by considering some contemporary comments about the use of 'modern' dress. As has been seen, an earlier actor taking the part of a gentleman of fashion might well have appeared in a suit which, in fact, was twenty years old, fashionable in its own time but now completely outmoded. Very few, if any, members of the audience objected. When, however, we go on to the fifties, sixties and later, queries and complaints begin to accumulate: more and more, the spectators wanted to see the interpreter of the fine gentleman looking like a real fine gentleman, while at least the more critical were beginning to ask for the introduction of nice distinctions. Thus, for example, in the past dramatic fops were once simply fops, but now there was an attempt to look upon them as individuals. 'Sir Courtly Nice,' we are told, 'is squeamish, affected, and formal. Lord Foppington, in the *Relapse*, a pert coxcomb, elated with large fortune, and proud of his person,' while 'Lord Foppington, in the *Careless Husband*,' is 'the most elegant and high-bred fop in all our modern Comedies', 'Clodio is a pert frenchified coxcomb', and 'Beau Clincher is most judiciously drawn by the author as a contrast to the real live gentleman, Sir Harry Wildair.'[18] Clearly, once these distinctions were being thought of, there was the demand that their clothes should visually reflect the differences of the characters.

Questions of another sort were also being asked. In the past Othello was Othello, and those watching the interpretation of an actor in the role were little concerned with his attire. Now, however, the same critic who discussed the nature of fops firmly objected to his appearance in modern dress. Othello, he stated, 'in modern cloaths' is a 'mistake', when such characters as Zanga and Oroonoko 'appear in their national habits'. In a manner at once similar and different Lichtenberg, when he first saw Garrick as Hamlet, started to puzzle out why the actor wore a contemporary suit in the part, instead of dressing himself in a manner more historically appropriate; there must, he thought, have been some reason for his choice. In thus cogitating, he observed that Garrick's costume was not merely contemporary; it was, in fact, 'a French suit', and of course this was a special kind of court dress, trim and tightly cut (plate 114). Suddenly, there came to him a final thought: Garrick had deliberately adopted the attire because its very tightness could support

114
Garrick as Hamlet, 1754.
Mezzotint by J. McArdell.

and strengthen the 'play of his features'. When, in a passion, the actor drew his sword on Horatio and partly turned his back to the audience, Lichtenberg saw that 'his exertions had produced that well-known diagonal crease from the shoulder to the opposite hip'; the effect, in his opinion, 'was, in truth, worth the play of facial expression twice over', and it would have been completely lost if Garrick, strictly following the text of the play, had donned a cloak.[19]

No doubt Lichtenberg and Samuel Derrick were peculiarly perceptive playgoers, yet their comments could not have been made, let us say, in 1710, and, although they were considering more curiously than most members of the audience, the same kind of thoughts were undoubtedly agitating the minds of many.

Obviously throughout these selected comments runs a definite train of thought—the actor's dress should be appropriate to his part, distinctions should be observed and traditional conventions should be abandoned if they conflicted with later concepts. Two related instances will serve as illustrations. A long-standing tradition had demanded that villainous characters, 'conspirators, traitors, and murderers', should have their dark thoughts revealed in dark costuming. Thomas Davies thus tells us that he once had seen John Hippisley as the First Murderer in *Macbeth*, probably about 1740: his face, he says, 'was made pale with chalk, distinguished with large whiskers, and a long black wig'.[20] 'This custom of dressing so preposterously the hateful implements of the tragic scene,' he adds, 'is now almost worn out', but outside of London the convention endured unaltered: at Dublin in 1782, just about the year when Davies was composing his *Miscellanies*, John Bernard saw the villainous Glenalvon, in John Home's *Douglas*, 'dressed in an entire suit of black, with a black wig, and a black velvet hat crowned with an immense plume of black feathers, which, bending before him, gave him very much the aspect of a mourning coach-horse.'[21] Although the convention thus endured, it seems clear that general taste in the metropolis had become aware that it clashed with what was being shown to the audience.

In drawing the character of Glenalvon, Home was apparently inspired by Shakespeare's Iago, and, while there is no evidence that the Venetian ensign commonly appeared in a black costume, it is certain that most actors made his villainy patent partly by their reading of the lines and partly by their dress. 'I think,' remarks Samuel Derrick, 'it was Mr Macklin who first dressed Iago properly; formerly he was dressed in such a manner, as to be known at first sight.'[22] Presumably Macklin introduced this alteration when he took the part at the Haymarket on 6 February 1744, and if so, there is added interest in noting that the Othello in this production was a 'Young Gentleman' described as making his first appearance on any stage—none other than Samuel Foote—and that his person was 'new dress'd after the Custom of his Country'.

This performance, therefore, has the double effect of showing one actor abandoning an ancient convention in a desire to make his role seem more credible and realistic, and another actor turning to an 'historical' or 'appropriate' costuming. And such historical costuming was one of the most notable innovations of the period.

During the years before 1740 only one single record has come down to us concerning an attempt to clothe the characters of a

115
William Powell as Posthumus. Oil painting by J. Zoffany.

drama in an authentic manner, and the attempt was one not conditioned by public demand but emanating from the mind of a theatrical enthusiast who was considerably in advance of his time. In the autumn of 1731 Aaron Hill succeeded in persuading the Drury Lane management to perform his tragedy of *Athelwold*. Even at that early date he had formed fixed ideas as to how such dramas should be 'correctly' put upon the stage, and he consequently addressed an urgent letter to the theatre pleading that the chief persons should be properly attired. Most of these characters, he points out, were Saxon, and 'Verstegan's Antiquities' was a source-book from which the costumier could derive information on what was worn in that period. Care, however, should be taken to see that one character, Leolyn, since he was a Briton, had an individually distinctive dress. Probably realising that the management might be rather suspicious of an historical approach so academic, Hill added two further notes: since this was to be a stage representation, the true dresses of that early period might well be given some 'Heightening', because '*beauty* must be joined to *propriety*, where the decoration of the stage, is the purpose to be provided for'; while the costs, he believed, could be kept suitably low. He had emphasised that 'Furrs' were 'a prime distinction in the *old Saxon* habits', but now he hastened to give the assurance that 'they need not be *real* furrs' and that 'many cheap *imitations* will have the same effect'.[23]

Hill's tragedy proved a dismal failure; it was a sport, an oddity, and maybe its only direct lasting influence on the stage was its adding another group of costumes to the theatres' stores; Posthumus' furry trimmings may well have come from this source (plate 115).

Nevertheless, the production of *Athelwold* in 1731 sets up a kind of warning sign-post; we are soon about to switch off onto another road. Already we have seen that, a short time after Garrick's advent, Charles Macklin took pains to devise an 'authentic' dress for Shylock and to treat that character in a manner new to the stage. One of Garrick's first actions on his assuming the management of Drury Lane was to revive the old Jacobean comedy of *Albumazar*, and playgoers were informed not only that it would be graced by '*Pieces of Music* before the Play, and between the Acts ... selected from the Old English Masters', but also that the characters would appear 'New Dress'd after the Manner of the Old English Comedy'. This production, however, seems also to have been before its time; no doubt it was responsible for adding still another category of costumes—the slashed 'Elizabethan'—to the wardrobe, but it seems to have remained a lonely experiment in its period. At the same time it indicates a new approach. Macklin's Shylock dress (see plate 8) was certainly a single actor's effort and presumably his companions on the stage wore ordinary 'modern' dress. In presenting *Albumazar*, there was clearly some sort of managerial direction: just how many of the characters were 'New Dress'd' we cannot tell, but at least an attempt was being made at concerted production.

The real movement forwards did not come until the formative sixties, but during the interim the way was at least being further prepared. On 29 November, 1751, Jonson's *Every Man in his Humour* was revived at Drury Lane, and the prompter's diary indicates that the persons, or at least some of them, were also 'Dress'd

in the Old English Manner' (plate 116). Quite probably these costumes were the same as those used in the production of *Albumazar* and consequently in themselves they are not of particular significance; but very significant is Thomas Davies' account of the care which Garrick took in the general planning and in the preparations for this venture. Evidently he was somewhat unsure as to whether the public would like the piece, and he took special pains in its casting: the part of Kiteley he took himself, Woodward was Bobadil, Yates Brainworm, Ross and Palmer Wellbred and Young Knowell, Shuter Master Stephen, Winston Downright, Berry Old Knowell, Mrs Ward Dame Kiteley, Miss Minors Bridget, Vaughan Master Matthew. Thus there was assembled 'such a groupe of original actors as were scarce ever collected before'. Distinguished as they might be, however, Garrick insisted on 'frequent rehearsal' and this became 'a matter of instruction'. During these rehearsals 'he took infinite pains' to stress upon the company that 'he expected an implicit submission' to his interpretation of the characters, even although he was prepared to allow Woodward to give an independent interpretation of Bobadil.[24] The whole description of his

116
Henry Woodward as Bobadil in Ben Jonson's *Every Man in his Humour*. (*Left*) engraving by Goldar dated 22 November 1776, and (*right*) engraving by Thornthwaite, 1776, after the water colour by J. Roberts.

procedure suggests a very close approach towards present-day methods, and it need hardly be repeated that such procedure was an absolute prerequisite for the attainment of that which the spectators—some consciously and some unconsciously—were beginning to seek.

The next forward movement came in the season of 1762–63, when the playbills of both Drury Lane and Covent Garden advertised many dramas dressed in the 'Habits of the Times': the latter theatre had its own *Every Man in his Humour* while Garrick was responsible for *2 Henry IV*, *Richard III*, and *Elvira*. The listing of these plays calls attention to the fact that, in scrutinising the productions during this and following seasons, we must be prepared to admit more than those specifically signalled out by the bills. *Henry IV*, for example, was so indicated, but the fact that *Richard III* was similarly 'dress'd in the habits of the times' is recorded only in the prompter's diary, and similar instances can be found in later years. Thus, when *The Royal Merchant* was presented at Covent Garden on 14 December 1767, the announcements made no allusion to its costuming, yet on that occasion one spectator, Sylas Neville, a man who had a connoisseur's interest in historical attire, approvingly noted in his diary that the performers wore 'the Flemish dresses of the times'. During the previous season there was no managerial announcement about Thomas Franklin's *The Earl of Warwick* when it was presented at Drury Lane on 13 December, yet this same spectator, attending a performance the following February, observed that 'the characters were very richly dressed in the dresses of the time'.

Obviously, therefore, a determined effort was being made to do what Aaron Hill had pleaded for thirty years before, and obviously, too, the effort was being greeted with approval. 'The beauty as well as the propriety of the dresses,' in *2 Henry IV*, it was said, gave 'great satisfaction', and there was even the more important comment that these 'Old English Habits' were 'indeed admirably suited to the style and manners of the plays of that time, in which a peculiarity prevails very remote from modern dialogue and the present fashions'.[25] We might readily have thought, therefore, that a complete change had come about and that the 'heterogeneous and absurd Mixtures' of the past had gone.

Many cooler reactions, however, soon confront us. When Nicholas Rowe's *Tamerlane* was revived at Drury Lane on 4 November 1767 Sylas Neville confided to his diary that the actor Holland as Bajazet 'was the only character in proper dress'; 'it hurt me,' he wrote, 'to see Tartars in ancient Greek dresses with ridiculous modern periwigs, and Greek Christians in English habits'.[26] Ten years later, in 1776, the Drury Lane prompter had noted that a revival of *Macbeth* was 'dressed in the Habits of the Times', but against this entry J. P. Kemble jotted down a caustic comment, declaring that he himself had 'seen some of these Habits, and very paltry and very improper they were'.[27] Even Garrick gives the game away: in 1750 William Shirley's *Edward the Black Prince* was presented at Drury Lane, and some contemporary allusions lead us to suppose that a serious attempt had been made to dress it in an 'historical' manner, one journal asserting categorically that 'the English characters, dress'd in the Habit of those Days, made an elegant Figure': yet from a letter which Garrick addressed to his fellow-manager a few months later it becomes apparent not only that the old and the new were mingled in this production, but also that this was done deliberately; the letter proposed that *King John* should be chosen for revival and costumed 'half old English, half modern, as in Edward the Black Prince'.[28] And if many of Garrick's newly-made costumes tended to be 'historical' in kind, he himself was capable of appearing in most inappropriate garments: Tate Wilkinson tells how he came forward in John Brown's *Barbarossa* (1754) 'in a glittering silver-spangled tissue shape'—evidently a fancifully designed 'Roman' costume—and with a blackened face; on catching sight of him, the irrepressible Mrs Clive, 'instead of court adulation', cried out, 'O my God! room! room! make room for the royal lamp-lighter'—a comment which 'disconcerted him much for the remaining part of the evening'.[29]

We might have supposed that when Quin, at the age of sixty, rolled his twenty-stone weight onto the stage as young Chamount in Thomas Otway's *The Orphan*, his suit 'heavy enough for Othello', with 'a pair of stiff-topped white gloves, then only worn by attendants at a funeral, an old fashioned major wig, and black stockings', he was simply a ridiculous relic of an older tradition;[30] but even at the close of this period not dissimilar absurdities can be discovered among the newer school of actors. And the actresses frequently persisted in picking their own dainty steps along paths of their own. In 1774 De Loutherbourg, after having carefully studied Bernard de Montfaucon's *L'Antiquité expliquée* (1722–24) for the purpose of setting Alexander Dow's *Sethona* in an authentic Egyptian milieu, designed special scenes and dresses for the whole production: these were praised as being 'much superior to those of any modern Tragedy', doing 'Honour to the Taste and Spirit of the Manager, who seems to have spared no Expence to furnish a splendid and rational Entertainment'; all was in keeping except for the heroine, Mrs Barry, who, determined to look her best, exercised her prerogative of wearing a gown cut in the latest mode. As a reviewer in the *St James's* Magazine bitingly remarked, she had 'always the liberty of making a mummy of herself'.

The balanced view we are seeking demands a setting of various pieces into the jig-saw puzzle. Already by 1755 the 'historical' concept was fully developed: in that year Roger Pickering, the author of *Reflections upon Theatrical Expression in Tragedy* told the actors that they must be 'conversant in the mode of dress ancient and modern in other countries as well as in our own' and they must, in addition, pay attention to the manners of these times and places— 'Alexander and Cato were not masters of the snuff box, nor Greek women of French heels'. Almost at the same time another author[31] was stating as an established truth that one of the accomplishments of an actor should be 'a judicious propriety in his dress', so that it might be 'adapted with sufficient exactitude to the age, time, and circumstances of his character'. This, he said, 'may be called the last colourings and finishings of his picture; and in this case, very much will depend on his knowledge of antient history and historical paintings'.

These words were being written some time before Drury Lane and Covent Garden launched their historical productions during the sixties; yet, as has been seen, even after De Loutherbourg had taken control at the former theatre in the early seventies older conventional methods were still operative. Although Thomas Jefferys in 1772 was giving the impression that Garrick was almost wholly responsible for the alteration in stage affairs and that in his playhouse a complete reformation had been effected, actually he was only one among many and there was much that still remained to be done. And here perhaps it may be profitable to end this general survey with reference to a production at the rival theatre which serves as a sort of epitome of what was happening during these years.

On Saturday 23 October 1773, Charles Macklin was responsible for a revival of *Macbeth* which created a considerable stir in its own time and was for long remembered. The story has been recounted more than once,[32] and consequently there is no need here to tell it again; but it would seem as though a brief listing of its main features, set against their background, can be of service.

(1)   The man, Charles Macklin, who fluttered the audiences in October 1773 had such a personality and behaved in such a way throughout his career that we might well have expected him to be an exponent of the old school, a companion of traditionally-minded Quin. Even on this occasion, when on the second performance of his *Macbeth* he harangued the spectators, claiming that there was a cabal against him, he displayed an egotistic and self-centered oddity which reminds us rather of conditions at the beginning of the century than of the atmosphere prevailing in later decades. Yet, as we well know, his concepts were those of the *avant garde*: many years before he had created the Shylock of his age and had recast Iago.

(2)   In this production of *Macbeth* he was obviously intent, not only on presenting his own part forcibly, as a performer of the old school might have done, but more importantly on being an overall director. A letter printed in *The London Evening Post* thus noted

'the improvement of Mrs Hartley's *thinking in Lady Macbeth*' and 'her manner of speaking', attributing this to the 'intelligence she had received' from him. His own preliminary jottings indicate the careful thought he was giving to the placement of supernumeraries and to the use of appropriate music: even 'bagpipes' are mentioned, and, although we cannot tell whether these Scottish instruments were actually added to the more familiar fifes and drums, the very thought itself has significance.

(3) He evidently planned the scenery, and, in doing so, his mind was clearly working in the new style. The 'Quadrangle of Macbeth's castle' had a 'door which is supposed to lead to Duncan's apartment', while another door 'through which Macbeth comes to the Weird Sisters, in the 4th act', was described by one reviewer as 'a better and more probable entrance than through the common stage portal'. It might have been expected that Macklin, with his long training in platform playing and in the use of the stage-doors, would have inclined towards keeping to the older practices, yet here he is shown accepting and indeed encouraging the movement which was leading the actors back into the midst of the scenery.

(4) The scenery attracted attention, but far more attention was given to the 'dresses and decorations, proper to the time, place and action . . . of a sort hitherto unknown to an English audience'. Eleven years afterwards, Thomas Davies referred to these as the 'old highland military habit' and in 1804 William Cooke called them 'the old Caledonian habit'.[33] And when we consider these, we realise that, in fact, they have at least three or four special aspects of interest for us.

In the first place, we note that the idea of dressing *Macbeth* in Scots habits was by no means unanticipated in preceding years. When this play appeared on the Edinburgh stage as early as 1757 the playbills had announced that the characters were 'entirely new dress'd, after the manner of the Ancient Scots'.[34] Exactly what was worn on this occasion cannot be determined, but it is reasonable to suppose that the production as a whole may have exerted an inspirational force on Macklin's; and, apart from this, the Edinburgh venture serves as a symbol of what was happening to the playhouses outside of London during those decades. The rapid growth of these theatres after the forties has already been noted, and here we have an excellent example of the way in which they were, at least occasionally, developing their own initiative. The London interest in 'habits of the time' soon was reflected in their efforts, and in this record we have a demonstration of how the historical appeal, travelling northwards and forming an alliance with Scots patriotic sentiment, created something entirely new.

Although we cannot be absolutely sure what Macklin's costumes for his Macbeth role looked like, there is sufficient evidence for us to believe that his accomplishment was relatively complex. At the beginning of the tragedy, when the thane appears as a victorious warrior, he evidently wore a costume suggestive of primitive life north of the border: he had a Scots bonnet and he was armed with a claymore; his plaid and stockings were almost certainly tartan; just possibly his main body attire may have been a belted plaid which in the seventeenth century, before the introduction of the separate kilt, gave a kilt-like effect, but it is equally possible that he went further in his attempt to secure historical accuracy by donning a plain belted tunic of the sort which the experts were describing as common wear among the 'Saxons'. The part of Macbeth, however, demands at least two dresses, for the warrior thane soon becomes a king; and it is significant that for his royal attire Macklin appears to have adopted a modified version of one of the older traditional groups of theatrical costumes, the 'Spanish'. True, Macklin might have claimed that a similar kind of suit had been familiar among the Scots nobility for some time, but the fact remains that one of his costumes inclined towards the archaeological and another was theatrically conventional.

A third point of interest is that in his *Macbeth* Macklin was intent upon more than his own clothes. Contemporary records amply demonstrate that often, when attempts were made at historical costuming, the chief performer and perhaps one or two of his close associates were clad in what was believed to be authentic manner, while the lesser characters presented themselves in a motley array of modern dress and conventional clothes. Among Macklin's jottings, especially important is his note that on Macbeth's first entrance he should have 'a body guard, in highland dresses, with targets &c.' In design—whatever actually was put upon the stage—the production was evidently conceived in over-all terms.

This *Macbeth*, then, includes within itself almost all the elements which contributed towards the development of theatre production during the course of the four decades from 1740 to 1780. It was tied to the past; it exhibited to the full the trends of the then present; and in its own way it prophesied the future. The Ultima Thule of Charles Kean, nearly a hundred years ahead, is at least dimly sighted.

It seems appropriate that such a short general survey as this, starting with David Garrick and necessarily paying special attention to his efforts, should come to a close with a reference to this last effort made by his one-time friend, associate, enemy and rival, the Irishman who, baptised as Charles McLaughlin, had already been acting for well over twenty years, under the name of Macklin, before the notable production of *Richard III* at Goodman's Fields in 1741, and who carried on his stage career until 1788, fully twelve years after Garrick's retirement. That the manager of Drury Lane was the great master of his age is certain, but it is essential to remember also the contributions made by his many companions, less fortunate and sometimes compelled to spend much of their time outside the fashionable metropolis, who in their several ways aided in creating this Georgian theatre.

NOTES TO CHAPTER SIX

[1] *Reminiscences* (1828), II [V] preface.

[2] Ellis Waterhouse, in *Painting in Britain* (1953), adroitly deals with this theme, and it forms the chief focus in Moelwyn Merchant's *Shakespeare and the Artist* (1959).

[3] *The Connoisseur*, August 1933, opposite p. 108.

[4] Byam Shaw, *Old Master Drawings*, vii, no. 28, March 1933, pp 60–61.

[5] F. Watson, 'An unfamiliar Conversation Piece by Alessandro Longhi' (*Bollettino dei Musei Civici Veneziani*, annata ix, n. 4, 1964, p 17–20).

[6] *Lichtenberg's Visits to England*, edited and translated by M. L. Mare and W. H. Quarrell (1938), pp. 70–1 and 26.

[7] Thomas Davies, *Life of David Garrick* (new edition, 1808), vol. i, p. 40.

[8] William Cooke, *The Elements of Dramatic Criticism* (1775), p. 195.

[9] Thomas Davies, *Life of David Garrick* (new edition, 1808), vol. i, p. 153.

[10] *The Letters of David Garrick*, edited by D. M. Little and G. M. Kahrl (1963), vol. i, p. 321.

[11] *Memoirs* (1790), vol. i, p. 33.

[12] Original letter in the 'Garrick Memorial' collection, Garrick Club. The conflicting nature of the available evidence on this subject is well summarised by C. B. Hogan in 'An Eighteenth-century Prompter's Notes' (*Theatre Notebook*, x, 1956, pp. 37–44). W. J. Lawrence discusses it in *Old Theatre Days and Ways* (1935), pp. 53–62.

[13] Lily B. Campbell has a very useful outline in 'A History of Costuming on the English Stage between 1660 and 1823' (*University of Wisconsin Studies in Language and Literature*, no. 2, 1918, pp. 187–223) and she examines the new ideas about acting in 'The Rise of a Theory of Stage Presentation in England during the Eighteenth Century' (*PMLA*, xxii, 1917, pp. 163–200): Donald T. Mackintosh discusses the innovations of the sixties in 'New Dress'd in the Habits of the Times' (*Times Literary Supplement*, 25 August 1927). The theme is also discussed in Dougald MacMillan's *Drury Lane Calendar*, 1747–76 (1938) and in the introductions, by E. L. Avery, A. H. Scouten and G. Winchester Stone, Jr., to parts 2, 3 and 4 of *The London Stage*. What research will be involved in exploring this whole subject detail by detail is strikingly illustrated in M. St Clare Byrne's 'The Costuming of *Macbeth* in the Eighteenth Century' (*Studies in English Theatrical History*, Society for Theatre Research, 1952, pp. 52–64), see pp. 201–3.

[14] For types of costume see also Cecil Price, *Theatre in the Age of Garrick*, pp. 48–58.

[15] Thomas Davies, *Dramatic Miscellanies* (1784), vol. iii, p. 449.

[16] Sybil Rosenfeld, 'The Wardrobes of Lincoln's Inn Fields and Covent Garden', *Theatre Notebook*, v, 1950, pp. 15–19.

[17] *Recueil des Habillements de Différentes Nations* (1757–1772), vol. ii, p. xiii.

[18] 'Thomas Wilkes (Samuel Derrick), *A General View of the Stage* (1759), p. 162.

[19] *Lichtenberg's Visits to England*, edited and translated by M. L. Mare and W. H. Quarrell (1938), pp. 20–3.

[20] Thomas Davies, *Dramatic Miscellanies* (1784), vol. iii, p. 93. Hippisley originally appeared in this role at Lincoln's Inn Fields in 1730 and was still playing it at Covent Garden in 1742. The tradition is discussed by W. J. Lawrence in *Old Theatre Days and Ways* (1935), pp. 124–9.

[21] *Retrospections of the Stage* (1830), I, p. 283.

[22] 'Thomas Wilkes (Samuel Derrick), *A General View of the Stage* (1759), p. 158.

[23] *Works* (1753), vol. i, pp. 89–91.

[24] Thomas Davies, *Dramatic Miscellanies* (1784), vol. iii, pp. 64–9.

[25] *Theatrical Intelligence*, 4 November 1762, quoted in *The London Stage*, IV, ii, p. 960.

[26] *The London Stage*, IV, iii, p. 1288.

[27] *Id.* V, i, p. 39.

[28] *The Letters of David Garrick*, edited by D. M. Little and G. M. Kahrl (1963), vol. i, p. 152.

[29] *Memoirs* (1790), vol. iii, p. 48.

[30] Francis Gentleman, *The Dramatic Censor* (1770), vol. ii, p. 58.

[31] 'Thomas Wilkes (Samuel Derrick), *A General View of the Stage* (1759), pp. 144–5 and 158.

[32] Muriel St Clare's Byrne's very important essay on the costuming has been cited above, note 13. W. W. Appleton, in his *Charles Macklin* (1961), discusses the production at length, and quotations from contemporary journals are given in *The London Stage*.

[33] Thomas Davies, *Dramatic Miscellanies* (1784), vol. iii, p. 83; William Cooke, *Memoirs of Charles Macklin* (1804), p. 284.

[34] J. C. Dibdin, *Annals of the Edinburgh Stage* (1888), p. 95.

Notes on illustrations

Frontispiece
'The Downfall of Shakespeare on a Modern Stage.' Oil painting by Philip Dawes, exhibited at the Free Society of Artists, 1765; while signed and dated that year, it may, of course, have been painted somewhat earlier. Although no doubt the artist did not attempt to depict the state of any particular theatre, the two statues at the side of the frontispiece, Satyr and Punch, seem to ridicule the two figures of Tragedy and Comedy at Covent Garden. The red-dressed person of Shakespeare lies dead at the front of the platform, having been stabbed by the operatic hero. On the two front wings of the frontispiece large scales are painted: stage-left, the works of Shakespeare, Jonson, Beaumont and Fletcher, and Congreve are weighed down by two scraps of paper, one inscribed 'Pantomime' and the other 'The Favourite Song'; stage-right, the tragic sceptre and crown are similarly weighed down by what seem to be musical instruments. The stage box left shows a dark-skinned spectator holding a libretto and having the story explained to him by a gentleman at his side: this recalls the visit of the Moroccan Ambassador to Drury Lane in 1756 (see p. 78), but no doubt there were later occasions when dignitaries from North Africa attended productions. *Oil painting in possession of Mrs Nicoll.*

1   page 1
Announcement of David Garrick's first appearance in London, at Goodman's Fields Theatre, on 19 October 1741. *The Trustees of the British Museum.*

2   page 2
David Garrick as Richard III in the tent scene, 1741–42. Oil painting by William Hogarth. Engraved by Hogarth and C. Grignion and published in 1746; it therefore shows Garrick at the beginning of his career and in the part which won him immediate fame. For description see Arthur Murphy, *Life* (1801), vol. 1, pp. 23–4. *Walker Art Gallery, Liverpool.*

3   page 5
Samuel Foote, in *The Diversions of the Morning or, A Dish of Chocolate*, as Instructor Puzzle, a part he created. Anonymous engraving, published 1747. *The Folger Shakespeare Library, Washington, D.C.*

4   page 5
Ipswich playbill announcing David Garrick's appearance there under the name of Lyddal, 1741. *Victoria and Albert Theatre Museum.*

5   page 11
David Garrick as Richard III. Oil painting by Francis Hayman, dated 1800 and exhibited at the Society of Artists that year. See R. Mander and J. Mitchenson, *The Artist and the Theatre* (1955), pp. 176–9. Like Quin as Falstaff, Garrick as Richard III proved a popular subject as a porcelain figurine: on this see *Theatre Notebook*, xi, 1957, pp. 53–5 and 128–30. *Victoria and Albert Theatre Museum.*

6   page 12
David Garrick as Abel Drugger in *The Alchemist*. Water-colour by J. Roberts, an engraving of this by Thornthwaite, dated 29 December 1777, appeared as the frontispiece to the play *The Provoked Wife* in Bell's *British Theatre* (1777). *British Museum.*

7   page 12
David Garrick as Sir John Brute in *The Provoked Wife*. Water-colour by J. Roberts, an anonymous engraving of this dated 1 June 1776, appeared as frontispiece to the play in Bell's *British Theatre* (1777). *British Museum.*

8   page 13
Charles Macklin as Shylock. Oil painting by J. Zoffany, on this and other representations of Macklin see R. Mander and J. Mitchenson, *The Artist and the Theatre* (1955), pp. 54–63. *Victoria and Albert Theatre Museum.*

9   page 15
David Garrick as Steward of the Shakespeare Jubilee at Stratford-upon-Avon, 1769. Mezzotint by J. Saunders, after a painting by B. Van de Gucht, published by J. Saunders, 1773. *British Museum.*

10   page 15
The Shakespeare Jubilee, Stratford-upon-Avon, 1769: procession of characters outside Shakespeare's Birthplace; ticket for the Oratorio and Ode. Anonymous water-colour from B. M. Burney Collection of Theatrical Portraits, Garrick folder. Folger.

11 *page 16*

The procession arranged for the Shakespeare Jubilee, 1769. The elaborately-planned display was not presented because of the pelting rain. The chief characters shown are: Mrs Ford, Falstaff, Pistol, the Witches, Hecate, Aguecheek, Caliban, Richard III, Edgar, Hamlet's Ghost, the Gravedigger, Friar Lawrence, the Apothecary, Shylock, Henry VIII, and Wolsey. Satirical engravings in the *Oxford Magazine* (1769), pp. 103 and 136. B. M. Burney Collection of Theatrical Portraits, Garrick folder. For details see *Catalogue of Personal and Political Satires*, vol. iv, pp. 551–3, nos. 5311–12. *British Museum.*

12 *page 17*

David Garrick reciting the Ode at the Shakespeare Jubilee, 1769. He repeated this at Drury Lane (see plate 13). Anonymous engraving in *The Town and Country Magazine* (1769), facing p. 473. *Victoria and Albert Theatre Museum.*

13 *page 17*

The stage of Drury Lane, 1769, 'Mr Garrick delivering his Ode ... on dedicating a Building and erecting a Statue, to Shakespeare'. Engraving by J. Lodge, 1769. *British Museum.*

14 *page 25*

A proscenium door from the Stamford Theatre, Lincolnshire. From Richard Southern: *The Georgian Playhouse* (1948), pl. 33. *Richard Southern Accession, University of Bristol Theatre Collection.*

15 *page 26*

Design by Robert Adam for the frontispiece or proscenium frame of Drury Lane, 1775. Original design, dated 8 May 1775, in Sir John Soane's Museum, vol. xxvii, no. 85. Inscribed 'Method proposed for finishing the Front of the Stage which covers the first Curtain and is never changed, The Apotheosis of Shakespear by the Tragic and Comic Muses'. *The Trustees of Sir John Soane's Museum.*

16 *page 27*

The intimacy between the performer and the audience in the boxes: an undated, anonymous eighteenth-century engraving (note should be taken of the stage-door beyond the boxes) from *The Georgian Playhouse*, fig. 9.

17 *page 27*

A coloured engraving by Thomas Rowlandson 'John Bull at the Italian Opera', published 1805 and 1811, *Victoria and Albert Museum.*

18 *page 28*

The interior of Covent Garden Theatre, 1763. Engraving by L. Boitard, published by E. Sumpter. This shows the progress of the notorious 'Fitzgiggo' riot during the performance on 24 February 1763, of T. A. Arne's opera, *Artaxerxes. British Museum.*

19 *page 29*

Performance of *Macbeth* at Covent Garden about 1765. An anonymous oil painting which was presented by the actor-manager J. A. Cave to F. B. Chatterton, lessee of Drury Lane; although described in his note as showing a performance at Drury Lane, the theatre is obviously Covent Garden. Note should be taken of the bold placing of Macbeth, the Witches and Banquo and of the stage grenadiers. *Mrs Nicoll.*

20 *page 31*

Ground-plan of the Comédie Française, Paris. Engraving by Benard in Denis Diderot's *Encyclopédie, Receuils des Planches,* vol. x, Theatres, V, 1772.

21 *page 31*

Ground-plan of the Theatre at Lyon. Engraved by Benard after Dumont in Diderot's *Encyclopedie, Receuils des Planches,* vol. x, Theatres, M, 1772.

22 *page 31*

Ground-plan of Theatre at Montpellier. Engravings in Dumont, *Parallele di plans des plus belles salles de spectacles* (1774), figs. 22 and 23.

23 *page 32*

Stage-boxes in the Theatre at Stuttgart. Engraving by Benard after de la Guépierre in Diderot's *Encyclopédie, Receuils des Planches,* vol. x, Theatres, GG, 1772.

24 *page 32*

Teatro Regio, Turin. Painting by P. D. Olivero *c.* 1740 showing forestage and stage-boxes, Museo Civico, Turin. *From Bamber Gascoigne, World Theatre pl. 213.*

25 *page 33*

Ground-plans and section of a theatre project by Pietro Bianchi, 1787. These three designs form part of an album in the Museo Correr, Venice. Dedicated to Lodovico Manin, they were for a theatre intended to be built at the entrance to the Grand Canal, close to the church of Santa Maria della Salute. Comparison of the three drawings shows clearly the deep elaborate 'proscenium' with its four tiers of stage-boxes. *Museo Correr,* Venice.

26 *page 38*

Drawing of section of playhouse, probably Drury Lane, by Christopher Wren, 1674. *The Warden and Fellows of All Souls College, Oxford.*

27 *page 38*

Model reconstruction of Wren's playhouse section by E. Langhans. *Theatre Notebook,* xviii, 3, 1963/4, pl. 3. *Professor E. A. Langhans.*

28 *page 39*

Adapted from Wren's 1674 playhouse section: line drawing; reconstructed plan (the top half is at upper level, the bottom half at stage level); and isometric reconstruction. *Mr R. Leacroft.*

29 *page 40*

Plan of the pit at Drury Lane; anonymous sketch showing Garrick's box and the seating of the musicians in the orchestra. *Folger.*

30 page 42
The stage of the Theatre Royal, Bristol. Photograph, 1941. *National Monuments Record.*

31 page 42
Side-boxes of the Theatre Royal Bristol. Photograph, 1941. *National Monuments Record.*

32 page 43
Auditorium of the Theatre Royal, Bristol. *National Monuments Record.*

33 page 43
Booking plan of the boxes at the Theatre Royal Bristol, 1773. From Kathleen Barker, *Theatre Royal Bristol 1766–1966* (1974) opposite p. 4. The original plan is in the Richard Smith Collection, Avon County Reference Library. *Miss Kathleen Barker.*

34 page 44
The Bridges Street front of Drury Lane as designed by Robert Adam, 1775. This oil painting adds to the evidence of plate 35 by indicating the pawnshop to the left of the entrance and a tavern to the right. *Mrs Nicoll.*

35 page 45
The Bridges Street front of Drury Lane as designed by Robert Adam, 1775. Engraving by Bagbie from *The Works in Architecture of Robert and John Adam* (1779), vol. ii, no. v, pl. vi.

36 page 46
Auditorium of Drury Lane by R. Adam, 1775. Engraving from *The Works in Architecture* (1779), vol. 2, set v, pl. vii.

37 page 47
'Design of ceiling for the Theatre Royal in Drury Lane', 1775 by Robert Adam. Dated 19 July 1775. Adam drawings vol. xiv, no. 17. *Sir John Soane's Museum.*

38 page 49
Exterior of Goodman's Fields Theatre, together with a plan showing its position. Engraving by Robert Wilkinson in *Londina Illustrata*, vol. 2, 1825.

39 page 49
Ground-plan of Goodman's Fields Theatre, drawn by William Capon. See n. 8, p. 76.

40 page 50
The ceiling of Goodman's Fields Theatre, drawn by William Capon after the painting by William Oram, 1816. An engraving after another drawing by Capon, 1786, said to be in the British Museum but not traceable, was published in Robert Wilkinson's *Londina Illustrata* 1825, vol. 2. It represents Apollo and the Muses which is first advertised as over the pit (*Daily Advertiser*, 12 September 1732) and three weeks' later as over the sounding board above the stage (*Daily Advertiser*, 4 October 1732); there is evidently some confusion with another painting of the King with allegorical figures. A new ceiling piece of Apollo and the Muses was announced in February 1733. *Folger.*

41 page 51
'Rich's Glory or his Triumphant Entry into Covent Garden', 1732. Satirical print from British Museum Crace portfolio. *British Museum.*

42 page 53
Cross-section and ground-plan of Covent Garden, 1774. Anonymous engraving in Dumont, *Parallèle de plans des plus belles salles de spectacles* (1774).

43 page 54
Frontispiece of proscenium frame designed by G. B. Cipriani for Covent Garden, 1777. Water-colour (see *Theatre Notebook*, vol. xiv, i, 1964, pl. 1). *Mr Robert Eddison.*

44 page 55
'The Modern Duel', a scene from Garrick's *Miss in her Teens*, Covent Garden 1747, in the only season when Garrick acted there. From left to right the characters seem to be Biddy Bellair (Miss Hippisley), Fribble (Garrick), Tag (Mrs Pritchard), Captain Flash (Henry Woodward). The print shows clearly the spiked railings, the footlights, the candelabra

and the stage-boxes but the artist has foreshortened the platform by omitting the stage-doors on each side. Another similar engraving was published in *The London Magazine*, April 1747, while a third, published by Samuel Lyne, depicts merely the actors, leaving out the scene and the spectators in the boxes. *British Museum.*

45 page 56
View from front-boxes of Covent Garden. Engraving reproduced by H. Saxe Wyndham, *Annals of Covent Garden Theatre*, 1906, vol. i, opposite p. 190, with the caption 'C. 1770. From an Old Print', but see Robert Eddison, *Theatre Notebook*, xiv, i, p. 20.

46 page 57
'The Triumphal Entry of the Red Kings with the Expulsion of their Black Majesties', 1768. Anonymous engraving about the quarrels of the patentees and the expulsion of Powell and Colman, the red kings, by Harris and Rutherford, the black kings. The protagonists have playing card emblems, Powell a heart, Colman a diamond, Harris clubs, and Rutherford spades. Harris has a crown of asses' ears and Rutherford a fool's cap and bells; Mrs Yates wears a coronet and heart on her shoulders and Mrs Lessingham is revealing an animal's leg marked 'Lust'. The rivalry between these actresses was a partial cause of the quarrel, see British Museum, *Political and Personal Satires*, vol. iv, 4209. *Harvard Theatre Collection.*

47 page 59
King's Theatre, Haymarket. Plan and section from Dumont, *Parallèle de plans des plus belles salles de spectacles* (1774).

48 page 62
'Delivering Playbills in the Country.' Anonymous engraving, late eighteenth century. *Harvard Theatre Collection.*

49 page 65
Theatre Royal, Orchard Street, Bath, interior. Reproduction of a

drawing by John Nixon in Mowbray Green, *The Eighteenth Century Architecture of Bath* (1902), the whereabouts of the original drawing are unknown. The Theatre was originally opened in 1750. The illustration shows a scene from *Hamlet*, with a back-drop of a castellated hill, tree-wings and column-wings.

50 *page 66*
Norwich Theatre, exterior, 1758. Anonymous engraving T. B.

51 *page 67*
Ground-plan of Queen's Theatre, Manchester. Plan in Ordnance Survey of Manchester, 1849. *Manchester Central Library.*

52 *page 68*
Theatre Royal, Liverpool, front elevation. Drawing by Robert Chaffers, 12 May 1773, reproduced in R. J. Broadbent; *Annals of the Liverpool Stage* (1908), frontispiece.

53 *page 69*
Ground-plan and side of stage of Frankfort Gate Theatre, Plymouth, 1758. Drawings by James Winston, see *Theatre Notebook*, i, 1947, pp. 93–5, *Harvard Theatre Collection.*

54 *page 69*
Richmond (Surrey) (opened 1765), stage of the Theatre. Frederick Bingham, *A Celebrated Old Playhouse: The History of Richmond Theatre (in Surrey) from 1765–1884* (1886), p. 15. *Richard Southern Accession, University of Bristol Theatre Collection.*

55 *page 70*
Richmond Theatre (Yorkshire). Showing the exterior; the interior before recent restoration; and a model reconstruction by Richard Southern. *Bristol.*

56 *page 71*
Richmond Theatre (Yorkshire), section and ground-plan. Reconstruction by J. Ravers. *Bristol.*

57 *page 72*
Theatre Royal, Scarborough, interior, 1813. Coloured aquatint by J. Green, published by R. Ackerman in *Poetical Sketches of Scarborough* (1813); the theatre was originally built in 1739.

58 *page 73*
Theatre at Sunderland, stage, 1785. Anonymous engraving in J. Cawdell, *Miscellaneous Poems* (1785).

59 *page 75*
Ipswich Theatre, exterior. A print from Suffolk Record Office. A similar view from the original water colour in the Folger Shakespeare Library.

60 *pages 80 and 81*
Side-boxes at the opera, 1785. Four pen and wash sketches by Thomas Rowlandson, dated 1785. *Fogg Art Museum, Harvard University, Grenville L. Winthrop Bequest.*

61 *page 82*
Covent Garden Audience in 1786. Coloured aquatint by Thomas Rowlandson. *British Museum.*

62 *page 82*
'The Weeping Audience.' Anonymous water colour. *Source unknown.*

63 *page 83*
'The Laughing Audience.' Engraving by Charles Corbet after William Hogarth, note should be taken of the orange girls, the spiked railings at the edge of the stage, and the orchestra pit. *Harvard Theatre Collection.*

64 *page 85*
'The Overflowing of the Pitt.' Anonymous engraving after S. H. Grimm, published by S. Sledge, 25 June 1771. This print has a bill advertising a performance of *Much Ado about Nothing*. After having spent some time in Bath recuperating from an illness, Garrick made his first appearance in London during the 1770–1 season on 13 November 1770, choosing *Much Ado* for the occasion: the play again presented as a benefit for the Theatrical Fund on 24 May

1771. One or other of these occasions, probably the latter, may have been the inspiration for Grimm's painting. *Bristol.*

65 *page 87*
James Cervetti, the cellist, nicknamed 'Nosey'. Engraving by A. Picto after 'Zofini', published 16 April 1771. Cervetti was also known as Cervetto and Ceruetto or Ceruetti, he came to England as an old man and was engaged to play the bass at Drury Lane, continuing there until a season or so previous to Garrick's retirement in 1776. He died on 14 January 1785 at the age of 102. (ms. note in 'Nixon Scrapbook', vol. i, p. 188. Garrick Club Library.) *British Museum.*

66 *page 89*
'The Theatrical Dispute', engraving. This depicts the riot at Drury Lane on 5 February 1776 over the performance of Henry Bate's *The Blackamoor washed White*, note should be taken of the apple and sticks thrown at the performers and lying on the stage; but the chief interest of the print is that it is apparently the only known illustration of the green baize curtain. *Bristol.*

67 *page 94*
The stage audience, 1728–29. Oil painting by William Hogarth showing a performance of *The Beggar's Opera* in 1728 or 1729. It was issued as an engraving by William Blake by J. and J. Boydell, 1790, together with a 'Key' listing the names both of the actors and of the spectators on each side. The earlier versions, of which this is one, are more authentic in depicting the audience at the back of the stage as well as at the sides, see Marvin Carlson, 'A Fresh Look at Hogarth's Beggar's Opera', *Educational Theatre Journal*, vol. 27 (1975), pp. 30–9. Mellon Collection, Yale University.

68 *page 98*
Garrick in the character of a Countryman, speaking the prologue to Brown's *Barbarossa* (first performed on 17 December 1754). The engraving by T. Cook after the

original drawing by D. Dodd which was published 29 October 1779. *British Museum.*

69 *page 98*

Thomas King as Fame, delivering the prologue to John Burgoyne's *The Maid of the Oaks*, 1774. Engraving by T. Cook after D. Dodd, published by Fielding and Walker, 25 October 1779. The play was presented at Drury Lane on 5 November 1774. *British Museum.*

70 *page 99*

John Palmer as Christmas, delivering the prologue to Garrick's *The Christmas Tale*, 1775. Engraving by T. Cook after D. Dodd, published by Fielding and Walker, 20 November 1779. This entertainment was presented at Drury Lane on 27 December 1773. *British Museum.*

71 *page 99*

Charles Macklin delivering his farewell epilogue to Colley Cibber's *The Refusal*. Engraving by J. G. Walker after D. Dodd, published by Fielding and Walker 20 November 1779. As this was spoken by Macklin at Drury Lane on 20 October 1753, the artist would not have actually seen the performance and the print is therefore suspect. *British Museum.*

72 *page 103*

The final scene in *L'Olimpiade*, a pasticcio, King's Theatre, 1769, designed by Francesco Bigari. Engraving by Walker after Gravelot, issued with the Italian-English libretto, January 1770. Bigari, the son of Vincenzo Bigari, served as a scene designer at the opera house 1766–72 (see 'Check-list' *Theatre Notebook*, xix, i, 1964, pp. 10–11 ... where, however, the opera is not mentioned). Apparently the present engraving is the only example of his scenic work extant. It is described in the English version of the text as 'The Temple of Olimpic Jove. A Fire on the middle of the altar. Licidas drest in white, between the Priests; Clistenes, Guards; then Megacles, next Argene, and afterwards Aristea.' *Bodleian Library.*

73 *page 103*

A scene in Milton's Comus, *c.* 1772. Engraving by W. Walker after R. Dighton, published by Lowndes, 22 November 1777, showing Miss Catley as Euphrosyne, her first recorded appearance in this alteration of Milton's masque seems to have been at Covent Garden on 17 October 1772. The chief interest of this print rests in the artist's 'realistic' drawing of the scene; this has four or five profiled wings, with the suggestion of a plain flat masking wing behind them, while a cut-out archway gives a view of a columned drop in the rear. *British Museum.*

74 *page 104*

William Thomas Lewis as Hippolytus in Edmund Smith's *Phaedra and Hippolytus*. Compare archway and drop with 73. Engraving, dated 27 July 1776, by G. Grignion after D. Dodd, *New English Theatre*, vol. 11. Lewis played the part at Covent Garden on 21 February 1775. *British Museum.*

75 *page 104*

A scene in John Burgoyne's *The Heiress*, 1786. Anonymous engraving in *The Lady's Magazine*, 1786. The play was first presented at Drury Lane on 14 January 1786, the print should be compared with that reproduced in plate 73 since the artist has again 'realistically' shown the components of the setting, with the wings used to suggest a domestic interior. *British Museum.*

76 *page 106*

A scene in Garrick's *Lethe*, 1766. Oil painting by J. Zoffany. From left to right the actors are Garrick as Lord Chalkstone, Ellis Ackman as Bowman, and Astley Bransby as Aesop. The picture seems to have been based on a command performance at Drury Lane on 23 January 1766, another version is in the Somerset Maugham Collection, National Theatre. At the Society of Artists in 1766 Zoffany also exhibited a picture of the single figure of Garrick: of this there are two versions, Garrick's own painting,

formerly in possession of William Randolph Hearst and in the Garrick Club no. 124. *Birmingham Museums and Art Gallery.*

77 *page 107*

A scene in Garrick's *Lethe*. Oil painting by J. Zoffany. From left to right the actors are Astley Bransby as Aesop, William Parsons as the Old Man, and Watkins as the Servant, a companion piece to plate 76. A study of the head and shoulders of Parsons is in the Garrick Club, no. 475, which was exhibited at the Society of Artists, 1766. The whole scene was issued as a mezzotint by John Young, in 1788. *Birmingham.*

78 *page 108*

The dagger scene in *Macbeth*, with Garrick and Mrs Pritchard by Henry Fuseli. Said to be sketched during a performance. They played these parts together at Drury Lane on 4 and 8 February and at Mrs Pritchard's farewell benefit on 25 April 1768. *Kunsthaus Zürich.*

79 *page 108*

Dagger scene in *Macbeth*, a later version dated 'Roma July 74' by Fuseli which is imaginary and has little to do with the actual performance. *British Museum.*

80 *page 109*

Macbeth and Banquo meeting the Witches. Oil painting by F. Zuccarelli. Another version dated 1760, was sold at Christie's in 1956. While manifestly it has no direct connection with the playhouse, it is an excellent example of the romantic landscapes which were being attached to, and indeed inspired by, Shakespeare's plays during the second half of the eighteenth century. *Governors of the Royal Shakespeare Theatre, Stratford-upon-Avon.*

81 *page 111*

Monument scene in *Romeo and Juliet*. Engraving by S. F. Ravenet after Benjamin Wilson, published by J. Boydell, 1765. A mezzotint of the same scene engraved by R. Laurie was published about the same time by

Sayer, and C. Sheppard issued a third engraving by Stayner. These three prints, although almost identical in design, vary somewhat in treatment of the setting, it would appear as though Ravenet conceived it in terms of a natural scene whereas Stayner thought of it more in terms of the stage. The performers are Garrick and Mrs Bellamy. *British Museum.*

82 *page 112*
Scene in Cymbeline, 1770. Oil painting by Edward Penny, exhibited at the Royal Academy, 1770. Although obviously not professing to be an exact delineation of a stage setting, the view into the cave suggests a cut-out piece of scenery, freely dealt with by the artist. Such views into caves and grottoes were popular among artists and stage designers during the seventies and even later. *Royal Shakespeare Theatre.*

83 *page 113*
Joseph Wright of Derby, The Cave of Salerno. Now in the Mellon Collection, Yale University. *Sotheby Parke Bernet.*

84 *page 113*
'Prospero's Cell with a Vision', after Joseph Wright engraved Robert Thew. The original painting for the Boydell Gallery is in the Earl of Crawford's Collection. It is another example of Wright's interest in grotto scenes, see plate 83.

85 *page 119*
The 'Eidophusikon' of P. J. De Loutherbourg, *c.* 1782, water colour by Edward Francis Burney: reproduced in *Theatre Notebook*, xviii, 2, 1964, pl. 2. *British Museum.*

86 *page 120*
Slanting wings from 'The London Theatres', 1769, shows Arthur Murphy's *The Citizen*. The engraving, dated 31 March 1767, presumably represents the Covent Garden revival on 31 December 1766 and 16 March 1767. The cast list on 7 October 1768 gives Woodward as Young Philpot, Michael Dyer as Young Wilding,

Edward Shuter as Old Philpot and Mrs Mattocks as Maria.

87 *page 121*
The Goodspeed Opera House, East Haddam, Connecticut, 1938, wings and flats of back-drop, and overhead grooves.

88 *page 122*
Machinery for moving wings in French Theatres. Engraving by Benard after Rudel in Diderot's *Encyclopédie*, *Receuil des Planches*, vol. 10, Machines de Theatre, T, 1772.

89 *page 122*
Plan of stage and machines in the theatre of the Seminary of the College Romain. Anonymous engraving in Dumont, *Parallèle des salles de spectacles* (1774).

90 *page 123*
A French stage being set. Anonymous engraving in Dumont, *Parallèle des salles de spectacles* (1774).

91 *page 127*
A scene in Ben Jonson's *Every Man in his Humour*, 1751. The anonymous engraving, though undated, seems to represent Edward Shuter as Stephen and Henry Woodward as Bobadil, in the revival of the play at Drury Lane on 29 November 1751. It is possible that the engraver has attempted to show these actors standing before a 'street' front-drop, but this print should be compared with the accompanying drawing. If the anonymous drawing of Shuter and Woodward in the same scene is the original sketch for the engraving then no background was provided by the artist for the performers. *Folger.*

92 *page 128*
Scene in William Whitehead's *The Roman Father* (Drury Lane, 24 February 1790). Anonymous engraving from *The Universal Magazine*, 1750; and an original drawing apparently that from which above print was executed. In the drawing from left to right, the

performers are Mrs Ward as Valeria, Mrs Pritchard as Horatia, Spranger Barry as Plobius and Garrick as Horatius. The engraving has been described as an important piece of evidence, showing a grouping of actors before a front-drop placed immediately behind the frontispiece. Comparison with the drawing, however, indicates that the evidence of the print is faulty in three ways: (i) the arrangement of the actors seems strained and awkward; (ii) if the print be taken as illustrating the histrionic gesture, it will lead us astray, again because of the reversal—Garrick uses his right arm to restrain Barry, and Mrs Ward raises her left hand, not her right; and (iii) examination of the drawing appears to indicate that the artist, although he has indulged in severe foreshortening, intended to delineate two or three columned side wings and a back shutter of or back-drop, and, if so, the actual stage setting was not a painted front-drop but an ordinary set scene. *Folger.*

93 *page 133*
Garrick and his mechanicals, 1772. Anonymous engraving on the title page of the 2nd edition of *The Theatres. A Poetical Dissection*, by 'Sir Nicholas Nipclose, Baronet'. The figure on the extreme right is identified, by the paper sticking out from his pocket, as James Messink who after starting as an acrobat and pantomime actor turned to devising scenes and machines in Dublin. He was engaged at Drury Lane by Garrick in 1767 and remained until 1777 (see Checklist in *Theatre Notebook*, vol. xix, 4, 1965, p. 136). The two men between him and Garrick are probably intended as stage hands. Messink's pantomime, *The Pigmy Revels*, produced on 26 December 1772, had a particularly successful run. *Harvard.*

94 *pages 134 and 135*
Scene in Murphy's *The Desert Island* and its French model. Engraving designed and executed by A. Walker, frontispiece to the first edition of the play, 1770, *Bodleian Library*. Mrs Pritchard played

Constantia. The accompanying engraving by N. le Mire after C. Cochin Filius, frontispiece to *L'Isle déserte* (1758) by Collet de Messine. Obviously Walker must have been influenced by the French engraving, but there is still a further possibility that, in fact, the new scene painted for the English production was also inspired from that source.

95 *page 135*

Scene in Murphy's *The Way to Keep Him*, 1760. Engraving designed and executed by A. Walker, frontispiece to the first edition of the play. It illustrates a scene in the third act when the duplicity of Lovemore (Garrick) is exposed; the Widow Bellmour (Miss Macklin) is on the left, Mrs Lovemore (Mrs Yates) on the right, and Sir Brilliant Fashion (John Palmer) stand behind. *Bodleian.*

96 *page 138*

Prison scene by P. J. De Loutherbourg, probably for *Robinson Crusoe*, 1781. Water colour maquette: *Robinson Crusoe, or Harlequin Friday*, for which R. S. Sheridan was said to have been responsible, was first presented at Drury Lane on 29 January 1781, and the 'inside of the prison of the Inquisition' was specially praised in *The Lady's Magazine*, February 1781. See 'Checklist', *Theatre Notebook*, xix, 3, 1965, pp. 105–12 for this and other records of De Loutherbourg's career. *Victoria and Albert Theatre Museum.*

97 *page 139*

Sea coast scene by P. J. De Loutherbourg. Water colour designs for wings, pieces, groundrows and backdrop. Set may have been intended for *Robinson Crusoe*. *Victoria and Albert Theatre Museum.*

98 *page 140*

'The First Scene of The Maid of the Mill', 1765. Engraved by William Woollett from the scene designed by John Inigo Richards, published by the former on 15 January 1768. Isaac Bickerstaffe's play was presented at Covent Garden, with 'New Scenes and Habits', on 31 January 1765.

Richards had been engaged at this Theatre in the season of 1759–60 and remained there until the beginning of the following century. See 'Checklist', *Theatre Notebook*, xix, 4, 1965, pp. 142–5.

99 *page 141*

Scene in Bickerstaffe's *The Maid of the Mill*. Engraving designed and executed by Isaac Taylor, frontispiece to a 'new edition' of the play, 1767. According to the stage direction, this shows '*a view of Lord* AIMWORTH'S *House, and improvements: a seat under a tree; and part of the garden wall, with a Chinese pavilion over it*'. *The John Rylands University Library of Manchester.*

100 *page 145*

Mezzotint by W. J. Ward, 1829, purporting to be of 'Garrick in the Greenroom' by Hogarth. Original in the Lady Lever Art Gallery. More probably this is from 'A poet declaiming his verses', the drawing of which, in the Museo Correr, Venice, is closely related to the mezzotint. See J. Byam Shaw, *Old Master Drawings*, vol. vii, no. 28, March 1933.

101 *page 146*

Mrs Massey as Christina in Henry Brook's *Gustavus Vasa*. Anonymous engraving, dated February 1778, after J. Roberts, *Bell's British Theatre* (1778). *Gustavus Vasa* was banned by the Lord Chamberlain in 1739, and, although it was acted at the Smock Alley Theatre, Dublin, on 3 December 1744, there is no record of its having been given in London. Just possibly, Mrs Massey might have taken the part in some Irish or provincial production, but most probably the picture is a fabrication. *British Museum.*

102 *page 146*

Anne Crawford (Barry) as Sophonisba? Engraving, dated 1 January 1778, by Thornthwaite after J. Roberts, *Bell's British Theatre* (1778). Appears as frontispiece to James Thomson's *Sophonisba* but that play was never performed in this period: interestingly the text is

preceded by a character list to which no performers' names are attached except for Mrs Barry's. It is impossible to determine whether (a) the print shows the actress as Roberts, in his own imagination, thought she might have appeared or (b) it depicts Mrs Barry clad in a dress which she would have considered inappropriate. *British Museum.*

103 *page 148*

Thomas Weston as Costard. Drawing by Robert Dighton. An engraving of this by C. Grignion, dated 23 September 1776, appeared as the frontispiece to *Love's Labours Lost* in *Bell's Shakespeare* (1776). This must be a studio portrait since at this period the play remained completely unknown to the stage. *British Museum.*

104 *page 149*

Garrick as Demetrius in Edward Young's *The Brothers* (1753). Engraving by Thornthwaite in *Bell's British Theatre* (1777) after an original drawing by J. Roberts. Garrick created the part at Drury Lane, 3 March 1753 but, after a short run, the play was not performed later in London, and by 1777 Garrick had retired.

105 *page 149*

David Garrick as Demetrius. Engraving dated 11 October 1777, by J. Collyer after D. Dodd, *New English Theatre*, vol. xii. Another anonymous engraving in similar costume was published by J. Wenman, 1778, see plate 104. *British Museum.*

106 *page 150*

Jane Lessingham as Ophelia. After the coloured drawing by James Roberts. Engraved by C. Grignion and published in *Bell's Shakespeare* (1775). Apparently her only recorded London appearance in the part was at Covent Garden, 21 April 1772. *British Museum.*

107 *page 150*

Miss Barsanti as Helena in *Midsummer Night's Dream*.

Engraving by C. Grignion after J. Roberts, dated 1 March 1776, frontispiece to the play in *Bell's Shakespeare* (1776). There appears to be no record of Miss Barsanti's having taken this role. *British Museum.*

108 *page 151*
Garrick as Abel Drugger. Water colour. This seems to be based on, or to be the original, of an engraving published by R. Sayer and J. Smith in their 'Dramatic Portraits', 1769, see plate 6. *Folger.*

109 *page 151*
Thomas Weston as Scrub and Garrick as Archer in *The Beaux' Stratagem.* Coloured engraving published by J. Smith and R. Sayer, 1771. Garrick first appeared as Archer 1742–43, Weston as Scrub during 1767–68; their duet became famous and they continued performing the roles up to the mid-seventies.

110 *page 152*
Garrick as Tancred in Thomson's *Tancred and Sigismunda*, 18 March 1745. Oil painting by Thomas Worlidge. Worlidge executed an etching of this picture, published by E. Jackson, 1752, and a smaller version published by himself. *Victoria and Albert Theatre Museum.*

111 *page 154*
The Weird Sisters in *Macbeth* by J. H. Fuseli. Oil painting. Two other versions are known, one in the North Carolina Museum of Art and the other in the Kunsthaus, Zürich, which is probably the canvas exhibited at the Royal Academy, 1783. A lithograph version was published by G. R. Smith in 1785. Fuseli's drawings

and paintings of Shakespearian scenes are numerous, their interest being of several kinds; sometimes he has sketched a scene which he must have seen on the stage, and such studies have obvious value as theatrical records; sometimes he has embellished the theatrical image so that, although the playhouse is not entirely forgotten, the effect becomes an imaginative impression; and sometimes, as in the present instance, he has allowed his fancy complete freedom (see plates 78 and 79). During his first sojourn in England, 1764–70, his studies were of a generally realistic kind; when he was in Italy, 1770–78, his Shakespearian pictures tended to become more formalised. His second period in England, 1779 until his death 1825 (years which fall outside the scope of the present volume) saw him actively associated with the vast Boydell project. *Royal Shakespeare Theatre.*

112 *page 155*
Shakespeare as seen by S. H. Grimm. Selected sketches from a magnificent series of about a hundred water colours by S. H. Grimm. Most of these are signed and dated, and apparently were executed over a period from 1769 to 1782. *Merchant of Venice*, act 3, scene 2; act 4, scene 2; *As You Like It*, act 1, scene 6; *Hamlet*, act 3, scene 6.

113 *page 157*
'Habit of Comus in the Masque of Comus.' Anonymous engraving in Thomas Jefferys, *Recueil des Habillements de Differents Nations*, 1757–72, vol. ii, no. ccxl. The description in the text, p. 83 reads; 'The Cap is decorated with Grapes and Vine Leaves. The Robe is Pink

Sattin puft with Silver Gauze, fastened over the Shoulder with a black Velvet Sash adorned with Jewels, The Jacket is of white curtain'd Sattin; the Collar is black Velvet set with Jewels: and the Boots are blue Sattin.' Colman's adaptation of *Comus* was brought out in 1772.

114 *page 163*
Garrick as Hamlet, 1754. Mezzotint by J. McArdell, after Benjamin Wilson, published by R. M. Laurie, 1754. A line engraved copy was published by R. Sayer and J. Smith in 1769.

115 *page 165*
William Powell as Posthumus. Oil painting by J. Zoffany, in possession of A. M. Davidson. Another slightly variant version is in the possession of Mrs Adrian Crombie. An anonymous engraving, undated, was published by R. Sayer and J. Smith. Powell first appeared in this part at Drury Lane on 1 December 1763, and apparently last acted it at Covent Garden on 16 May 1769. *The Leger Galleries Limited.*

116 *page 167*
Henry Woodward as Bobadil in Ben Jonson's *Every Man in His Humour.* The engraving dated 2 November 1776 by J. Goldar formed the frontispiece to the play in Lowndes' *The New English Theatre*, vol. v. The original water colour on vellum by J. Roberts was engraved by Thornthwaite and appeared as the frontispiece to the play in *Bell's British Theatre* (1776). Woodward first took the part at Drury Lane on 29 November 1751 and the character in the above illustration is shown 'Dress'd in the Old English Manner'. *British Museum.*

Index